Biblical
Building Blocks

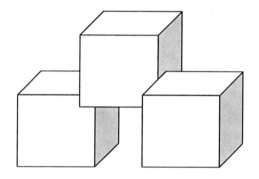

A Manual for Teaching Christian Biblical Doctrine

Donald E. Grondwalski, D.D

Biblical Building Blocks
by Donald E. Grondwalski

Printed in the United States of America

ISBN 9781609571368

www.xulonpress.com

DEDICATED

To my wonderful wife, whose inspiration, patience, and experience have made this book possible.

Acknowledgements

My deep appreciation and thanks goes to those who have made this book possible.

First to my Lord and Savior Jesus Christ and His sacrifice for all mankind and the Holy Spirit's guidance in this work, I am eternally grateful.

A big thank you to retired teacher, Pat Marcos and my sister-in-law, Special Needs teacher, Susan Draxinger for the many hours they put into editing the draft of this book.

And finally, my thanks go to Juan Garnica and the entire Xulon Press team's guidance and help in producing this book.

My prayer is that we will come to know the truth and that the truth will set us free.

Preface

To discover truth has been my life-long desire. When I made the choice to explore the whole Bible, the truth that I had been seeking became a reality. Life experiences prior to my Christian walk never seemed to satisfy my longing and desire to understand truth. Truth was a slippery slope without absolutes. If a concept of truth fit into my immediate lifestyle, I would accept it and walk within it until some new concept came into my life, living a worldly life of truths conceived by mankind. As I came to what I call the cross-road of my life, the Bible was introduced to me and I needed to make a conscience choice to continue on with my life as normal or make that critical turn of experiencing what the Bible had to offer, challenging my hypocrite manner of stating I am a Christian yet knowing very little about it. As I read the Bible from Genesis to Revelation, I began to sense a feeling of fullness and satisfaction. I realized that only in the Bible is real truth found. Even today, I continue to rely on the truth found in God's Living Word the Bible.

To be successful in any career, one must build a solid foundation of knowledge and skills. Living the Christian life is much the same. We must know what we believe and why we believe it. The Bible alone is the source needed to discover the truths and build a solid life here on earth and in eternity. Writing this book is my attempt to help guide those who are searching for the truth according to God and His Word. I believe that God's love found in His Word, the Bible, will do the rest.

Contents

Begin
With
Prayer

Bible Theology & Doctrine Defined

Biblical Building Block # 1

(1 John 4:16 HCSB)

16 And we have come to know and to believe the love that God has for us. God is love, and the one who remains in love remains in God, and God remains in him.

God is love and of all the doctrines, love is the greatest, and in which all other doctrines are established. The Bible is a Love story between God and mankind. If one approaches the Holy Scriptures as such they will enjoy the enlightenment of God's desire to have a relationship with each individual person as well as all of mankind. To begin this journey we must open the Holy Bible, our minds and hearts and allow the words of God to penetrate our being. Only then can we see and hear what God has for his creation and that is His Love.

1. What does Theology mean to you, can you define it?

2. What sources do we use to develop Biblical Theology?

3. How would you define doctrine?

4. Why is teaching Biblical doctrine important?

5. How significant is it to know and understand what you believe in?

6. What kinds of doctrine/teachings are found in the Bible?

7. Can you name some of the characteristics of sound Biblical Doctrine?

The Definition of Theology

The word **theology** means the study of God and religious truth; rational inquiry into religious questions of religious doctrines/teachings and of matters pertaining to Divinity (God).

There are two Greek words that make up the word 'theology.' "theos" meaning "God" and "logos" meaning "word" or discourse." Discourse is defined as a formal lengthy discussion of a subject either written or spoken.

So, theology is the study of God through the use of doctrine (something taught). We recognize the Holy Bible as being the Source of information for Christianity today. Along with our study of theological truths, we must consider "religion" which denotes the practice of the truths we believe in. The two should be integrated and united in the life of the believer and the church. Therefore, all believers are in some way 'theologians' who must specialize in the teachings of God presented to them through the Holy Bible. If no effort is put into studying of doctrine/teaching of God then one will not be properly rooted and grounded in what they believe and why they believe in it. Seeking and understanding the truth should be a priority to everyone.

(2 Timothy 2:15 KJV) ¹⁵ Study to shew thyself approved unto God, a workman that needeth not to be ashamed, rightly dividing the word of truth.

Characteristics of Theology

Theology can be considered a science, falling under the category of behavior science. However theology has it own unique characteristics. As an example, in theology God is the unique subject. Another example is the consideration of the relationship between people and God. So, Christian Theology is the careful, systematic, study, analysis, and statement of Christian Doctrine/teaching using the Holy Bible as its source of information to gain knowledge about God and how mankind is impacted.

Characteristics of Theology can be categorized as being **"Biblical"** which would use primarily the contents from the Holy Bible, both Old and New Testaments. As **"Systematic"** which is the drawing together into one coherent whole, what the Old and New Testaments say on any given topic such as God and His plan for mankind, rather than looking at each book of the Bible separately. As what is done in the context of **"Human Culture"** which relates teachings of data found in other disciplines that deal with the same subject matter. Also, categorized as **"Contemporary"** which is aimed at restating timeless Biblical truths in a form that is understandable to people in today's world and finally, **"Practical"** which is both the giving of information, with the intention that the doctrine/teaching be applied to everyday life.

Sources of Knowledge That May be Used

The Bible which is the Word of God and authored by God only allows God to make changes and amendments. No person has been given this right. Mankind can and should only express the Word of God in all matters of the faith in Jesus Christ. Biblical Theology should use first of all the Scriptures of the Bible to be the defining statement on all matters. Nature, the created universe and mankind can also be studied to determine certain truths. Another source can be traditional theology where inquiry is made into what has been taught and practiced by peoples stating to be Christians and believers in Jesus Christ so that what they believe can be proven stable against the Scriptures. The Scriptures specify what is to be believed and practiced in a believer's life.

The Methods or Divisions of Theology

Collection of Biblical Material

The collection of Biblical material identifies all the relevant biblical passages dealing with a particular topic being investigated is called *exegesis* and means "to lead out – guide out, to draw out". In theology it refers to the analysis and interpretation of Scripture and is concerned with Biblical language, Biblical archeology, Biblical introduction and Biblical hermeneutics (the science of interpretation of the Bible).

Dogmatic

Dogmatic refers to the study of dogma, creeds and other writings that mankind has assembled from their study of the Scriptures. It is a principle, statement of idea, belief, or opinion that is considered to be absolute truth. There is a major difference between dogma and doctrine. Dogma is a principle or belief written by men. Doctrine refers to the teaching of truth given to mankind from the Scriptures of God, being God's revelation.

Biblical Theology

Biblical Theology is the study of the contents within the Bible itself. It takes into consideration who wrote the particular passage, when it was written, to whom it was written, why it was written, and compares it to the progression of truth throughout the whole Bible. An example would be the study of the doctrine of sin. Biblical Theology would view its description in the Old Testament, track it to the New Testament, and compare the findings, its impacts to mankind, and link to other aspects of the Bible to establish the doctrine and teachings of how the entire Word of God, the Bible speaks about it.

Historical Examination

Historical examination studies Biblical history, church history, the history of doctrine and the history of the world. This would include comparing, testing, analyzing, and determining historical information against each other. It is a study of chronological records and/or events of mankind.

Systematic

Systematic Theology is a step by step manner of study. It takes each topic in an orderly fashion and studies that doctrine until it exhausts all of its findings. It studies Biblical Theology doctrines in a systematic manner.

Pastoral or Practical

This is the practical application of theology to mankind in everyday living and how to apply it to ones life and how to act as the Church. The Bible is full of practical application for the believer and should be studied and acted upon.

The Word Doctrine Defined

The word "Doctrine" has a meaning of, teachings, or something taught, instructions, and when related to religion or a belief system it is the teachings and instructions that one would base their beliefs and actions of life on. Also, this could be considered the communication of knowledge that should be incorporated into a person's life style.

In the Old Testament the word doctrine is used and translated from the word l*eqah,* which means "what is received". The word *tora,* which is rendered "law", is used in expressing the idea of a body of revealed teaching.

The word 'doctrine' is found about 51 times in the KJV, and about 37 times in the NKJV. The word teaching(s) has been substituted for the word doctrine in other modern versions. In the New Testament two words are used for doctrine. The word *Didaskalia* which means both the act and the content of teaching and the word *didache* is used in more parts of the New Testament and it too can mean either the act or the content of teaching. (Matthew 7:28; John 7:16-17; Acts 2:42; Romans 6:17)

The early church converts stayed loyal and constant in using the apostle's Doctrine (Teachings) as seen in Acts 2:42. This should set the stage for the Church today, which also should continue in the Doctrines. The Doctrines must be understood and then taught and acted on.

(Acts 2:42 KJV) And they continued steadfastly in the apostles' Doctrine, and fellowship, and in breaking of bread, and in prayers. (Doctrine is the verb for Teaching).

The Purpose

There is a two fold purpose for theological studies of doctrine/teachings pertaining to the believer. One is to make sure that the believer is rooted and grounded in the Word of God and in the understanding of what is taught from the Scriptures. This is essential for clearly understanding God and His makeup as the Father, Son and Holy Spirit, the Atonement and Salvation, Jesus Christ His works and commission to the church, sin, mankind, and the spiritual aspect such as angels and demons. The second purpose is to instruct the believer that they may know the certainty of these Truths which will give them guidance, wisdom, hope, and increase their faith. This is needed to be well equipped to face this life and overcome the adversary, the devil, and his deception as his only desire is to kill, steal and destroy. There is no other wisdom on earth that can protect mankind from the adversary except the Word of God and acting upon it. It is to encourage the believer to contend and strive for "the faith" once delivered to the saints. Luke 1:1-4 implies the purpose of doctrine and theology.

(Luke 1:1-4 NKJV) Inasmuch as many have taken in hand to set in order a narrative of those things which have been fulfilled among us, ² just as those who from the beginning were eyewitnesses and ministers of the word delivered them to us, ³ it seemed good to me also, having had perfect understanding of all things from the very first, to write to you an orderly account, most excellent Theophilus, ⁴ that you may know the certainty of those things in which you were instructed.

God has revealed Himself in the Bible which is made up of 66 separate writings given to mankind by God, Who is the author. One must understand that God is not confined or limited to just the writings or doctrines or any article of faith, but at this time the Bible is the source that has been issued to mankind to use, study, understand and act upon. It is His revelation that He has desired to give and He will be the source to illuminate its use and meaning. So the Bible is the Word of God which is the source of measure to be used for all Theological studies and all writings, creeds, sermons, and teaching should be tested against it. It is God's infallible Word. No one has the right to change any of the meanings but only to seek the understanding of what has been given, being instructed by it, not defining it.

(Acts 18:25 KJV) ²⁵ This man was instructed in the way of the Lord; and being fervent in the spirit, he spake and taught diligently the things of the Lord, knowing only the baptism of John.

Necessity of Doctrine

There is a serious issue within the church today and that is ignorance of the Scriptures. It is really important to understand what one believes and why they believe it. There is also an attack on Biblical doctrine from within the church. We are in a time when churches are trying and experimenting in finding a new and different church model that will work for this current generation, with a priority of gaining numbers of people at the cost of water down teachings. They want to be careful of what they say and how they say it. They prefer to say things that make people feel good instead of presenting sound doctrine/teaching. Turning away from doctrinal matters and moving to philosophies of men and doctrines of devils (being deceived). Many churches have no time for doctrinal preaching or teaching and have congregations that do not even carry or use a Bible during the service. They have tuned to oratory, politics, ethics, book-sermons or a social gospel saying that doctrine is useless and obsolete. (Note - even the word doctrine is being replaced because it makes some uncomfortable)

The Apostle Paul prophesied in (2 Timothy 4:3-4 KJV) ³ For the time will come when they will not endure sound doctrine; but after their own lusts shall they heap to themselves teachers, having itching ears; [4] And they shall turn away *their* ears from the truth, and shall be turned unto fables.

> Text Message → If we give the Word of God in Truth and sound doctrine it will do the work of reaching people and increasing the church
> Text Message → Don't go outside of Scripture stay within it!!

There is Need for Doctrine to be Taught

God indeed has absolutes. His Truths are pure and perfect. But today it seems we are in a world of no absolutes concerning one's faith and how to conduct his/her life. There is a rise in beliefs that are outside of sound doctrine such as relativism, the theory that truth is an ethical relation to the individual or group that holds it. Making their own truths and have no accountability to God with no absolutes to live by. So it is and always has been a necessity to teach the doctrine of the Bible that has God's absolutes. His Word reflects His Truth and Laws as eternal absolutes, which are unchanged and unchanging forever pure, perfect and reliable.

The following are examples of beliefs that support the need for Biblical doctrine to be studied first within the church then outwardly to the world. A theory that does not deny God but denies the possibility of knowing God is *Atheism/agnosticism. Situation ethics* is a system of ethics based on brotherly love in which acts are morally evaluated within a situation context rather than by application of morale absolutes. *Existentialism* is a philosophy that emphasizes in a hostile or different universe, regards human existence as unexplainable and stresses freedom of choice and responsibility for the consequences of one's acts. All of these beliefs bypass the truths in the Holy Bible drawing people away from the truth that the doctrine in the Bible illuminates.

False Religions, counterfeit Christianity, incorrect teachings within the church, Pluralism (the doctrine that reality is composed of many ultimate substances and believing that no single explanatory system or view can be right) and believing that all faiths can be right – is growing within the Christian Church and other philosophies of men have saturated this generation causing a real need for sound doctrine.

Beliefs in any religion, cult, and philosophy have their own teachings/doctrine and what ever a person receives, believes, obeys and practices will definitely determine a person's attitude and character. So your character is what you are, and will drive your behavior in what you do and this will ultimately decide your destiny, where you go. What you believe in will become what you obey and what you obey will be what you practice and all of this will determine your character.

> Text Message → Character → what we are → Behavior → what we do → Destiny → where we go

To build a character pleasing to God, one must be built on the Word of God and to accomplish this must believe, study, and obey His Word, which hold His truths and laws as absolutes. Sound doctrine/teaching must be the foundation used to establish this. If there are no absolutes then there can never be truths because truth becomes what ever mankind wants them to be. Mankind being accountable to their creator must trust and obey the absolutes of God, His Word and the doctrine within it.

By knowing the truth you shall be made free. (John 8:32 NKJV) [32] and you shall know the truth, and the truth shall make you free." Truth is what will bring you peace, joy, contentment, love and fulfillment in this life. Truth is to be used to dispel error and confusion. You are able, by God's truth, to combat and defeat false teachings which use deception, denying truth, because truth is the light that will dispel darkness and set you free.

(2 Timothy 3:15-17 KJV) [15] and that from childhood you have known the Holy Scriptures, which are able to make you wise for salvation through faith which is in Christ Jesus. [16] All Scripture *is* given by inspiration of God, and *is* profitable for doctrine, for reproof, for correction, for instruction in righteousness, [17] that the man of God may be complete, thoroughly equipped for every good work.

(2 Timothy 4:1-4 KJV) [1] I charge *you* therefore before God and the Lord Jesus Christ, who will judge the living and the dead at His appearing and His kingdom: [2] Preach the word! Be ready in season *and* out of season. Convince, rebuke, exhort, with all longsuffering and teaching. [3] For the time will come when they will not endure sound doctrine, but according to their own desires, *because* they have itching ears, they will heap up for themselves teachers; [4] and they will turn *their* ears away from the truth, and be turned aside to fables.

Classification of Doctrine

All doctrine seems to come from three areas or types of sources within the Scriptures and can be classified as **God, Satan/Devil and Man**. In Matthew 16:13-23 these sources are illustrated. The **thought of God** concerning Christ is seen in verses (Matthew16:16-17 NKJV) *[16] Simon Peter answered and said, "You are the Christ, the Son of the living God." [17] Jesus answered and said to him, "Blessed are you, Simon Bar-Jonah, for flesh and blood has not revealed* this *to you, but My Father who is in heaven.* – Peter confessed that Jesus was the Christ, the Son of God – This surely was revelation from God. The **thought of Man** – is seen in verses (Matthew16:13-14 NKJV) *[13] When Jesus came into the region of Caesarea Philippi, He asked His disciples, saying, "Who do men say that I, the Son of Man, am?" [14] So they said, "Some* say *John the Baptist, some Elijah, and others Jeremiah or one of the prophets."* - Where people thought that Jesus might be Elijah. The **thought of Satan** – is seen in verses (Matthew 16:22-23 NKJV) *[22] Then Peter took Him aside and began to rebuke Him, saying, "Far be it from You, Lord; this shall not happen to You!" [23] But He turned and said to Peter, "Get behind Me, Satan! You are an offense to Me, for you are not mindful of the things of God, but the things of men."* - Where Peter, confessed a thought he received from Satan.

Doctrine of God (God, Christ, Apostles)

When we speak about the doctrine of God we see the areas that are linked in nature and spoken of in Scripture. They are the Doctrine of God, Doctrine of Christ, and Doctrine of the Apostles. All are God given doctrine.

Doctrine of God

The Word of God simply declares that the Scriptures are His Doctrine and He gives them out to mankind. He will rain upon mankind His Words so that the truths are available to them.

(Deuteronomy 32:2 KJV) ² My doctrine shall drop as the rain, my speech shall distil as the dew, as the small rain upon the tender herb, and as the showers upon the grass:

(1 Timothy NKJV) ¹ Let as many bondservants as are under the yoke count their own masters worthy of all honor, so that the name of God and *His* doctrine may not be blasphemed.

Doctrine of Christ

In Mark 4:2, it states that Jesus taught many things in parables and doctrine. In (2 John 1:9-11) it tells believers to reject any one who teaches false doctrine and does not bring the doctrine of Christ. Jesus taught His Father's doctrine, the doctrine of God, the Father, and Son were one in doctrine. (John 7:16-17 NKJV) ¹⁶ Jesus answered them and said, "My doctrine is not Mine, but His who sent Me. ¹⁷ If anyone wants to do His will, he shall know concerning the doctrine, whether it is from God or *whether* I speak on My own *authority.*

(Mark 4:2 KJV) ² And he taught them many things by parables, and said unto them in his doctrine,

(2 John 1:9-11 NKVJ) Whoever transgresses and does not abide in the doctrine of Christ does not have God. He who abides in the doctrine of Christ has both the Father and the Son. ¹⁰ If anyone comes to you and does not bring this doctrine, do not receive him into your house nor greet him; ¹¹ for he who greets him shares in his evil deeds.

(1 Timothy 6:3 KJV) ³ If any man teach otherwise, and consent not to wholesome words, *even* the words of our Lord Jesus Christ, and to the doctrine which is according to godliness;

Doctrine of the Apostles

When we speak of the Doctrine of the Apostles we identify the New Testament writings. These were given to the Apostles by God through the Holy Spirit and also through their personal experience with the living Word Jesus Christ. The Church, those who are believers in the Gospel of Jesus Christ, is to read, study, and exercise these doctrines until the second coming of our Lord Jesus Christ. The Church is not to become students of this world's doctrines but to avoid them and stay on the course of the doctrine stated in the Holy Bible. We are to be careful not to add, subtract or water down these doctrine/teachings but hold them up and teach them to all who will hear. The early church converts practiced and stay within the Doctrine of the Apostles.

(Acts 2:24 NKJV) [42] continued steadfastly in the apostles' doctrine and fellowship, in the breaking of bread, and in prayers.

In Hebrews 6:1-2 we have a brief summary of some of the Apostles doctrine. They are repentance from dead works, faith towards God, of Baptisms, of lying on of hands, resurrection of the dead and eternal judgment.

(Hebrews 6:1-2 KJV) [1] Therefore leaving the principles of the doctrine of Christ, let us go on unto perfection; not laying again the foundation of repentance from dead works, and of faith toward God, [2] Of the doctrine of baptisms, and of laying on of hands, and of resurrection of the dead, and of eternal judgment.

Doctrine of Men and Satan/Devil

When we speak of Doctrine of Men and Satan/Devil we see that there will be false doctrine introduced to mankind, both having its links to Satan. His intent is to cause the gap between mankind and God to deepen. This is the battle for the mind. What we believe will be what we do and will determine out future in eternity. Satan is out to take away as many creations of God as he can. We must speak, teach and focus on the Doctrine of God daily and use the only source of information that is proven to be truth that is found in the Bible. We are not to turn to the best sellers list of books to build our faith on, but keep a balance in what one reads and studies.

(Colossians 2:8 NKJV) Beware lest anyone cheat you through philosophy and empty deceit, according to the tradition of men, according to the basic principles of the world, and not according to Christ.
Doctrine of Men

The church composed of the believers of the Gospel of Jesus Christ need to be rooted and grounded in the Scriptures to avoid being tricked by doctrines and teachings that will be created by mankind or the world. These doctrines/teachings are not of God and will create division in organized church bodies. There will be confusion and worse, spiritual disaster in the one who accepts and practices them. They are called hypocrites, trusting in mankind's knowledge and bypassing Gods Word. We must avoid certain doctrine/teachings and speak the truth, Gods Word, in love.

(Ephesians 4:14-15 NKJV) [14] that we should no longer be children, tossed to and fro and carried about with every wind of doctrine, by the trickery of men, in the cunning craftiness of deceitful plotting, [15] but, speaking the truth in love, may grow up in all things into Him who is the head--Christ—

(Matthew 15:7-9 NKJV) ⁷ Hypocrites! Well did Isaiah prophesy about you, saying: ⁸ *'These people draw near to Me with their mouth, And honor Me with their lips, But their heart is far from Me. ⁹ And in vain they worship Me, Teaching as doctrines the commandments of men.' "*

(Mark 7:6-7 NKJV) ⁶ He answered and said to them, "Well did Isaiah prophesy of you hypocrites, as it is written: *'This people honors Me with their lips, But their heart is far from Me. ⁷ And in vain they worship Me, Teaching as doctrines the commandments of men.'*
Doctrines of Satan/Devil and His Deceiving Spirits/Demons

The Scriptures warn us that in the latter times doctrines of deceiving spirits, and demons would be spread and that some will leave the faith and follow them. These will be lies, untruths that will probably sound good but not be of God causing mankind to feel good about what they want to believe in. They will be deceived which will lead them to the destruction of the their souls. Deception is Satan's major attack weapon which started against humanity in the Garden of Eden (Genesis 3:1-6).

(1 Timothy 4:1-3 NKJV) ¹ Now the Spirit expressly says that in latter times some will depart from the faith, giving heed to deceiving spirits and doctrines of demons, ² speaking lies in hypocrisy, having their own conscience seared with a hot iron, ³ forbidding to marry, *and commanding* to abstain from foods which God created to be received with thanksgiving by those who believe and know the truth

(2 Timothy 4:3-4 NKJV) ³ For the time will come when they will not endure sound doctrine, but according to their own desires, *because* they have itching ears, they will heap up for themselves teachers; ⁴ and they will turn *their* ears away from the truth, and be turned aside to fables.

TEXT MESSAGE → The only sure and infallible test of all doctrine is the Word of God, the complete body of Scriptures, working from the part to the complete, and the complete to the part.

Symbols of Doctrine

Is like Leaven – Leaven is an ingredient that works subtly and silently within a whole, such as in dough for making bread. This has the power to animate something imparting interest, spirit, and encouragement. Leaven is a symbol here of the evil influence of false teachings/doctrine that once injected into a persons being will cause corruption within. It will go against the pure Word of God and create conflict. It is critical that one protect all that they allow within, what they read, what they study and meditate on. All of these can impact a persons direction of belief and faith.

(Luke 12:1 NKJV) ¹ In the meantime, when an innumerable multitude of people had gathered together, so that they trampled one another, He began to say to His disciples first *of all*, "Beware of the leaven of the Pharisees, which is hypocrisy."

Is Like Wind – Believers in Jesus Christ, the Church must become mature in their faith to know the doctrines of the Word of God so that they are not tossed around by false teaching. "Wind" in the following verse represents doctrine of the world and not of God. Believers need to be rooted and grounded with the Word of God in love to sustain the strong winds of false teaching that will be blowing about.

(Ephesians 4:14-15 NKJV) [14] that we should no longer be children, tossed to and fro and carried about with every wind of doctrine, by the trickery of men, in the cunning craftiness of deceitful plotting, [15] but, speaking the truth in love, may grow up in all things into Him who is the head--Christ--

Is Like Rain – This has the meaning of doctrine/teachings coming from God being sent from a heavenly place. Water in itself is necessary for life. Symbolically rain represents what is necessary for spiritual life, God's own Word.

(Deuteronomy 32:2 NKJV) [2] Let my teaching drop as the rain, My speech distill as the dew, As raindrops on the tender herb, and as showers on the grass.

The Nature of Doctrine

In 1 and 2 Timothy of the New Testament there are several specific references concerning doctrine/teachings. A study of these and others from the Gospels, Acts, and other epistles, identifies the nature of Doctrine. Two elements are identified, Instructing or teaching the truth, and Substance or sound words. These two elements can not be separated. Instructing or teaching involves the substance or content of what is taught (sound word).

(1 Timothy 4:6 NKJV)_ If you instruct the brethren in these things, you will be a good minister of Jesus Christ, nourished in the words of faith and of the good doctrine which you have carefully followed.

(2 Timothy 1:13 NKJV) [13] Hold fast the pattern of sound words which you have heard from me, in faith and love which are in Christ Jesus.

(Titus 1:9 NKJV) [9] holding fast the faithful word as he has been taught, that he may be able, by sound doctrine, both to exhort and convict those who contradict.

> TEXT MESSAGE → The believer must be instructed and taught the Word of God which is the substance of doctrine.

Nature of True Doctrine- Must be Sound

Sound Doctrine is free from defect, without error and is derived from the Word of God. It alone is to be used for instruction and teaching of the Church. It is essential for the spiritual health and development of the believer but most of all it will lead one in the proper path to salvation and a relationship back to God. It will also root and ground the individual into the truths giving them the ability to withstand all things in Christ.

(2 Timothy 4:2-3 NKJV) ² Preach the word! Be ready in season *and* out of season. Convince, rebuke, exhort, with all longsuffering and teaching. ³ For the time will come when they will not endure sound doctrine, but according to their own desires, *because* they have itching ears, they will heap up for themselves teachers;

(1 Timothy 4:6-7 NKJV) ⁶ If you instruct the brethren in these things, you will be a good minister of Jesus Christ, nourished in the words of faith and of the good doctrine which you have carefully followed. ⁷ But reject profane and old wives' fables, and exercise yourself toward godliness.

(Galatians 1:6-9 NKJV) ⁶ I marvel that you are turning away so soon from Him who called you in the grace of Christ, to a different gospel, ⁷ which is not another; but there are some who trouble you and want to pervert the gospel of Christ. ⁸ But even if we, or an angel from heaven, preach any other gospel to you than what we have preached to you, let him be accursed. ⁹ As we have said before, so now I say again, if anyone preaches any other gospel to you than what you have received, let him be accursed.

Must be Pure

Religious beliefs outside of Christianity, such as those found in cults, and philosophies of mankind believe, teach and practice false doctrines. Job said, "My doctrine is pure". It is free from defilement or pollution. It is without fault, and is sinless.

(Job 11:4 NKJV) For you have said, 'My doctrine *is* pure, And I am clean in your eyes.'

Must be Scriptural

All Scripture is the inspired Word of God. This includes both the Old and New Testament of the Holy Bible. It is what God wants mankind to use for instruction, for rebuking, for correcting, and training in righteousness and truth. There is no other source. No best seller book can replace what the Scriptures are intended to do. Everything must be tested by the infallible Word of God. Scripture must be interpreted by proper principles, including the guidance of the Holy Spirit, in order to arrive at proper exposition.

(2 Timothy 3:14-17 NKJV) ¹⁴ But you must continue in the things which you have learned and been assured of, knowing from whom you have learned *them,* ¹⁵ and that from childhood you have known the Holy Scriptures, which are able to make you wise for salvation through faith which is in Christ Jesus. ¹⁶ All Scripture *is* given by inspiration of God, and *is* profitable for doctrine, for reproof, for correction, for instruction in righteousness, ¹⁷ that the man of God may be complete, thoroughly equipped for every good work.

Must be Obeyed/Obedience

Doctrine in itself is only useful if put to work and becomes action in a persons life. Knowing the truth and doing nothing with it renders it useless. We must be obedient to what we are taught from God's doctrine and so once learned we are obligated to make it come to life in our own acts of living. Knowing about love, holiness, righteousness, unity of the body of Christ, the Holy Spirit, the plan of salvation and not exemplifying these truths in life leaves one with a lifeless theory until they actually practice it, becoming a doer of the Word of God. There is no affect on mankind's life unless they obey and put into action/practice the doctrine of God. Lead and teach by example and your fruits will bear witness of your heart whether they be good or spoiled.

(Romans 6:17 NKJV) [17] But God be thanked that *though* you were slaves of sin, yet you obeyed from the heart that form of doctrine to which you were delivered.

(John 7:16-17 NKJV) [16] Jesus answered them and said, "My doctrine is not Mine, but His who sent Me. [17] If anyone wants to do His will, he shall know concerning the doctrine, whether it is from God or *whether* I speak on My own *authority.*

(2 Timothy 3:10-17 NKJV) [10] But you have carefully followed my doctrine, manner of life, purpose, faith, longsuffering, love, perseverance, [11] persecutions, afflictions, which happened to me at Antioch, at Iconium, at Lystra--what persecutions I endured. And out of *them* all the Lord delivered me. [12] Yes, and all who desire to live godly in Christ Jesus will suffer persecution. [13] But evil men and impostors will grow worse and worse, deceiving and being deceived. [14] But you must continue in the things which you have learned and been assured of, knowing from whom you have learned *them,* [15] and that from childhood you have known the Holy Scriptures, which are able to make you wise for salvation through faith which is in Christ Jesus. [16] All Scripture *is* given by inspiration of God, and *is* profitable for doctrine, for reproof, for correction, for instruction in righteousness, [17] that the man of God may be complete, thoroughly equipped for every good work.

Determines Character

Following false doctrine will bring about a corruption of character and form rebellion in attitudes and decision making. Our beliefs will undoubtedly form our behavior and what we become. What we believe affects our being and our being affects our doing. If we follow sound doctrine it will bring about a development of the Divine nature and the character of Christ within us. Paul warns that people will turn from the truth, affecting their being and do things that are not related to God's truth, which affects their doings.

(1 Timothy 4:1-3 NKJV) [1] Now the Spirit expressly says that in latter times some will depart from the faith, giving heed to deceiving spirits and doctrines of demons, [2] speaking lies in hypocrisy, having their own conscience seared with a hot iron, [3] forbidding to marry, *and commanding* to abstain from foods which God created to be received with thanksgiving by those who believe and know the truth.

Affects Fellowship

Doctrine will be a factor in good fellowship. If both individuals are sharing the same faith, beliefs and understanding of doctrine they will most likely have fewer conflicts in activities. But if one is claiming something that they are not either faithful in or actually believe in, it will be noticed by the other. This can become a determining factor in the kind and extent of fellowship experienced. A person living a life by the Word of God will soon collide with others who are not, and one can not exist in both, for they will either compromise their faith or be constantly at odds within the fellowship. One must make a choice to follow the Lord or the world.

Apostle John wrote to the believers telling them not to receive any who came to their house if they did not bring the doctrine of the Father and Son (2 John 9-10) - He said not to bid them God-speed, lest they become partakers of their evil teaching and deeds. John taught that believers should not have fellowship with those who spread false doctrine.
However, we must keep in mind what type of doctrinal issues he is telling us to break fellowship over. He is not giving us permission to stop fellowship over minor areas of doctrine – rather only when the most foundational truths are at stake – such as the person of Christ and salvation through Jesus Christ.

(2 John 1:9-11 NKJV) [9] Whoever transgresses and does not abide in the doctrine of Christ does not have God. He who abides in the doctrine of Christ has both the Father and the Son. [10] If anyone comes to you and does not bring this doctrine, do not receive him into your house nor greet him; [11] for he who greets him shares in his evil deeds.

(1 John 1:1-7 NKJV) [1] That which was from the beginning, which we have heard, which we have seen with our eyes, which we have looked upon, and our hands have handled, concerning the Word of life-- [2] the life was manifested, and we have seen, and bear witness, and declare to you that eternal life which was with the Father and was manifested to us-- [3] that which we have seen and heard we declare to you, that you also may have fellowship with us; and truly our fellowship *is* with the Father and with His Son Jesus Christ. [4] And these things we write to you that your joy may be full. [5] This is the message which we have heard from Him and declare to you, that God is light and in Him is no darkness at all. [6] If we say that we have fellowship with Him, and walk in darkness, we lie and do not practice the truth. [7] But if we walk in the light as He is in the light, we have fellowship with one another, and the blood of Jesus Christ His Son cleanses us from all sin. [42] And they continued steadfastly in the apostles' doctrine and fellowship, in the breaking of bread, and in prayers.

(Acts 2:42 NKJV) [42] And they continued steadfastly in the apostles' doctrine and fellowship, in the breaking of bread, and in prayers.

> TEXT MESSAGE →Fellowship is the condition of being together or sharing similar interests and friendships. Pertaining to a believer in Jesus Christ these fellowships should be centered on the Doctrines of the Bible.

Determines Destiny

Our eternal destiny is affected by what and who we believe. It is a fruitless statement to say that it does not matter what a person believes, as long as they are sincere. This is exemplified in cults (false teachings/false Doctrine), inside and outside of Christian environments, who are sincere, but sincerely WRONG. Our eternal destiny is decided by what we believe and do concerning Jesus Christ. "What do you think about the Christ? Whose Son is He?" and ""What then shall I do with Jesus who is called Christ?" How you answer these questions and most of all how you react to them is your destiny.

(Matthew 22:42 NKJV) ⁴² saying, "What do you think about the Christ? Whose Son is He?" They said to Him, "*The Son* of David."

(Matthew 27:22 NKJV) ²² Pilate said to them, "What then shall I do with Jesus who is called Christ?" *They* all said to him, "Let Him be crucified!"

(2 Peter 3:14-17 NKJV) ¹⁴ Therefore, beloved, looking forward to these things, be diligent to be found by Him in peace, without spot and blameless; ¹⁵ and consider *that* the longsuffering of our Lord *is* salvation--as also our beloved brother Paul, according to the wisdom given to him, has written to you, ¹⁶ as also in all his epistles, speaking in them of these things, in which are some things hard to understand, which untaught and unstable *people* twist to their own destruction, as *they do* also the rest of the Scriptures. ¹⁷ You therefore, beloved, since you know *this* beforehand, beware lest you also fall from your own steadfastness, being led away with the error of the wicked;

Doctrine and Love

If theologically and scripturally we are correct in our doctrine but we do not have LOVE we are nothing (1 Corinthians 13:1-6). This is not to say that prophecy, faith, knowledge, or spiritual gifts are nothing. What is meant is that I am nothing without LOVE. God's nature is love and all of His doctrine is based on it. So should it be with the people of God. If Gods people, who often uphold their own doctrines, would constantly remember that **LOVE is the Greatest Doctrine** in the Bible, then all other doctrine would take their appropriate place in relation to it. One's Love of the Doctrine and the Love of the Doctrine (within it) will produce Gods Love.

(1 Corinthians 13:1-6 NKJV) ¹ Though I speak with the tongues of men and of angels, but have not love, I have become sounding brass or a clanging cymbal. ² And though I have *the gift of* prophecy, and understand all mysteries and all knowledge, and though I have all faith, so that I could remove mountains, but have not love, I am nothing. ³ And though I bestow all my goods to feed *the poor,* and though I give my body to be burned, but have not love, it profits me nothing. ⁴ Love suffers long *and* is kind; love does not envy; love does not parade itself, is not puffed up; ⁵ does not behave rudely, does not seek its own, is not provoked, thinks no evil; ⁶ does not rejoice in iniquity, but rejoices in the truth; ⁷ bears all things, believes all things, hopes all things, endures all things.

(1 John 4:16 HCSB) **16** And we have come to know and to believe the love that God has for us. God is love, and the one who remains in love remains in God, and God remains in him.

Conclusion - Progress of Doctrine

God progressively revealed Truth in Scripture from the Old Testament to the New Testament. This may suggest the way in which the believer in the faith should handle the doctrines of Scripture by bringing together all that the Bible/Scripture has to say on the subject to establish the doctrine within it. God did not give the full revelation of Him immediately but precept upon precept, line upon line, here a little, there a little. This pattern is the pattern we should take in our study/learning of the doctrines, a piece at a time until we have a solid foundation that will support our faith. One building block at a time.

The period between Genesis and the book of Deuteronomy written by Moses covered approximately 2500 years. These writing are called the Pentateuch and were inspired by God and given to Moses. Before this the patriarchs spoke and kept within their hearts the promises of redemption and the Gospel story was declared in the heavens. (Genesis 1:14-19; Psalm 19:1-6)

Under the leadership of Joshua, Judges, Samuel and the Kings of Israel/Judah the writings of the prophetic and historical books, Joshua through Malachi were written. It took approximately 1100 years to record the Old Testament. The whole doctrine of God was not ever received by just one patriarch, prophet, priest, king or saint. It was given in a progressive manner as God saw fit to do.

Between the Old Testament and the New Testament there was a period of approximately 400+ years. This period of silence set up the coming of Jesus Christ. The timing needed to be perfect and in line with the will of God. Mankind and the universe were now ready to receive their savior.

Within 100 years the New Testament was recorded in 27 Books. God inspired men to write His words. It must be noted that all of the Books make up one completed revelation of God. They are all to be considered equal in that each builds upon and within each other. They are not to be considered old in the way of useless or done, but they compliment each other and unite the Word of God as a single message, a living message to be spoken of, taught, given out, and acted upon. Each book is part of the whole. The New Testament period was given the Living Word, Jesus Christ, and through the Apostles it was recorded.
(John 1:1-3: 14-18; Acts 2:42; Ephesians 3:1)

(Hebrews 1:1-2 NKJV) ¹ God, who at various times and in various ways spoke in time past to the fathers by the prophets, ² has in these last days spoken to us by *His* Son, whom He has appointed heir of all things, through whom also He made the worlds;

(Ephesians 3:1-5 NKJV) [1] For this reason I, Paul, the prisoner of Christ Jesus for you Gentiles-- [2] if indeed you have heard of the dispensation of the grace of God which was given to me for you, [3] how that by revelation He made known to me the mystery (as I have briefly written already, [4] by which, when you read, you may understand my knowledge in the mystery of Christ), [5] which in other ages was not made known to the sons of men, as it has now been revealed by the Spirit to His holy apostles and prophets:

NOTE: The word doctrine must be understood because of the depth of its meaning. The word Doctrine is used in some modern translations as teaching(s). So in this document and documents linked to this study the following will pertain; → "Doctrine" will refer to, the Truth's of God's Word - that are to be taught understood and applied.

TEXT MESSAGE → All Doctrine must arise out of and be founded firmly upon the only absolute authority in man's possession, the inspired and infallible 'Word of God'.

Begin With Prayer

The Biblical Teaching/Doctrine of Revelation

Biblical Building Block # 2

(John 14:9-11 HCSB)

⁹ Jesus said to him, "Have I been among you all this time without your knowing Me, Philip? The one who has seen Me has seen the Father. How can you say, 'Show us the Father'? ¹⁰ Don't you believe that I am in the Father and the Father is in Me? The words I speak to you I do not speak on My own. The Father who lives in Me does His works. ¹¹ Believe Me that I am in the Father and the Father is in Me. Otherwise, believe because of the works themselves.

God so loves His creation that He became flesh so that mankind could have a personal relationship with God, which was Gods intent all along for mankind. Knowledge of God was seen in all that was created upon the earth and in the heavens but mankind could not know God from only the physical creations of God. A more intimate and personal relationship would be needed for God to reveal Himself to mankind and the Bible is a story that guides and teaches us about a personal God, one who Loves us enough to experience death, to provide a plan of salvation for all of mankind.

1. Define Biblical Revelation.

2. How can mankind understand God and His will?

3. List several ways that the revelation of God has been given to mankind.

4. Is mankind accountable for knowing about God?

5. What one historical event shows God's revelation to mankind?

6. Why is the revelation of God necessary?

7. What is the importance of knowing God's revelation to a Believer?

8. What is the importance of knowing God's revelation to a non-believer?

9. Explain general revelation.

10. Define special revelation.

The Definition of Revelation

In the New Testament the Greek word *Apokalupsis* is defined as an uncovering or to uncover or unveil; an act of revealing or making someone or something known. It best represents what is meant by "Revelation"' in Scriptures. Revelation is also defined as a manifestation of divine will or truth. This is God's own self-disclosure or manifesting of Himself and things concerning Him. Revelation is necessary for people to know God. Unless God gives revelation mankind will not know the truths about God.

There are two factors to be considered, the <u>revealer</u> (God), who manifest Himself through the spoken word, writings, visions, miracles, nature/universe, history and through Jesus Christ in person. The 2nd factor to be considered is the <u>receiver</u> (Mankind). The Scriptures/Holy Bible, being a product of this revelation of God.

In Theology revelation refers to God unveiling Himself to mankind, and communicating Truth to the mind and heart of mankind, which they could not discover in any other way. ***Natural reasoning of man alone can not discover or be aware of the Truth of God, only God can give it.***

(Ephesians 1:17-19 NKJV) ¹⁷ that the God of our Lord Jesus Christ, the Father of glory, may give to you the spirit of wisdom and revelation in the knowledge of Him, ¹⁸ the eyes of your understanding being enlightened; that you may know what is the hope of His calling, what are the riches of the glory of His inheritance in the saints, ¹⁹ and what *is* the exceeding greatness of His power toward us who believe, according to the working of His mighty power

(Galatians 1:12 NKJV) ¹² For I neither received it from man, nor was I taught *it, but it came* through the revelation of Jesus Christ.

(1 Samuel 3:21 KJV) ²¹ And the LORD appeared again in Shiloh: for the LORD revealed himself to Samuel in Shiloh by the word of the LORD.

Revelation is an ACT of God

Revelation is God's knowledge and truths given to mankind about God and coming from God. This is called the act of revelation which was forever settled in heaven before it was even recorded on earth. Although Scripture was written by mankind God was the actual author using the Holy Spirit to guide mankind to write the revelation of God, the Holy Bible.

(Psalms 119:89 KJV) ⁸⁹ For ever, O LORD, thy word is settled in heaven.

Necessity of Revelation

God created mankind in the image of His likeness and they have certain abilities or capacities which enables them to receive "revelation" from God. These abilities or capacities have been created in mankind's body, soul, and spirit. Mankind possesses a will, intelligence, conscience and a spirit which can know and worship God and have a relationship with Him. This is not so with animals which mankind has been given rule over. Because of these abilities/capacities mankind has a need for the truths and if not filled with the truth then they will be filled with untruths, imaginations, and philosophies of mankind that are useless/worthless and corrupted thoughts.

Because of mankind's sin their God given abilities/capabilities, were weakened. They were unable to recognize God's revelation. Adam and Eve's action of sin caused the fall of mankind into a state of **spiritual ignorance and a separation from God**. Due to this fall mankind became totally corrupt in spirit, soul, and body. Their mind, reasoning and understanding became evil and darkened. They were separated and alienated from God becoming an enemy of God in their minds by wicked works.

That mankind is a created but fallen being indicates the need of revelation from God. If God does not take the initiative in revealing Himself to mankind, it is virtually impossible for mankind through their own initiative to discover or know God.

(Ephesians 4:17-18 NKJV) [17] This I say, therefore, and testify in the Lord, that you should no longer walk as the rest of the Gentiles walk, in the futility of their mind, [18] having their understanding darkened, being alienated from the life of God, because of the ignorance that is in them, because of the blindness of their heart;

(Colossians 1:21 NKJV) [21] And you, who once were alienated and enemies in your mind by wicked works, yet now He has reconciled

Paul declared that the world with all its wisdom could not know God.

(1 Corinthians 1:21 NKJV) [21] For since, in the wisdom of God, the world through wisdom did not know God, it pleased God through the foolishness of the message preached to save those who believe.

(1 Corinthians 2:11-16 NKJV) [11] For what man knows the things of a man except the spirit of the man which is in him? Even so no one knows the things of God except the Spirit of God. [12] Now we have received, not the spirit of the world, but the Spirit who is from God, that we might know the things that have been freely given to us by God. [13] These things we also speak, not in words which man's wisdom teaches but which the Holy Spirit teaches, comparing spiritual things with spiritual. [14] But the natural man does not receive the things of the Spirit of God, for they are foolishness to him; nor can he know *them,* because they are spiritually discerned. [15] But he who is spiritual judges all things, yet he himself is *rightly*

judged by no one. [16] For *"who has known the mind of the LORD that he may instruct Him?"* But we have the mind of Christ.

Revelations Importance

For a believer in Jesus Christ to live a life pleasing to God, he or she must understand His revelation which is the Scriptures/Holy Bible and be rooted and grounded in the teaching/doctrine that it provides. It should be used as a measuring tool against all other writings, philosophies, beliefs, teachings and oracles/sermons of mankind. The one and only way of salvation is clearly stated within it and there is no other way of salvation for mankind. The Scriptures are also for instruction in righteousness, reproof and correction so that all believers can be prepared to do what God would want them to do in everyday living. Success in this life depends on the revelation of God. This success is not worldly success, but spiritual in nature, pleasing God.

(2 Timothy 3:16-17 NKJV) [16] All Scripture *is* given by inspiration of God, and *is* profitable for doctrine, for reproof, for correction, for instruction in righteousness, [17] that the man of God may be complete, thoroughly equipped for every good work.

(1 Corinthians 15:3-4 NKJV) [3] For I delivered to you first of all that which I also received: that Christ died for our sins according to the Scriptures, [4] and that He was buried, and that He rose again the third day according to the Scriptures,

(Joshua 1:8 KJV) **8** This book of the law shall not depart out of thy mouth; but thou shalt meditate therein day and night, that thou mayest observe to do according to all that is written therein: for then thou shalt make thy way prosperous, and then thou shalt have good success.

Progressive Revelation

Progressive Revelation denotes something moving in steps, continuing steadily by increments. God has revealed His revelation in a steady pattern within the Scriptures and time. Line upon line and precept upon precept was given to mankind. The Scriptures/Bible provides this progressive action within it. In various times and in various ways God spoke to mankind through prophets and then through Jesus Christ the living Word. It should be noted that this does NOT mean that it is being changed with each additional line or precept, but that it is moving or has moved to fullness in the Living Word, Jesus Christ.

(Isaiah 28:9-13 KJV) **9** Whom shall he teach knowledge? and whom shall he make to understand doctrine? *them that are* weaned from the milk, *and* drawn from the breasts. **10** For precept *must be* upon precept, precept upon precept; line upon line, line upon line; here a little, *and* there a little: **11** For with stammering lips and another tongue will he speak to this people. **12** To whom he said, This *is* the rest *wherewith* ye may cause the weary to rest; and this *is* the refreshing: yet they would not hear. **13** But the word of the LORD was unto them precept upon precept, precept upon precept; line upon line, line upon line; here a little, *and* there a little; that they might go, and fall backward, and be broken, and snared, and taken.

(Hebrews 1:1-2 NKJV) [1] God, who at various times and in various ways spoke in time past to the fathers by the prophets, [2] has in these last days spoken to us by *His* Son, whom He has appointed heir of all things, through whom also He made the worlds;

General Revelation of God in Nature

Through General Revelation God revealed Himself to mankind in nature, conscience and history. Creation in itself suggests that there is a creator and intelligence behind the entire splendor of creation. The engineering and design of order, law, control, the magnificence of nature, the world and the universe all declare intelligence greater than mankind. It is God who is the architect, designer, engineer, and the One who holds it all together in harmony and order. This in itself declares a creator and that creator is God, Who is being revealed in the heavens and upon the earth.

(Genesis 1:1 KJV) [1] In the beginning God created the heaven and the earth.

(Psalm 19:1 HCSB) **1** The heavens declare the glory of God, and the sky proclaims the work of His hands.

(Romans 10:17-18 NKJV) [17] So then faith *comes* by hearing, and hearing by the word of God. [18] But I say, have they not heard? Yes indeed: *"Their sound has gone out to all the earth, And their words to the ends of the world."*

Since the creation of the world God has been visible throughout the earth. We see Him in the rain which causes the earth to be fruitful. We also see Him maintaining the balance of all created things on earth and in the heavens. It can be said that nature is God's book by creation, and it has a language of its own which may be heard in every nation. All mankind is held accountable for their knowledge of the revelation of God in nature and are without excuse.

(Romans 1:19-20 NKJV) [19] because what may be known of God is manifest in them, for God has shown *it* to them. [20] For since the creation of the world His invisible *attributes* are clearly seen, being understood by the things that are made, *even* His eternal power and Godhead, so that they are without excuse,

(Acts 14:15-17 NKJV) [15] and saying, "Men, why are you doing these things? We also are men with the same nature as you, and preach to you that you should turn from these useless things to the living God, who made the heaven, the earth, the sea, and all things that are in them, [16] who in bygone generations allowed all nations to walk in their own ways. [17] Nevertheless He did not leave Himself without witness, in that He did good, gave us rain from heaven and fruitful seasons, filling our hearts with food and gladness."

However this revelation through nature has limitations and is inadequate on its own because God cannot personally be known through it. Creation reveals the existence of God but can not bring mankind into contact with Him. Nature reveals His power but does not reveal His person. Being insufficient for a personal knowledge of God, nature was meant to direct mankind towards further revelation of Him. It was designed to arouse in mankind a desire to seek beyond it for the one who made it. They were to look at creation and then beyond for their creator.

Unfortunately, the majority of mankind has chosen not to do so. They have turned to the created things of this world, including the works of their own hands and have exalted them to be gods over themselves.

Paul referred to those "who changed the Truth of God into a lie" worshiping and serving the created more than the creator. Mankind corrupted the Truth of God making their own god/s from their own imaginations and with their hands crafting images to worship.

(Romans 1:21-23 NKJV) [21] because, although they knew God, they did not glorify *Him* as God, nor were thankful, but became futile in their thoughts, and their foolish hearts were darkened. [22] Professing to be wise, they became fools, [23] and changed the glory of the incorruptible God into an image made like corruptible man--and birds and four-footed animals and creeping things.

(Romans 1:25 NKJV) [25] who exchanged the truth of God for the lie, and worshiped and served the creature rather than the Creator, who is blessed forever. Amen.

General Revelation of God in Conscience

Conscience is defined as inner thought, the ability of recognizing the distinction between what is right and wrong in regard to one's conduct, coupled with a sense that one should act accordingly, and a knowing within oneself of right conduct.

That mankind has the ability of conscience is a universally accepted fact. Mankind is a mortal creature, capable of knowing right from wrong. However the question is, where did this moral sense come from? Some may suggest that conscience is socially acquired meaning, that it is received from others by their instruction and example. *The error here is* in stating that mankind's moral sense is received from people. It is God who equipped mankind with a conscience and God's laws and order will naturally awaken its senses. Making mankind accountable and without excuse for their actions in this life.

According to the Apostle Paul the Gentiles, though never taught the law, had the law written in their hearts, their conscience, and their thoughts, bearing witness to accuse or excuse them.

(Romans 2:14-15 NKJV) [14] for when Gentiles, who do not have the law, by nature do the things in the law, these, although not having the law, are a law to themselves, [15] who show the work of the law written in their hearts, their conscience also bearing witness, and between themselves *their* thoughts accusing or else excusing *them*)

(1 Corinthians 8:7-10 NKJV) ⁷ However, *there is* not in everyone that knowledge; for some, with consciousness of the idol, until now eat *it* as a thing offered to an idol; and their conscience, being weak, is defiled. ⁸ But food does not commend us to God; for neither if we eat are we the better, nor if we do not eat are we the worse. ⁹ But beware lest somehow this liberty of yours become a stumbling block to those who are weak. ¹⁰ For if anyone sees you who have knowledge eating in an idol's temple, will not the conscience of him who is weak be emboldened to eat those things offered to idols?

(1 Timothy 4:2 NKJV) ² speaking lies in hypocrisy, having their own conscience seared with a hot iron,

(Titus 1:15 NKJV) ¹⁵ To the pure all things are pure, but to those who are defiled and unbelieving nothing is pure; but even their mind and conscience are defiled.

General Revelation of God in History

The history of the world is a revelation of God. Examining the rise and fall of nations indicates that somewhere behind the scenes is a sovereign hand, guiding, governing, controlling, rising up and casting down the rulers of these nations and directing their future or end. The empire of Rome is a great example. It was in a position of building roads and linking cultures because of its power in the world at the time. This empire was used by God to spread the Gospel of Jesus Christ. The timing was perfect.

(Deuteronomy 32:8 KJV) "When the most high divided to the nations their inheritance, when he separated the sons of Adam, he set the bounds of the people according to the number of the children of Israel."

(Romans 13:1 NKJV) ¹ Let every soul be subject to the governing authorities. For there is no authority except from God, and the authorities that exist are appointed by God.

Examples of God in mankind's history	
In Egypt	Exodus 9-12; Romans 9:17; Jeremiah 46:14-26 Ezekiel 29:30
God caused the Assyrian Empire to fall.	Isaiah 10:12-19; Ezekiel 31; Nahum 3:1-7
God judged Babylonian kingdom according to His prophets' word.	Daniel 1-5; Jeremiah 50-51; Isaiah 47-48; 45: 1-5
Medo-Persian Empire came under the judgment of God	Isaiah 44:24-45; 1-7; Daniel 2; Daniel 7
Grecian Empire collapsed	Daniel 8:1-25; 11: 1-35

Special Revelation

Special Revelation refers to these acts of God where He reveals Himself and His Will to specific people/persons. Examples would be Abraham, Moses, Jacob, Daniel, and the Apostles. It can also refer to the use of miracles to demonstrate His presence and power or show mercy and love. Prophecies are another type of Special revelation that God used. Jesus Christ is the Living Word, the total sum of revelation given to mankind.

Special Revelation in Miracles

A miracle is an event that is unexplainable by the laws of nature and so is held to be a supernatural event of God. God's miracles are legitimate but there are also illegitimate or counterfeit miracles by Satan. In the course of the world's history God has revealed Himself, His power and His love for mankind in miracles. The Scriptures identify and are a record of many miracles from God ranging from creation to the final Book of the Bible, Revelation with the greatest miracle being the Resurrection of Jesus Christ.

The purpose of God's legitimate miracles is to bless and direct mankind to God. Miracles, both ancient and modern are specific revelations of God's power and motivation in dealing with mankind. These miracles are used by God for a purpose that is in line with His nature and that is Love. He uses them to reach fallen mankind not to impress but to prove a point, which is, that God is in control, not mankind and we must seek God for our salvation and eternal existence.

Examples of Miracles	
The Plagues in Egypt.	Exodus 4-12
Miracles of the magicians were satanic counterfeits.	Exodus 7:12,22
Opening of the Red Sea and Jordon.	Exodus 14-15; Joshua 4-5
Manna from heaven and water from the rock.	Exodus 16-17; I Corinthians 10:1-6
Acts records numerous miracles; spiritual, physically, and materially in the ministry of Christ and His Apostles.	Matthew 8; Acts 3-4
The anti-Christ will perform miracles to deceive the people of the earth.	Matthew 24:24; 2 Timothy 2:9; Revelations 13:13; Acts 8:9-11

Special Revelation of God in Prophecy

Preaching and predictions are types of prophecy used by God. Both are inspired by God and reveal the Word of God. The fulfillment of prophecy is a revelation of God and His Knowledge.
Prophecies played a role in the prediction/foretelling of nations and the birth of Jesus.

Fall of nations were foretold	
Babylon	Jeremiah 50:5; Isaiah 47-48
Egypt	Ezekiel 30-31
Assyria	Ezekiel 31
Grecian Empire	Daniel 8

Coming of Christ was foretold (some examples)	
There were about 300 prophecies to be fulfilled within the short life time of Christ. These prophecies had been foretold over a 1000 year time span by different people. (all were fulfilled)	
Be the seed of a woman	Genesis 3:15; Isaiah 7:14; Matthew 1: 20-23
Be the seed of Abraham	Genesis 12: 1-3; Matthew 1:1
To be of the Tribe of Judah	Genesis 49:10; Hebrews 7:14
To be born in Bethlehem	Micah 5:2; Matthew 2:6
Anointed by the Spirit	Isaiah 61:1-2; Luke 4:18-20
To minister life and healing	Isaiah 35; Matthew 8
To be sold for 30 pieces of silver	Zachariah 11:12-13; Matthew 26:15
Ride into Jerusalem upon an ass	Zachariah 9:9; Matthew 21:4-5
Suffer crucifixion	Psalms 22; Isaiah 53; Matthew 27
Christ was to rise from the dead	Psalms 16; Psalms 110; Matthew 22:43-45

Special Revelation of God in Christ

The special revelations of God in both miracles and prophesy are insufficient in that they only reveal certain of His attributes but not His entire personhood. With all this, there still existed the need for a more personal revelation of God. *This need God has met in Jesus Christ.*

Jesus Christ is the fulfilling of God's revelation that includes His will, His nature, His person and His character. He is in human form, the complete expression of God's revelation to mankind. He is the Living Word of God.

(John 14:9-11 NKJV) [9] Jesus said to him, "Have I been with you so long, and yet you have not known Me, Philip? He who has seen Me has seen the Father; so how can you say, 'Show us the Father'? [10] Do you not believe that I am in the Father, and the Father in Me? The words that I speak to you I do not speak on My own *authority;* but the Father who dwells in Me does the works. [11] Believe Me that I *am* in the Father and the Father in Me, or else believe Me for the sake of the works themselves.

Revelation of God in Scripture

The revelation of God in Scripture is the inspired written Word. The Word was made flesh-Jesus Christ, and He is the Living Word, and a living revelation of God. This revelation is contained in the 66 books of the Bible. The Scriptures were inspired by the Holy Spirit and in them we have an infallible revelation of the truth, nature, being and will of God. There is no other source that one should use and all other communication pertaining to God should always be tested against the Scriptures.

(John 1:14 NKJV) [14] And the Word became flesh and dwelt among us, and we beheld His glory, the glory as of the only begotten of the Father, full of grace and truth.

Revelation of God in Personal Experience

God has revealed Himself through a series of revelations through the ages and His intent was for mankind to know Him. Mankind, who has been made in the image of God, has been given intellectual, mental and spiritual capacity to receive revelation from their creator. However, the intellectual and spiritual parts of mankind's being have to come under the illuminating influence of the Holy Spirit in order to be able to receive and fully understand the revelation of God.

Mankind must seek to understand God's revelation to gain a personal relationship with God. God has unveiled the knowledge of Himself and made it available to all mankind. So one must take the initiative now to know and have a personal relationship with God. God has already taken the first initiative by giving His Revelation to mankind.

Old Testament examples of people who have known God in a personal way	
Enoch walked with God.	Genesis 5:21-24
Noah walked with God.	Genesis 6:9-13
God revealed Himself to Abraham.	Genesis 12:1-3
Isaac knew God.	Genesis 26:24
God revealed Himself to Moses in the burning	Exodus 3:1-15

bush.	
Joshua met the Lord as the captain of the host.	Joshua 1:1; 5:13-15
The Lord revealed Himself to Samuel in a vision.	1 Samuel 3:2-4
New Testament examples of people who have known God in a personal way	
Apostles receive a personal experience of God in Christ.	Matthew 10:10
Jesus is the revelation of God to man personally.	Matthew 11:27; 16: 17-18
Paul had a personal revelation of Jesus Christ.	Acts 9:4-6; 18:9
The beloved Apostle John knew Jesus experientially.	John 13:23; 1 John 4: 7-11; Revelation 1: 1-12

(1 Corinthians 2:12-13 NKJV) [12] Now we have received, not the spirit of the world, but the Spirit who is from God, that we might know the things that have been freely given to us by God. [13] These things we also speak, not in words which man's wisdom teaches but which the Holy Spirit teaches, comparing spiritual things with spiritual

The disciples understanding was opened to allow them to comprehend the Scriptures. So God through the Holy Spirit can and will open the understanding to all who believe in Jesus Christ as their Savior.

(Luke 24:44-45 NKJV) [44] Then He said to them, "These *are* the words which I spoke to you while I was still with you, that all things must be fulfilled which were written in the Law of Moses and *the* Prophets and *the* Psalms concerning Me." [45] And He opened their understanding, that they might comprehend the Scriptures.

The transformation power of the Gospel today is alive and well. It is continually bringing lost souls to the saving grace of the Gospel of Jesus Christ, through the Word of God, powered by the Holy Spirit. Scripture is THE Revelation, the unveiling of the truths of God. They continue everyday to prove themselves true in the lives of people all over the world, every tongue, every race, every nation - and all will proclaim that **Jesus Christ is Lord**.

(John 20:22 NKJV) [22] And when He had said this, He breathed on *them,* and said to them, "Receive the Holy Spirit.

TEXT MESSAGE → Revelation is not given to mankind so that they can be lifted up above other people – It is to bring mankind to know God – and to assist others in their walk with God – Any person preaching/claiming new revelation of God and bringing glory to themselves is not truly being used by God.

Begin With Prayer

Biblical Teaching/Doctrine of Scripture

Biblical Building Block # 3

(John 14:23 HCSB)

23 *Jesus answered, "If anyone loves Me, he will keep My word. My Father will love him, and We will come to him and make Our home with him.*

Our Father in heaven loves us so much that He made a way for mankind to learn about Him by making His Word become flesh, Jesus Christ. The Word became flesh to bear witness of God and to make a way of salvation for all of mankind. God wants you and me to be a family with a real relationship of caring for one another, talking to one another, trusting one another, and loving one another. He has opened up His home to us if we just allow our hearts to believe in the resurrected Lord, Jesus Christ and ask Him into our heart. By opening your heart to God and believing and trusting Him, He will make His home with you.

1. Define the word Scriptures.

2. Describe "revelation" as it pertains to the Bible.

3. Explain why we teach that the Bible is inspired.

4. How are the Holy Spirit and "illumination" related?

5. Make a list of proofs that the Bible is God's Word.

6. How many books are in the Bible?

7. State the difference between the Old Testament and the New Testament?

8. Explain the meaning of "canonicity".

9. Why is the Apocrypha not considered part of the Bible?

Names and Titles of the Inspired Book

A number of names and titles refer to the Holy Bible. Some of them are the Bible or Holy Bible, Scriptures, Old and New Testaments, The Word of God and the Oracles of God. They are all one and the same. The Greek word *"biblios"* simply means book – from which our English word "Bible" is derived. Though the word "Bible" is not used in Scripture, the Greek work *"Biblios"* is used often. There are many books referred to as "Bibles" in the Scriptures.

Example of books being referred to as Bibles	
The Book of Moses	Mark 12:26
The Book of Isaiah	Luke 3:4; 4:17-18
The Book of Psalms	Luke 20:42; Acts1:20
The Book of Prophets	Acts 7:42
The Book of the Law	Galatians 3:10
The volume of the book	Hebrews 10:7
The blood sprinkled Book	Hebrews 9:19
The book to the 7 Churches	Revelations 1:11
The little Book	Revelation 10:5-10; 5:1-10; and 22:7,9-10,18

The Bible is the Divine library, consisting of 66 separate yet related books with 2 divisions, the Old Testament which has 39 books and the New Testament, which contains 27 books.

The Bible is the only authoritative written revelation of God.

TEXT MESSAGE → Remember revelation is from God. It is God unveiling Himself, and communicating Truth to the mind and heart of mankind which they could not discover in any other way. *It is imparted Truth which could not be discovered by natural reasoning alone.*

NOTE → There are false Bibles/Books such as those used by the Mormons and Jehovah Witnesses stating that they are Christian doctrine, but teach false doctrine. All of these new revelation claims came well after the last written book of the Bible, the book of Revelation. The Mormons claimed new revelation between 1830 AD – 1835 AD and seven new writings of the Jehovah Witnesses were claimed between 1886 AD-1917 AD.

The Word of God

God inspired His Word to be written by men, and although the Bible was written by men it must be recognized that their minds, hearts and the spirit within them was directed by God.

The term "the Word of God" as pertaining to the Scriptures is stated or alluded to about 2000 time in the Bible. It is the Living Word, Jesus Christ, which is the Word made flesh.

The self revealing thought and will of God as set forth in the Gospel of John is often associated with the second person of the Trinity. The Living Word is revealed within the Written Word and the Written Word guides us to the Living Word. **They are one.**

Examples of how the Scriptures are spoken of or alluded to as "the Word of God".	
The Word of God	1 Thessalonians 2:13; Hebrews 4:12; Ephesians 6:17; Mark 7:13;Colossians 1:25; John 10:35; Luke 8;11
The Word of the Lord	Jeremiah 1:2,11; Ezekiel 1:3; Isaiah 1:10; Hosea 1:1; Acts 8:25; 2 Thessalonians 3:1; 1 Peter 1:23-25; Isaiah 40:8; 1 Thessalonians 1:8;4:15; Acts 13: 48
The Word of Christ	Colossians 3:16
The Word of Life	Philippians 2:16
The Word of Truth	Ephesians 1:13
The Word of Faith	Romans 10:8
The Word	James 1:21-23; John 1:1-3; Luke 4:4; 1 Timothy 4:5; Romans 10:17; Acts 4:31

The Scriptures

The Greek term *"graphai"* means writings. This term is used in the New Testament by Paul (Romans 1:2) as 'Holy Scriptures'. Jesus referred to the books of the Old Testament as "the Scriptures" (Matthew 21:42). So the Scriptures are the writings contained in the Bible. This word is used about 34 times in the Gospels and 28 times in the rest of the New Testament and found once in the Old Testament.

Some examples of the word "Scripture/s" as found in the Bible.	
The Scriptures of Truth	Daniel 10:21
The Scripture	Mark 12:10; 15:28: Luke 4:21: John 2:22; 7:38: 10:35;Romans 4:3; 2 Timothy 3:16; Galatians 3:8,22; 4:30; Acts 1:1,6; John 19:24,28,36,37; 20:9

The Scriptures	Matthew 21:42; 22:29; 26:54; 56; Mark 12:24; Luke 24:27; John 5:39; Romans 16: 26; Acts 13:27; 17:11; 2 Timothy 3:15; 1 Corinthians 15:3
The Holy Scriptures	2 Timothy 3:15; Romans 1:2

The Oracles of God

The expression "oracles of God" means speaking of God's Word. The word "oracle" in the Greek expression *logion* means "the speaking place. So, the Oracles of God as spoken concerning the Bible means – God's Words being spoken. Indeed the Bible is the Oracle of God, a place where He speaks. It is divine revelation being communicated. In Romans 3:2 it is referred to also as the law in the Old Testament. As we see in Romans 3:2, believers are told that they should speak and teach as the Oracles of God, speaking God's Word as they are given ability by God. (Romans 3:2 NKJV) *² Much in every way! Chiefly because to them were committed the oracles of God.*

(Hebrews 5:12 NKJV) ¹² For though by this time you ought to be teachers, you need *someone* to teach you again the first principles of the oracles of God; and you have come to need milk and not solid food

(1 Peter 4:11 NKJV) ¹¹ If anyone speaks, *let him speak* as the oracles of God. If anyone ministers, *let him do it* as with the ability which God supplies, that in all things God may be glorified through Jesus Christ, to whom belong the glory and the dominion forever and ever. Amen.

The Old and New Testaments

The word 'Testament' means "Covenant". The Bible is divided into 2 sections the covenant of the Law (the Old Testament) and the covenant of Grace (the New Testament). The Hebrew word *"berit"* means covenant which is an agreement or treaty. The Greek word for covenant is "diatheke" and has a meaning of "obligation of a promise", as the New Testament is a promise on the part of God.

While the Old Testament focuses on God's dealings with Israel under the Law Covenant given through Moses, the New Testament focuses on God's dealings with the world under the Grace Covenant given through Jesus Christ. Jeremiah 'under the Old Law Covenant', foretold the coming of the New Covenant (Grace).
(Jeremiah 31:31-34 KJV) ³¹ Behold, the days come, saith the LORD, that I will make a new covenant with the house of Israel, and with the house of Judah: ³² Not according to the covenant that I made with their fathers in the day *that* I took them by the hand to bring them out of the land of Egypt; which my covenant they brake, although I was an husband unto them, saith the LORD: ³³ But this *shall be* the covenant that I will make with the house of Israel; After those days, saith the LORD, I will put my law in their inward parts, and write it in their hearts; and will be their God, and they shall be my people. ³⁴ And they shall teach no

more every man his neighbour, and every man his brother, saying, Know the LORD: for they shall all know me, from the least of them unto the greatest of them, saith the LORD: for I will forgive their iniquity, and I will remember their sin no more.

The New Testament is mentioned as a better covenant in Hebrews. Note that the word promises is used to describe the New Covenant. The New Covenant makes the old obsolete, meaning that we are not to dismember the Old Testament but that the Old Testament should be considered fulfilled and is superseded by the New Testament.

(Hebrews 8:6-13 NKJV) [6] But now He has obtained a more excellent ministry, inasmuch as He is also Mediator of a better covenant, which was established on better promises. [7] For if that first *covenant* had been faultless, then no place would have been sought for a second. [8] Because finding fault with them, He says: *"Behold, the days are coming, says the LORD, when I will make a new covenant with the house of Israel and with the house of Judah-- [9] not according to the covenant that I made with their fathers in the day when I took them by the hand to lead them out of the land of Egypt; because they did not continue in My covenant, and I disregarded them, says the LORD. [10] For this is the covenant that I will make with the house of Israel after those days, says the LORD: I will put My laws in their mind and write them on their hearts; and I will be their God, and they shall be My people. [11] None of them shall teach his neighbor, and none his brother, saying, 'Know the LORD,' for all shall know Me, from the least of them to the greatest of them. [12] For I will be merciful to their unrighteousness, and their sins and their lawless deeds I will remember no more."* [13] In that He says, *"A new covenant,"* He has made the first obsolete. Now what is becoming obsolete and growing old is ready to vanish away.

Jesus, in establishing the New Covenant fulfilled the Old Covenant. He became the revelation of the Old Testament and unveiled the Truths of God as the Living Word establishing the New Testament as promised.

(Luke 22:20 NKJV) [20] Likewise He also *took* the cup after supper, saying, "This cup *is* the new covenant in My blood, which is shed for you.

(2 Corinthians 3:6-14 NKJV) who also made us sufficient as ministers of the new covenant, not of the letter but of the Spirit; for the letter kills, but the Spirit gives life. [7] But if the ministry of death, written *and* engraved on stones, was glorious, so that the children of Israel could not look steadily at the face of Moses because of the glory of his countenance, which *glory* was passing away, [8] how will the ministry of the Spirit not be more glorious? [9] For if the ministry of condemnation *had* glory, the ministry of righteousness exceeds much more in glory. [10] For even what was made glorious had no glory in this respect, because of the glory that excels. [11] For if what is passing away *was* glorious, what remains *is* much more glorious. [12] Therefore, since we have such hope, we use great boldness of speech-- [13] unlike Moses, *who* put a veil over his face so that the children of Israel could not look steadily at the end of what was passing away. [14] But their minds were blinded. For until this day the same veil remains unlifted in the reading of the Old Testament, because the *veil* is taken away in Christ.

(Matthew 26:26-28 KJV) **26** And as they were eating, Jesus took bread, and blessed *it*, and brake *it*, and gave *it* to the disciples, and said, Take, eat; this is my body. **27** And he took the cup, and gave thanks, and gave *it* to them, saying, Drink ye all of it; **28** For this is my blood of the new testament, which is shed for many for the remission of sins.

Symbols of the Inspired Book	
The Word is Like	*Verse*
A **Fire** - it burns cleanses and purges all that is contrary to its holy standard.	(Jeremiah 23:29)
A **Hammer** - It smashes and demolishes evil.	(Jeremiah 23:29)
A **Lamp** - It's an instrument of light and illumination in the darkness.	(Psalms 119:105)
A **Mirror** - It reveals to us what we are and what we can be in God.	(James 1:23)
Milk - It nourishes the young in Christ.	(1 Peter 2:2)
A **Rod** – As a measuring instrument it is the Divine Standard in all matters of faith, truth and practice.	(Revelations 11:1-2)
A **Seed** - It is germinating, life producing word, having the potential of eternal life.	(1 Peter 1:23; Luke 8:11; James 1:18)
A **Sword** - It is sharp and two-edged in its operation, separating the things of the flesh and the spirit.	(Hebrews 4:12)
Water – It is life giving, refreshing, and cleansing agent.	(Ephesians 5:26; John 15:3; 17:17; Psalms 119:5,9)
Gold - It is of priceless value. The Bible is an inexhaustible gold mine where one can dig out treasures.	(Psalms 19:10; Job 28:1; Proverbs 25:2)
Honey - It is sweet & refreshing to the taste.	(Psalm 19:10; Revelations 10:10)
An **Ox-goad**– It is an instrument which prods the oxen into fulfilling its duties.	(Ecclesiastes 12:11)
A **Nail** – It is fastened in a sure place. We can safely hang things on it.	(Ecclesiastes 12:110)
Bread – It is the staff of life, ever fresh and meant for daily consumption.	(Matthew 4:4; Deuteronomy 8:3; Psalms 119:103; Isaiah 55:10: Exodus 16)
A **Pearl** – It is a precious gem.	(Matthew 7:6)
An **Anchor** – It holds the believer in safety through every storm.	(Hebrews 6:18-19)
A **Star** – It guides the believer to Christ	(2 Peter 1:19; Revelations 2:28)

and salvation.	
Meat– It is strength-giving found food for the mature Believer.	(Hebrews 5:14)

The Definition of Inspiration

Inspiration concerning Scripture is the influence of God giving Scripture to mankind. All Scripture has been given by inspiration. The word itself means "breathing into". So naturally speaking, inspiration is breathing the truths of God into mankind's ability to understand spiritual truths. The writers of the Books of the Bible had been inspired (breathed into) and instructed by God to write His Words. It is God speaking through mankind to give His revelation to the world. Paul states;

(2 Timothy 3:16 KJV) "All Scripture is given by inspiration of God, and is profitable for doctrine, for reproof, for correction, for instruction: that the man of God may be perfect, thoroughly furnished unto all good works."

In this verse the Greek word "Theopneustos", translated 'inspiration' simply means 'God breathed'. God breathed into Adam the breath of life and he became a living soul.

(Genesis 2:7 NKJV) **7** And the LORD God formed man *of* the dust of the ground, and breathed into his nostrils the breath of life; and man became a living being.

(Job 32:8 KJV) **8** But *there is* a spirit in man: and the inspiration of the Almighty giveth them understanding.

Jesus "breathed" upon His disciples on the morning of the resurrection, telling them to receive the breath receiving the Holy Spirit to guide them, strengthen them and guide them.

(John 20:22 NKJV) **22** And when He had said this, He breathed on *them,* and said to them, "Receive the Holy Spirit.

Inspired Guidance

Inspiration is the supernatural work of the Holy Spirit upon the writers. The Bible says "holy men of God spoke as they were moved by God/Holy Spirit".

(2 Peter 1:21 NKJV) **21** for prophecy never came by the will of man, but holy men of God spoke *as they were* moved by the Holy Spirit.

(1 Corinthians 2:12-13 NKJV) **12** Now we have received, not the spirit of the world, but the Spirit who is from God, that we might know the things that have been freely given to us by God. **13** These things we also speak, not in words which man's wisdom teaches but which the Holy Spirit teaches, comparing spiritual things with spiritual.

Mode/Methods of Inspiration
(Revelation, Inspiration, Illumination, Plenary- Verbal – Inspiration)

Revelation

Revelation is God communicating His Truth to mankind, which they could not discover by their own natural reason. This is an unveiling of God's Person and Purpose to mankind.
The Bible itself is not of mankind's wisdom or thoughts, but those thoughts of God's inspiration given to mankind. Divine knowledge was communicated by the Spirit of God to selected people who recorded it as they were led to by God. All that may be known of God in the written revelation of God He has revealed; His nature, character and being. He has revealed the purpose of mankind's existence and his redemptive plan for them.

Inspiration

While revelation has to do with impartation of Divine Truth, inspiration has to do with the recording of the Truth from God. Inspiration concerning Scripture is the influence of God giving Scripture to mankind. All Scripture has been given by inspiration. (*As stated previously in 'The Definition of Inspiration)* - The word itself means "breathing into", so naturally speaking inspiration is the breathing into as regards to the truths of God entering mankind's ability to understand these spiritual truths. The writers of the Books of the Bible had been inspired and instructed by God to write His Words.

Inspiration was the power which enabled the men of God to write the Divine revelation without error or defect. (2 Peter 1:21 NKJV) *[21] for prophecy never came by the will of men, but holy men of God spoke as they were moved by the Holy Spirit*

God commanded men to write things in a Book. - Example → Moses received the 10 Commandments on stone (written) and he recorded them in a book. (Exodus 17:14 KJV) *[14] And the LORD said unto Moses, Write this for a memorial in a book, and rehearse it in the ears of Joshua: for I will utterly put out the remembrance of Amalek from under heaven.*

(2 Timothy 3:15-17 NKJV) *[15]* and that from childhood you have known the Holy Scriptures, which are able to make you wise for salvation through faith which is in Christ Jesus. *[16]* All Scripture *is* given by inspiration of God, and *is* profitable for doctrine, for reproof, for correction, for instruction in righteousness, *[17]* that the man of God may be complete, thoroughly equipped for every good work.

Illumination

Illumination describes the process of the Holy Spirit to enlighten mankind's ability to understand and receive God's Revelation. It is the work of the Holy Spirit to bring revelation, inspiration, and illumination. Revelation is the reception/discovery of Truth. Inspiration is the recording/communication of Truth. Illumination is the perception/understanding of Truth brought about by the influence of the Holy Spirit.

Illumination is the supernatural opening of the understanding to receive that which is revealed in God's Word. The Holy Spirit knows what He meant when He inspired the Word. We, therefore, need His illumination to be enlightened. It should be remembered that there is absolutely nothing to be added to the completed Biblical revelation and anyone who dares to add comes under the curse of God. This excludes all other books including 'best sellers'. The Bible stands alone, as the only inspired revelation of God.

(1 Corinthians 2:11-14 NKJV) [11] For what man knows the things of a man except the spirit of the man which is in him? Even so no one knows the things of God except the Spirit of God. [12] Now we have received, not the spirit of the world, but the Spirit who is from God, that we might know the things that have been freely given to us by God. [13] These things we also speak, not in words which man's wisdom teaches but which the Holy Spirit teaches, comparing spiritual things with spiritual. [14] But the natural man does not receive the things of the Spirit of God, for they are foolishness to him; nor can he know *them,* because they are spiritually discerned.

This is promised to us by the Lord Jesus, the Holy Spirit - (John 15:26 NKJV) [26] "But when the Helper comes, whom I shall send to you from the Father, the Spirit of truth who proceeds from the Father, He will testify of Me. – The Holy Spirit, who is the agent of revelation and inspiration, also becomes the agent of illumination.

Plenary- Verbal – Inspiration

Plenary-Verbal Inspiration means that the Bible is complete/full in every part (plenary) and by the means of words (verbal). The words used in the Scriptures are words directed by God to the writers. This revelation is Divine using mankind to complete the written word. It is God's Word wrapped with humanity.

The Bible was written by 40 different men completing 66 books in three (3) languages over a period of approximately 1600 years eventually becoming one harmonious book. This unity and progression of thought together with the absence of contradiction indicates the Bible had ultimately one author, God. The phrase "God Said" is found within the Bible about 3800 times.
The fact that the writers themselves claimed that God directed and guided their writings supports the Scriptures as being God's revelation and inspiration.

(2 Peter 1:20-21 NKJV) [20] knowing this first, that no prophecy of Scripture is of any private interpretation, [21] for prophecy never came by the will of man, but holy men of God spoke *as they were* moved by the Holy Spirit.

Proofs of Inspiration - Miracles of the Bible

A miracle is an event that is unexplainable by the laws of nature and so is held to be a supernatural event of God. In the course of the world's history God has revealed Himself, His power and His love for mankind in miracles. The Scriptures identify and are a record of many miracles from God ranging from Creation to the final Book of the Bible, Revelation. The Bible itself is a result of a miracle 'Inspiration'. This is an act of power, a supernatural deed brought about by God. There are many accounts in the Bible pertaining to miracles and most were confirmed by eye witnesses.

Miracles under Moses	
Books of Exodus & Numbers record miracles under the ministry of Moses,10 Plagues in Egypt.	Exodus 4-12
Opening of the Red Sea.	Exodus 14-15
Manna from heaven for 40 years, the water out of the rock.	Exodus 16-17
Healing of the people by faith in the lifted serpent of brass.	Numbers 21
Miracles under Joshua	
Jordan was opened.	Joshua 3-5
Walls of Jericho collapsed.	Joshua 6
The sun stood still for Israel's victory over their enemies.	Joshua 10
Under Sampson	
Slaying of the Lion.	Judges 14:6
Water from the jawbone of the ass.	Judges 15:15
Collapse of the temple in Sampson's death was miracles of strength.	Judges 16:30
Under Elijah and Elisha	
Book of Kings records miracles of the healing of the waters.	2 Kings 2:21-22
Multiplying of the oil.	2 Kings 4:1-7
Resurrection of the child.	2 Kings 4:8-37
Under Christ	
Numerous miracles are recorded in the Gospels; in physical realm, healing of the sick and diseased; in the spiritual realm, exorcism, and raising of the dead, in the cosmic realm, walking on the water and stilling the storms.	Matthew 8-9
Under the Apostles	
The Apostles carried on the ministry of Christ performing various miracles of healing and exorcism.	Acts 4:16-22; 6:8; 15:12; 19:11
The greatest of all miracles is that of the resurrection of Jesus Christ	

Prophecies and Their Fulfillment

Prophecy is Divine Knowledge being stated and seen to fulfillment. It is God giving a message to be revealed, predicting the future. Miracles are the evidence of Divine Power. Prophecy is evidence of Divine Knowledge. Studying Biblical prophecy can provide some of the greatest proofs of inspiration. Men in the Bible were given knowledge-prophecies, that accurately predicted events generations before they happened, is proof of God's involvement.

NOTE → <u>Predictive prophecy must measure up to 4 tests to be approved of as valid:</u>
    1. Must be stated before the events come to past.
    2. Must be explicit and specific in its predictions, so that there could be no possibility of accidental or coincidental fulfillment.
    3. Those who state the prophecies should have no part in their fulfillment.
    4. The events of fulfillment should correspond exactly or accurately with the details of the prophecy in all points.

Bible prophecy has met these qualifications and has been proven to be entirely genuine.

Some Examples	
The prophecy of judgment on Egypt and its fulfillment.	(Genesis 15 with Exodus 4:12; Ezekiel 29:30)
The Prophesy that was fulfilled concerning the rise and fall of Assyria also illustrates Divine inspiration.	(Isaiah 10 with Ezekiel 31-32)
Israel's history and dispersion is a remarkable fulfillment of the prophecy.	(Deuteronomy 28)

The greatest example of prophecy and fulfillment is that which pertains to the Messianic Prophecy. The only man ever to have explicit detail given beforehand of His birth, life, ministry, death, burial, and resurrection was the Lord Jesus Christ.

TEXT MESSAGE → This was foretold by 30 different persons, over a period of 4,000 years before Jesus was even born. There were approximately 330 Old Testament prophecies that were fulfilled in the first coming of Christ.

The Unity of the Bible

The unity of the Bible is unsurpassed by any other writing on earth. The Bible is composed of 66 books that were written by approximately 40 different people, who lived in different cultures and countries, ranging from Egypt to Babylon to Rome. They were a diverse group of statesmen, peasants, prophets, kings, herdsmen, tradesmen, prisoners and fishermen and used three (3) different languages. There are different kinds of literature in the Bible. They are history, law, poetry, prophecy, biography, songs, letters, parables and proverbs. With all of this the Bible withstands all of the critic's tests and challenges and stands as one of the most unique books ever written. It is the most published book and most studied book. All of this is not just a coincidence. It is a Divine work of God.

The Harmony of the Divisions of the Books

OLD Testament		
The Law - Related to History (17)		
Historical Books (12)		Pentateuch (5)
Pre-Exile History (9)	Post-Exile History (3)	Historical Pentateuch (5)
Joshua	Ezra	Genesis
Judges	Nehemiah	Exodus
Ruth	Esther	Leviticus
1 Samuel		Numbers
2 Samuel		Deuteronomy
1 Kings		
2 Kings		
1 Chronicles		
2 Chronicles		
The Psalms – Poetry/Poetical Books (5)		
Job		
Psalms		
Proverbs		
Ecclesiastes		
Song of Solomon		
The Prophets – Prophecy (17)		
Minor Prophets (12)		Major Prophets (5)

Post Exile Prophecy (3)	Pre-Exile Prophecy (9)	Pentateuch Prophetical (5)
Haggai	Hosea	Isaiah
Zechariah	Joel	Jeremiah
Malachi	Amos	Lamentations
	Obadiah	Ezekiel
	Jonah	Daniel
	Micah	
	Nahum	
	Habakkuk	
	Zephaniah	

New Testament			
Doctrinal Epistles (22)			History (5)
Hebrew/Christian Epistles (9)	Pastoral & personal Epistles (4)	Christian Church Epistles (9)	Historic Foundations (5)
Hebrews	1 Timothy	Romans	Matthew
James	2 Timothy	1 Corinthians	Mark
1 Peter	Titus	2 Corinthians	Luke
2 Peter	Philemon	Galatians	John
1 John		Ephesians	Acts
2 John		Philippians	
3 John		Colossians	
Jude		1 Thessalonians	
Revelation		2 Thessalonians	

The Harmony of Themes through the Bible

Though the Bible has one primary message it intends to communicate, there are other themes that are developed consistently through its books beginning in Genesis and ending in the New Testament. The greatest theme in the Bible centers on the person and work of Christ. The Bible as the written 'Word of God' was meant to reveal Jesus Christ, the **Living Word.**

The Harmony Between the Old and New Testaments

The Bible consists of two (2) major divisions, the Old and New Testaments, both of which have their own unique emphasis. However, each is incomplete without the other and each perfectly compliments the other. There are approximately 6,600 cross references between them with support interrelatedness.

The New is within the Old Testament → *The Old is within the New Testament*
The New is in the Old contained → *The Old is in the New opened*
The New is in the Old concealed → *The Old is in the New revealed*

The Bible Itself Claims Inspiration

Writers of the Old and New Testaments both state that the words they wrote or spoke were not from themselves but came from God. They claimed that God had spoken to them and directed them to write what they had been given. So, the writings themselves declare inspiration because they came from those who profess that God Himself gave it to them to be written and these men did not claim any credit for the words, thus being inspired.

(Deuteronomy 4:2 NKJV) ² You shall not add to the word which I command you, nor take from it, that you may keep the commandments of the LORD your God which I command you.

(Luke 1:70 NKJV) ⁷⁰ As He spoke by the mouth of His holy prophets, Who *have been* since the world began,

(1 Chronicles 28:19 KJV) ¹⁹ All *this, said David*, the LORD made me understand in writing by *his* hand upon me, *even* all the works of this pattern.

(2 Timothy 3:16 NKJV) ¹⁶ All Scripture *is* given by inspiration of God, and *is* profitable for doctrine, for reproof, for correction, for instruction in righteousness,

(1 Corinthians 2:12-13 NKJV) ¹² Now we have received, not the spirit of the world, but the Spirit who is from God, that we might know the things that have been freely given to us by God. ¹³ These things we also speak, not in words which man's wisdom teaches but which the Holy Spirit teaches, comparing spiritual things with spiritual.

Results of Inspiration

Inspiration produces results that solidify it's claim; genuineness, credibility, canonicity, infallibility and authority of the Scriptures. This results in the only credible resource for Christians/Believers in Jesus Christ to be used in support of their faith in Jesus Christ and in which they should study → so that the man of God may be complete, equipped for every good work. (2 Timothy 3:17)

Genuineness – Not being counterfeit, but authentic and also free from hypocrisy or dishonesty and being considered pure. It is in fact true and what it claims to be. Both Jews and Christians/Believers in Jesus Christ, whose theological views are at variance, agree on the genuineness of the Bible/books.

Credibility – Being worthy of belief, and deserving praise. The Lord Jesus Himself confirmed the writings of the Old Testament, spoke of them as the law, the Psalms, and the Prophets.

(Luke 24:44-45 NKJV) ⁴⁴ Then He said to them, "These *are* the words which I spoke to you while I was still with you, that all things must be fulfilled which were written in the Law of Moses and *the* Prophets and *the* Psalms concerning Me." ⁴⁵ And He opened their understanding, that they might comprehend the Scriptures.

Jesus Christ endorsed Old Testament Books	
Genesis	Mark 13:19; Matthew 19:4-5; Genesis 2:24; John 8:44: Luke 17:26-28; Luke 17:28-30
Exodus	Mark 12:26; Matthew 22:31-32; Matthew 5:21,27,15:4;22:23; Luke 24:27; John 6:32; Luke 6;3-4
Leviticus	Matthew 5:33,43; 19:19; 22:39; Mark 12:31; Luke 10:27
Deuteronomy	Matthew 22:37; Mark 12:29; Luke 10:27; Matthew 4:1-11
Numbers	Matthew 5:33,43; 19;19; 22:39; Mark 12:31; Luke 10:27; John 3:14
Psalms	Matthew 22:42-44; 21:16; 27:46; Luke 24:44-45; John 13:18; 10:34; Mark 15:34; Luke 23:46
Isaiah	Mark 4:12; Luke 4:17-18; Matthew 8:17; Luke 8:10; 22:37
Jeremiah	Mark 11:17; Matthew 21:13; Luke 19:46
Hosea	Matthew 9:13; 12:7
Zechariah	Mark 14:27
Jonah	Matthew 12:39-40
Malachi	Luke 7:27; Matthew 11:10

The Apostles also endorsed the Old Testament.

(Romans 3:2 NKJV) Much in every way! Chiefly because to them were committed the oracles of God.

(Acts 1:16 NKJV) ¹⁶ "Men *and* brethren, this Scripture had to be fulfilled, which the Holy Spirit spoke before by the mouth of David concerning Judas, who became a guide to those who arrested Jesus;

(Hebrews 1:1-2 NKJV) ¹ God, who at various times and in various ways spoke in time past to the fathers by the prophets, ² has in these last days spoken to us by *His* Son, whom He has appointed heir of all things, through whom also He made the worlds;

Both History and Archeology have provided evidence to confirm the proof of the credibility of the Scriptures in numerous cases.

> Text Message → The Historical book 'Complete Works of Flavius Josephus' – The Antiquities of The Jews – written during his life time 37 AD – died sometime after 100 AD. He was commissioned to write a history of the Jewish people by the Romans. He identifies Jesus as a historical figure and his work includes statements about His miracles.

Canonicity - The word "canon" means "a basis for judgment" and refers to a standard rule. Canonicity means that the Biblical books have been measured by a standard, have stood the test and have been approved and recognized as being inspired of God. There where four broad principles used to test the New Testament Books. (Stated from Henry C. Thiesson in 'Lectures in Systematic Theology')

1. *As to Apostolicity* → Was the book written by an apostle, and if not, was it written by someone in close relation to an apostle to raise it up to apostolic level?

2. *As to Contents* → Were the Contents of such spiritual character to warrant a place in Scripture?

3. *As to Universality* → Was the book universally accepted by the church in that time?

4. *As to Inspiration* → Was the book inspired? Did it have internal evidence? Infallibility - By "infallibility" it meant incapable of error, exemption from any liability to making mistakes.

The Old Testament Canon is in the Westminster Confession of Faith of 1647 which is in agreement with most historic Protestant denominations. It reads : "Under the name of Holy Scripture, or the Word of God written are now contained all the Books of the Old and New Testaments, which are these…," and there follow the thirty-nine books of the OT and the twenty-seven of the NT, "all which are given by inspiration of God to be the rule of faith and life".

> Text Message → The Church did not produce the Word, the Word produced the Church.

The Word is not subject to authority of the fallible Church, but the Church is subject to the infallible inspirational authority of the Word.

Authority → The Scriptures have been given the authority over all believers and the church on a whole. They alone have the power to command, enforce and exact obedience and judgment on mankind. Being infallible, inspired, and authoritative of God the Scripture must be used, taught and obeyed by all Christians concerning their faith and actions in life. Reason, conscience, and the Church must be subjected to the authority of the Word without hesitation or without feeling the need to make changes.

> Text Message → No Change Control approved for the Old Testament or New Testament.

(2 Timothy 3:14-17 NKJV) [14] But you must continue in the things which you have learned and been assured of, knowing from whom you have learned *them,* [15] and that from childhood you have known the Holy Scriptures, which are able to make you wise for salvation through faith which is in Christ Jesus. [16] All Scripture *is* given by inspiration of God, and *is* profitable for doctrine, for reproof, for correction, for instruction in righteousness, [17] that the man of God may be complete, thoroughly equipped for every good work.

(Galatians 1:8-9 NKJV) [8] But even if we, or an angel from heaven, preach any other gospel to you than what we have preached to you, let him be accursed. [9] As we have said before, so now I say again, if anyone preaches any other gospel to you than what you have received, let him be accursed.

The Apocrypha

The Apocrypha comes from a Greek word that means "hidden books". In theology the term "Apocrypha" refers to the 15 books/parts or 14 books/parts if you include the Letter of Jeremiah in Baruch. The writing dates range from 200 BC to 100 AD. Some were written in Hebrew and some in Greek and others in Aramaic. These were added to the Old Testament by the Roman Catholic Church in 1546 A.D. Most of the rest of Christendom rejects these books from having a place in the canon Scriptures.

The books are; Esdras, 2 Esdras, Yobit, Judith, Book of Esther, Wisdom of Solomon, Ecclesasticus, Baruch (Letter of Jeremiah), Song of the three Holy Children, History of Susanna, Bel and the Dragron, The prayer of Manasses, I Macabees and II Macabees.

Reasons They Are Not Accepted

Universally acknowledge that they never had a place in the Hebrew canon.

They were written in the 400 years between Malachi and John the Baptist when there were no inspired prophetic utterances. This is why the Jews reject them.

They are never quoted in the New Testament by Jesus or the Apostles.

They are not found in any catalogue of canonical Books during the first four centuries of the Church.

Divine Inspiration and authority is claimed by none of the writers and is disclaimed by some of them.

The books contain many historical, geographical, and chronological errors, at times contradicting themselves, the Bible and history.

They teach doctrines and uphold practices which are contrary to the Canonical Scriptures. In these writings, lying is sanctioned, suicide and assassinations are justified, magical incantations and prayers for the dead are taught and approved.

Text Message → Remember Scripture is imparted Truth from God which could not be discovered by natural reasoning alone. So, when mankind tries to add their reasoning without the aid of the Holy Spirit it becomes corrupted.

Begin With Prayer

The Biblical Teaching/Doctrine of God

Biblical Building Block # 4

(Exodus 34:6 HCSB)

6 *Then the LORD passed in front of him and proclaimed: Yahweh— Yahweh is a compassionate and gracious God, slow to anger and rich in faithful love and truth,*

God is love. He is true to His nature of love by reaching out to mankind with His entire being. The Father sent the Son who sent the Holy Spirit to be with mankind. This love was not a mere simple act but it was a giving act. God became man to suffer for all of mankind through death and resurrection. He knew in advance of what He was going to face, and that, even more strengthens the act of His love to mankind by death on the cross and shedding His blood. What more can one give? This is real, true love. So we must ask 'what less can I give'?

1. Make a list of some arguments that explain the existence of God.

2. Explain the nature of God?

3. What are some attributes of God that only He can have?

4. What are some attributes of God that He has and wants mankind to exemplify?

5. Define the righteousness of God.

6. Describe the holiness of God.

7. Explain the trinity.

8. What does the Godhead mean?

9. What is meant when we say "God is love"? List some examples of how God shows His love to mankind.

The Existence of God

The Existence of God Stated

The existence of God is not something that the Bible tries to prove; it declares it as fact. God does not need to defend His existence. He desires to enlighten mankind to the fact that He is what He says He is, the one and only God. The opening line of the Bible reads "In the beginning God…" (Genesis 1:1 NKJV). Also from Genesis 1:3-29 you will see the words "God said" nine times again declaring His existence.

For any person to believe in God they must have that belief within their mind, heart and soul without doubt but truly seeking after Him. Believing is a prerequisite to having and putting your faith in God. Accepting the existence of God is the beginning of one's ability to have faith and one must believe and allow God, in His Word and Spirit, to work within the individual. In Hebrews 11:6 we see that one must believe in God's existence first. This would mean that one needs to put his/her faith into action by believing.

(Hebrews 11:6 NKJV) [6] But without faith *it is* impossible to please *Him,* for he who comes to God must believe that He is, and *that* He is a rewarder of those who diligently seek Him.

By faith mankind must come to the belief in God. Without taking this step, nothing can be received or known of God in any manner that makes sense. One's faith is the linkage between mankind and God, the creation and the creator. (Hebrews 11:1 KJV) *"Faith is the substance of things hoped for, the evidence of things not seen".* Through one's faith the existence of God becomes real, and then it can become a substance of hope; the reality to which one's faith is directed.

God has provided physical and visible proofs that shed light of His existence in the world and universe that He created. These physical things that can be seen also reflect the invisible attributes of God. So mankind really has no excuse for not believing in the existence of God. (Romans 1:20 KJV) *"For the invisible things of Him from the creation of the world are clearly seen, being understood by the things that are made, even His eternal power the Godhead; so that they are without excuse."*

David wrote in the OT - "The fool hath said in his heart, there is no God." (Psalm 53:1 KJV)

Existence of God and Arguments for His Existence

Cosmological Argument

The Cosmological Argument questions "how did it come to be"? In other words "how did it get here?" This argument looks at the existence of an effect (the universe) and then identifies the existence of its cause (God, the creator). And if the universe exists, someone or something must have put it there, which leads back to a creator, God.

(Genesis 1:1 KJV) **1** In the beginning God created the heaven and the earth.

(Psalms 19:1-6 KJV) **1** The heavens declare the glory of God; and the firmament sheweth his handywork. **2** Day unto day uttereth speech, and night unto night sheweth knowledge. **3** *There is* no speech nor language, *where* their voice is not heard. **4** Their line is gone out through all the earth, and their words to the end of the world. In them hath he set a tabernacle for the sun, **5** Which *is* as a bridegroom coming out of his chamber, *and* rejoiceth as a strong man to run a race. **6** His going forth *is* from the end of the heaven, and his circuit unto the ends of it: and there is nothing hid from the heat thereof.

Teleological Argument

The Teleological Argument refers to purpose and design. There seems to be a purpose of the universe and the planet earth and the design of it is perfect. The operation of the planets is in harmony with each other indicating a design that has a reason or purpose. Note that the world and planets are in the perfect shape, they are round.

Anthropological Argument

The Anthropological Argument refers to the creation of mankind. *Anthropos* is a Greek word for man/mankind. The creation of mankind was performed by God. God is the designer and engineer of this creation and mankind was made in the image (likeness) of God.

(Genesis 1:26-27 KJV) **26** And God said, Let us make man in our image, after our likeness: and let them have dominion over the fish of the sea, and over the fowl of the air, and over the cattle, and over all the earth, and over every creeping thing that creepeth upon the earth. **27** So God created man in his *own* image, in the image of God created he him; male and female created he them.

> Text Message → The Greek word that pertains to only a male person, adult, husband or opposite a female is '*Aner*' – the Greek work '*anthropos*' primary designates a human being regardless of sex. It is male and female that bears the image of God.

Dominion (control or the exercise of control) was given to mankind at their creation by God. They are superior to all other created living things on earth. One of the strongest arguments for the existence of an intelligent God is that mankind was given the greatest intelligence over all of the other created living things on earth by their creator and the dominion over them. Human beings, who are all distinct and unique from each other, argue the existence of a creator of no limits on His ability to continue to create and sustain life in all of its complexities. Evolution theories are mankind's attempt to escape from the accountability and responsibility to God their creator. It is also a lie of the deceiver, Satan, who deceives us into believing that mankind is a god himself or equal to God. The acceptance of this will kill, destroy and steal one's eternal life in paradise with God their creator.

Ontological Argument

The Ontological Argument and the Anthropological Argument are similar. Mankind who is a created intelligence also has an intuition with the understanding of knowledge without the process of reasoning. They know intuitively that there is a God. This is knowledge that they are born and created with. The fact that there is a universal belief in a god or gods in every nation on earth substantiates this argument. If people do not accept or find the true God, they will make a deity of their own to worship such as money, movie stars, and philosophies of mankind, gods made of statues and technology/science, to satisfy this intuitive knowledge. Belief in God is not just the result of cultural conditioning. It is intuitive.

(Acts 17:23-25 NKJV) [23] for as I was passing through and considering the objects of your worship, I even found an altar with this inscription: TO THE UNKNOWN GOD. Therefore, the One whom you worship without knowing, Him I proclaim to you: [24] God, who made the world and everything in it, since He is Lord of heaven and earth, does not dwell in temples made with hands. [25] Nor is He worshiped with men's hands, as though He needed anything, since He gives to all life, breath, and all things

(Romans 1:18-20 NKJV) [19] because what may be known of God is manifest in them, for God has shown *it* to them. [20] For since the creation of the world His invisible *attributes* are clearly seen, being understood by the things that are made, *even* His eternal power and Godhead, so that they are without excuse,

Moral Argument

The Moral Argument concerns that aspect of mankind's inner sense of right and wrong. People have an internal sense of knowing and feeling right and wrong, mostly adhering to the right and avoiding the wrong. The Bible calls this conscience and considers it a God-given sense. Being universal, it is a witness to the existence of a supreme law-giver and judge who built into mankind this sense of responsibility for the right and for understanding wrong.

(John 8:9 NKJV) Then those who heard *it,* being convicted by *their* conscience, went out one by one, beginning with the oldest *even* to the last. And Jesus was left alone, and the woman standing in the midst.

Biological Argument

Biological pertains to biology, which is the science of living things. The Greek word "*bios*" means "life". The outstanding characteristic of living things is that they can make life and it is a scientific fact that life can only come from pre-existent life, not from matter alone. Therefore to trace all life back to its source, we must eventually come back to God Himself. This life-source is God.

(John 1:1-5 NKJV) [1] In the beginning was the Word, and the Word was with God, and the Word was God. [2] He was in the beginning with God. [3] All things were made through Him, and without Him nothing was made that was made. [4] In Him was life, and the life was the light of men. [5] And the light shines in the darkness, and the darkness did not comprehend it.

Historical Argument

The Historical Argument links points of history to a power beyond governing, guiding, and controlling the destinies of the nations of the world. History itself argues the existence of God who watches over and controls its outcome. An example would be the fall of Babylon; it fell on a night when soldiers forgot to close the gates in the wall through which the great river Euphrates flowed. God's prophets had foretold this over one hundred years before it took place (Isaiah 45:1-5; Daniel 5). There are many other illustrations of the fact that behind it all we see the hand of God moving to accomplish His will. A study of history can help identify these.

Christological Argument

The Christological Argument can be considered one of the strongest arguments. History of Jesus Christ is a fact and it is impossible to explain His person apart from the existence of God. Jesus Christ is the greatest revelation of God's existence. All that He was, did, and said attests to the existence of God.

(John 1:14-18 NKJV) [14] And the Word became flesh and dwelt among us, and we beheld His glory, the glory as of the only begotten of the Father, full of grace and truth. [15] John bore witness of Him and cried out, saying, "This was He of whom I said, 'He who comes after me is preferred before me, for He was before me.' " [16] And of His fullness we have all received, and grace for grace. [17] For the law was given through Moses, *but* grace and truth came through Jesus Christ. [18] No one has seen God at any time. The only begotten Son, who is in the bosom of the Father, He has declared *Him.*

Biblical Argument

The Biblical Argument is just that, the Bible is its witness to the existence of God. These writings which are inspired by God and the harmony and consistency of them argue the existence of a higher intelligence than mankind.

Non-Believer Philosophies of God

A review of the non-Believer's philosophies, concerning God show two groups: Theistic and Non-Theistic. The Theistic view believes that there is a god or gods. The Non-Theistic view believes that there is no god at all.

Theistic Views

Pantheistic View

The Pantheistic view is the belief that God is all and all is God. The words "*pan*" meaning "all" and "*theo*" meaning "God" make up the term Pantheism. This view regards all finite things as aspects or parts of one eternal self-existence being. This view also believes that there is no God apart from nature, and that everything in nature is a part or manifestation of God.

Materialistic Pantheism - This is the belief in the eternity of matter and the spontaneous generation of life. The universe and nature are the only gods that mankind can worship. This theory ignores and misreads all the evidence in the material realm that there is a God who exists beyond it.

Hylozoism or Panpsychism - These are the same beliefs under different names. They state that all matter has both physical properties and the principle of life in it. This theory extends beyond materialistic pantheism in a search for a non-material god. But it still denies the existence of a supreme personal being.

Neutralism - This belief states mind and matter are only pieces of reality and that reality is a neutral substance missing and denying an existence of God.

Idealism - This theory states that the ultimate reality is of the nature of the mind. It says that the world is the product of the mind, either of the individual mind or of the infinite mind. It is the theory that everything exists only in the mind.

Philosophical Mysticism - This is any philosophy that seeks to discover the nature of reality through the process of thought or spiritual intuition, making man god or gods. This belief claims that the only god is the god within. This is deification and worship of self.

Summarizing

Pantheism	Believes nature is god and misses the God of Mankind.
Materialistic Pantheism	Believes matter is eternal and misses the God who made matter.
Hylozoism	Believes in a principle of life god and misses the God who is the source of life.
Neutralism	Believes some neutral substance god and misses God the creator of all substance.
Idealism	Believes the mind god and misses the God who is a real person having a perfect mind.
Philosophical Mysticism	Believes that mankind, himself is god and misses the God who made all of mankind.

Polytheistic View

The Polytheistic view is the worship of many gods. Most ancient religions were polytheistic and some still exist today. The Bible denounces polytheism. There are no gods other than God Himself. Mankind has been given a warning by God not to turn to idols or make images of the heathen gods. (This includes worshiping others in place of God, such as worshipping Mary who was the earthly mother of Jesus. She is only a created being and not to be worshipped). Even mentioning other gods was not acceptable and should never be done. The worship or acceptance of their being is called idolatry and will come under the curse and wrath of God. There is only one true God.

(Exodus 20:3 NKJV) You shall have no other gods before Me.

(Leviticus 19:4-5 KJV) **4** Turn ye not unto idols, nor make to yourselves molten gods: I *am* the LORD your God. **5** And if ye offer a sacrifice of peace offerings unto the LORD, ye shall offer it at your own will.

(Joshua 23:7 NKJV) **7** *and* lest you go among these nations, these who remain among you. You shall not make mention of the name of their gods, nor cause *anyone* to swear *by them;* you shall not serve them nor bow down to them,

(Deuteronomy 7:4-5 NKJV) **4** For they will turn your sons away from following Me, to serve other gods; so the anger of the LORD will be aroused against you and destroy you suddenly. **5** But thus you shall deal with them: you shall destroy their altars, and break down their *sacred* pillars, and cut down their wooden images, and burn their carved images with fire.

Dualistic View

The Dualistic view is a belief that there are two separate values or gods of eternal and equal power who are at war with each other. The early Gnostics held this view of two Gods in conflict in the universe and that this conflict is generally fought out in and among human beings. Examples would be good and evil, right and wrong, mind and matter, thought and thing. This is contradictory to God's revelation of Himself; He is one God over all. There is no contest.

Deistic View

The Deistic View believes that God is only present in creation by His power, not in His person. This view believes that God set the various laws of nature in motion during creation and left the universe to maintain itself by these laws. It believes that pertaining to mankind also. This belief states an absentee God. Teaching that truth concerning God can be known by reason. It rejects the Bible as Gods Word or revelation of Himself. This view believes that only principles of natural religion are identified in the book.

Summarizing

Pantheism	Makes all god and misses the one and only God of all.
Polytheism	Makes many gods and misses the one true God.
Dualism	Makes good and evil two equal gods in conflict and fails to discover a good God who will judge all evil.
Deism	Presents an absentee god, a god who has nothing to do with anything he created, an existence of no God missing a Loving God.

Non-Theistic Views (Atheistic and Agnostic Views)

The Atheistic View

Practical - This thought teaches that there may be a God but lives as if there is none. They have no interest in religion because of hypocrisy among the professors of religion.

Dogmatic – One who is dogmatic, will openly declare his/her disbelief in the existence of any god.

Virtual - This idea generates abstract definitions of God to try and account for the world and life, such as "social consciousness" or "the unknowable" or "moral order of the universe". In making God so obscure it is virtually atheistic.

Critical – This thought denies the existence of God on the grounds that no one can prove or demonstrate the existence of God.

Classical – This concept is aimed at denying the god or gods of some particular religion.

Rationalistic - Enthrones reason and dethrones faith in the existence of God. It claims reason as the only source of knowledge.

Atheism is unreasonable and arrogant in that it ignores all the facts and evidences of the existence of God and then makes a universal conclusion that He does not exist. As David said in (Psalm 14:1 KJV) *"the fool hath said in his heart, there is no God."*

Agnostic View

The Agnostic view believes that one cannot know whether God exists or not. This thought neither denies nor affirms the existence of God. An Agnostic is one who says "I cannot know" or "I know nothing". This belief holds that we cannot have knowledge as to the existence or nature of God and the universe. – **It is willful ignorance–not plain ignorance.**

(Acts 17:23-24 NKJV) [23] for as I was passing through and considering the objects of your worship, I even found an altar with this inscription: TO THE UNKNOWN GOD. Therefore, the One whom you worship without knowing, Him I proclaim to you: [24] God, who made the world and everything in it, since He is Lord of heaven and earth, does not dwell in temples made with hands.

Nature of God

Unless God takes the initiative and reveals Himself to us, he/she will stumble on in the darkness of insufficient reason. Mankind's wisdom is foolishness when it comes to knowing God. However, God has revealed Himself in the Scriptures. Mankind must accept this self-revelation or else he/she will not be able to know God. We must rely on the Bible's description of God. The Scriptures gives us 4 basic definitions/descriptions of God in His own eternal and essential nature and being (Love, Spirit, Light, and Fire).

(Ephesians 4:17-18 NKJV) [17] This I say, therefore, and testify in the Lord, that you should no longer walk as the rest of the Gentiles walk, in the futility of their mind, [18] having their understanding darkened, being alienated from the life of God, because of the ignorance that is in them, because of the blindness of their heart;

(1 Corinthians 1:19-21 NKJV) [19] For it is written: *"I will destroy the wisdom of the wise, And bring to nothing the understanding of the prudent."* [20] Where *is* the wise? Where *is* the scribe? Where *is* the disputer of this age? Has not God made foolish the wisdom of this world? [21] For since, in the wisdom of God, the world through wisdom did not know God, it pleased God through the foolishness of the message preached to save those who believe.

God is Love

Love refers to the very heart of God's nature. God does not just have love, He is love. Love involves the grace, mercy, kindness, goodness and benevolence of God toward all His creatures and He showed His love through Jesus Christ.

(1 John 4:8-12 NKJV) [8] He who does not love does not know God, for God is love. [9] In this the love of God was manifested toward us, that God has sent His only begotten Son into the world, that we might live through Him. [10] In this is love, not that we loved God, but that He loved us and sent His Son *to be* the propitiation for our sins. [11] Beloved, if God so loved us, we also ought to love one another. [12] No one has seen God at any time. If we love one another, God abides in us, and His love has been perfected in us.

(John 3:16 NKJV) [16] For God so loved the world that He gave His only begotten Son, that whoever believes in Him should not perish but have everlasting life.

God is Spirit

God is a spirit being. This is why God is spoken of as being invisible. It is also one reason why God forbade Israel to make any visible images or similitude of Himself. God is also a personal being. When we speak of God as being a Spirit, this does not mean that He is some impersonal force or entity. He is a person with self-consciousness, self-determination, will, intelligence and feelings. In His personhood He is essentially spiritual. He can not be restricted to any particular place or in any sense be brought under control as a physical thing.

(John 4:24 NKJV) ²⁴ God *is* Spirit, and those who worship Him must worship in spirit and truth."

(1 Timothy 1:17 NKJV) ¹⁷ Now to the King eternal, immortal, invisible, to God who alone is wise, *be* honor and glory forever and ever. Amen.

(1 Corinthians 2:11-13 NKJV) ¹¹ For what man knows the things of a man except the spirit of the man which is in him? Even so no one knows the things of God except the Spirit of God. ¹² Now we have received, not the spirit of the world, but the Spirit who is from God, that we might know the things that have been freely given to us by God. ¹³ These things we also speak, not in words which man's wisdom teaches but which the Holy Spirit teaches, comparing spiritual things with spiritual.

God is Light

Light reflects the majesty or the glory of God. God is light, and He dwells in unapproachable light that no one has seen, nor can see. God does not just have light; He is light. Light is absolutely pure, impossible to defile. As light, God is eternal, immortal and invisible.

(1 John 1:5-7 NKJV) This is the message which we have heard from Him and declare to you, that God is light and in Him is no darkness at all. ⁶ If we say that we have fellowship with Him, and walk in darkness, we lie and do not practice the truth. ⁷ But if we walk in the light as He is in the light, we have fellowship with one another, and the blood of Jesus Christ His Son cleanses us from all sin.

(1 Timothy 1:17 NKJV) ¹⁷ Now to the King eternal, immortal, invisible, to God who alone is wise, *be* honor and glory forever and ever. Amen.

(1 Timothy 6:16 NKJV) ¹⁶ who alone has immortality, dwelling in unapproachable light, whom no man has seen or can see, to whom *be* honor and everlasting power. Amen.

God is a Consuming Fire

A consuming fire identifies the holiness of God's nature. Fire is not God, but God's holiness is a consuming fire. This relates to the definition that God is light. The most frequent symbol used of God in the Bible is that of fire. It is always significant of His holiness and absolute righteousness manifested in judgment against sin. (Hebrews 12:29 KJV) *29 For our God is a consuming fire.*

Examples	
Lamp of Fire	Genesis 15:17
Tongues of fire	Acts 2:1-4
Coals of fire	Isaiah 6:6,7
Alter of fire	1 Kings 18:24,38
Burning bush of fire	Exodus 3:1-6
Lake of Fire	Revelation 20:15

Attributes of God

The Attributes of God are those qualities or characteristics that make up God. These attributes are what makes God what and who He is. These can be divided into two different groupings; essential, those that only belong to God and moral, those that pertain to God and His creatures that are capable of having these attributes.

(Romans 1:20 NKJV) *20 For since the creation of the world His invisible attributes are clearly seen, being understood by the things that are made, even His eternal power and Godhead, so that they are without excuse,*

Essential Attributes

The essential attributes belong only to God and are what separate God from His creatures. This is what makes God who he is, the one and only God. These can never become attributes of mankind, because these attributes are what makes God unique from anything else, and only belong to God. These are also spoken of as being non-moral or incommunicable attributes of God, which separates God from His creatures.

God is Eternal

God is eternal, having no beginning or end, the everlasting one. There never was a time when God was not. He has always been and will always be. This concept is sometimes hard for mankind to understand since we live in "time" that consists of a beginning and an end. This is not so with God. He exists in eternity. In the creation of mankind God's intent was for them to be eternal beings with Him. Then sin entered the world, separating mankind and God, bringing death. But God has provided salvation through Jesus Christ and this salvation brings with it an eternal life with God, Who is eternal.

(Isaiah 43:10-12 NKJV) *10 "You are My witnesses," says the LORD, "And My servant whom I have chosen, That you may know and believe Me, And understand that I am He. Before Me there was no God formed, Nor shall there be after Me. 11 I, even I, am the LORD, And besides Me there is no savior. 12 I have declared and saved, I have proclaimed, And there was no foreign god among you; Therefore you are My witnesses," Says the LORD, "that I am God.*

The following Scriptures confirm the truth that God is eternal. He is not limited to or by time. He is timeless. Although the saints receive eternal life and will live forever, as God does, such eternal life is given by God. Eternity of being can never be ascribed to mankind, as it is only an essential attribute of God.

Exodus 3:14 KJV	[14] And God said unto Moses, I AM THAT I AM: and he said, Thus shalt thou say unto the children of Israel, I AM hath sent me unto you.
Genesis 21:33 NKJV	[33] Then *Abraham* planted a tamarisk tree in Beersheba, and there called on the name of the LORD, the Everlasting God.
Hebrews 1:10 NKJV	[10] And: *"You, LORD, in the beginning laid the foundation of the earth, And the heavens are the work of Your hands.*
Genesis 1:1 KJV	[1] In the beginning God created the heaven and the earth
Deuteronomy 33:27 NKJV	[27] The eternal God *is your* refuge, And underneath *are* the everlasting arms; He will thrust out the enemy from before you, And will say, 'Destroy!'
Romans 1:20 HCSB	[20] Then God said, "Let the waters abound with an abundance of living creatures, and let birds fly above the earth across the face of the firmament of the heavens."
Isaiah 44:6 KJV	[6] Thus saith the LORD the King of Israel, and his redeemer the LORD of hosts; I *am* the first, and I *am* the last; and beside me *there is* no God.
Revelation 1:8 KJV	[8] I am Alpha and Omega, the beginning and the ending, saith the Lord, which is, and which was, and which is to come, the Almighty.

God is Self-Existent

God is self-existent and does not owe His existence to any other; neither does he depend on any other to sustain it. He is the source of all life and all life depends on Him. He is absolutely independent of anything outside of Himself. This is not so with mankind who is totally dependent upon God for their existence. The following Scriptures pertain to God's self-existence:

1 Timothy 1:17 NKJV	[17] Now to the King eternal, immortal, invisible, to God who alone is wise, *be* honor and glory forever and ever. Amen.
Exodus 3:14 NKJV	[14] And God said to Moses, "I AM WHO I AM." And He said, "Thus you shall say to the children of Israel, 'I AM has sent me to you.' "
John 1:4 NKJV	[4] In Him was life, and the life was the light of men.
Revelation 1:8 KJV	[8] I am Alpha and Omega, the beginning and the ending, saith the Lord, which is, and which was, and which is to come, the Almighty.

75

Isaiah 41:4 NKJV	[4] Who has performed and done *it*, Calling the generations from the beginning? ' I, the LORD, am the first; And with the last I *am* He.' "

God is Immutable

God is immutable meaning constant, endless, and unchangeable, pertaining to His character and being. The laws and principles that He has set forth are eternal and constant. He is one God in three persons. The Father, Son and Holy Spirit will never change. His holiness and righteousness of being will always be. He is not susceptible to change, and is eternally the same. This is the bonding agent that holds together truth. Mankind, however, must change and repent to be what God intends them to be. Following are some Scriptures stating his immutability.

James 1:17 NKJV	[17] Every good gift and every perfect gift is from above, and comes down from the Father of lights, with whom there is no variation or shadow of turning.
Hebrews 13:8 NKJV	Jesus Christ *is* the same yesterday, today, and forever.
Malachi 3:6 NKJV	[6] "For I *am* the LORD, I do not change; Therefore you are not consumed, O sons of Jacob.
Hebrews 6:18 NKJV	[18] that by two immutable things, in which it *is* impossible for God to lay, we might have strong consolation, who have fled for refuge to lay hold of the hope set before *us*.
Romans 11:29 NKJV	[29] For the gifts and the calling of God *are* irrevocable.

God is Omnipotent

God is omnipotent. He is all powerful and nothing is impossible for Him to do. His power is under the control of His holy and righteous nature that dictates His wisdom in using this unlimited power. Being all powerful God has absolute right to govern, judge and award His creatures as He sees fit. His will be done, not mankind's. The following Scriptures identify His omnipotence:

Jeremiah 32:17 KJV	[17] Ah Lord GOD! behold, thou hast made the heaven and the earth by thy great power and stretched out arm, *and* there is nothing too hard for thee:
Revelation 4:11 NKJV	[11] "You are worthy, O Lord, To receive glory and honor and power; For You created all things, And by Your will they exist and were created."
Job 42:2 NKJV	[2] "I know that You can do everything, And that no purpose *of Yours* can be withheld from You.
Revelation 19:6 NKJV	[6] And I heard, as it were, the voice of a great multitude, as the sound of many waters and as the sound of mighty thundering, saying, "Alleluia! For the Lord God Omnipotent reigns!

Luke 1:37 NKJV	[37] For with God nothing will be impossible."

God is Omniscient

God is omniscient. He is all knowing, and knows all things at all times. God has the ability to know what is going on throughout the universe and in all of His creation and spans the past, present, and future. Perfect knowledge is the accurate possession of all facts, perfect understanding is the full perception and interpretation of the fact and perfect wisdom is the correct application of the facts. These all are part of the omniscience of God. This makes God infallible, incapable of error in any action or judgment. The following Scriptures reveal God's omniscience:

Jeremiah 23:23-24 KJV	[23] *Am* I a God at hand, saith the LORD, and not a God afar off? [24] Can any hide himself in secret places that I shall not see him? saith the LORD. Do not I fill heaven and earth? saith the LORD.
Hebrews 4:12-13 NKJV	[12] For the word of God *is* living and powerful, and sharper than any two-edged sword, piercing even to the division of soul and spirit, and of joints and marrow, and is a discerner of the thoughts and intents of the heart. [13] And there is no creature hidden from His sight, but all things *are* naked and open to the eyes of Him to whom we *must give* account.
1 Timothy 1:17 NKJV	[17] Now to the King eternal, immortal, invisible, to God who alone is wise, *be* honor and glory forever and ever.
Proverbs 15:3 KJV	[3] The eyes of the LORD *are* in every place, beholding the evil and the good.
1 John 3:20 NKJV	[20] For if our heart condemns us, God is greater than our heart, and knows all things.

God is Omnipresent

God is omnipresent, all-present. He is unlimited by space or time. He is everywhere present at all times. He is present universally and simultaneously in the entire universe, always. This characteristic involves immensity, which means that God is present even beyond space. Finite space depends upon Him for its existence.

Isaiah 66:1-2 KJV	[1] Thus saith the LORD, The heaven *is* my throne, and the earth *is* my footstool: where *is* the house that ye build unto me? and where *is* the place of my rest? [2] For all those *things* hath mine hand made, and all those *things* have been, saith the LORD: but to this *man* will I look, *even* to *him that is* poor and of a contrite spirit, and trembleth at my word.
Exodus 3:14 KJV	[14] And God said unto Moses, I AM THAT I AM: and he said, Thus shalt thou say unto the children of Israel, I AM hath sent

	me unto you.
Acts 17:27-28 NKJV	[27] so that they should seek the Lord, in the hope that they might grope for Him and find Him, though He is not far from each one of us; [28] for in Him we live and move and have our being, as also some of your own poets have said, 'For we are also His offspring.
2 Chronicles 2:6 KJV	[6] But who is able to build him an house, seeing the heaven and heaven of heavens cannot contain him? who *am* I then, that I should build him an house, save only to burn sacrifice before him?
Psalms 139:7-12 KJV	[7] Whither shall I go from thy spirit? or whither shall I flee from thy presence? [8] If I ascend up into heaven, thou *art* there: if I make my bed in hell, behold, thou *art there*. [9] *If* I take the wings of the morning, *and* dwell in the uttermost parts of the sea; [10] Even there shall thy hand lead me, and thy right hand shall hold me. [11] If I say, Surely the darkness shall cover me; even the night shall be light about me. [12] Yea, the darkness hideth not from thee; but the night shineth as the day: the darkness and the light *are* both alike *to thee*.

Moral Attributes

The qualities and characteristics that relate to God in relation to His creatures are called Moral Attributes. God intends mankind to acquire the attributes such as holiness, righteousness, love and faithfulness. They are also called communicable attributes or ones that can be obtained. Because of Gods nature, these attributes are perfect.

Holiness

Holiness is perfect in God. His holiness is pure sinless, and has no tolerance for sin. The holiness of God is His natural character and is not derived but constant and always present. God is perfectly holy in all that He does. Holiness is the balance to live consistent with the nature of life. This is a major theme through out the Scriptures.

Scripture samples of the Holiness of God	
Leviticus 19:2 NKJV	[12] And you shall not swear by My name falsely, nor shall you profane the name of your God: I *am* the LORD.
Mark 1:24 NKJV	[24] saying, "Let *us* alone! What have we to do with You, Jesus of Nazareth? Did You come to destroy us? I know who You are--the Holy One of God!"
Exodus 15:11 KJV	[11] Who *is* like unto thee, O LORD, among the gods? who *is* like thee, glorious in holiness, fearful *in* praises, doing wonders?
Isaiah 57:15 KJV	[15] For thus saith the high and lofty One that inhabiteth

	eternity, whose name *is* Holy; I dwell in the high and holy *place*, with him also *that is* of a contrite and humble spirit, to revive the spirit of the humble, and to revive the heart of the contrite ones.
Revelation 4:8 NKJV	[8] *The* four living creatures, each having six wings, were full of eyes around and within. And they do not rest day or night, saying: "Holy, holy, holy, Lord God Almighty, Who was and is and is to come!"
The Holy Spirit is sent to the believer to make them holy.	
John 14:26 NKJV	[26] But the Helper, the Holy Spirit, whom the Father will send in My name, He will teach you all things, and bring to your remembrance all things that I said to you.
1 Peter 1:15-16 NKJV	[15] but as He who called you *is* holy, you also be holy in all *your* conduct, [16] because it is written, *"Be holy, for I am holy."*
Acts 1:7-8 NKJV	[8] But you shall receive power when the Holy Spirit has come upon you; and you shall be witnesses to Me in Jerusalem, and in all Judea and Samaria, and to the end of the earth."

Righteousness

God is righteous. He is just and correct. His perfect righteousness means that He is without sin or guilt. Righteousness is His holy attribute in action against sin and all that is contrary to doing the right thing. This holiness of God will demand that sin be judged and the sinner punished. So this action of judgment is the righteousness of a just God in action. The righteousness of God is to be exemplified by the believers in Jesus Christ living holy and righteousness lives so that their actions will be a guiding light to help lead others to the saving grace of Jesus, leaving judgment to God.

Ephesians 4:24 NKJV	[24] and that you put on the new man which was created according to God, in true righteousness and holiness.
2 Chronicles 12:6 NKJV	[6] So the leaders of Israel and the king humbled themselves; and they said, "The LORD *is* righteous.
Isaiah 11:4-5 NKJV	But with righteousness He shall judge the poor, And decide with equity for the meek of the earth; He shall strike the earth with the rod of His mouth, And with the breath of His lips He shall slay the wicked. [5] Righteousness shall be the belt of His loins,
Deuteronomy 32:4 NKJV	[4] *He is* the Rock, His work *is* perfect; For all His ways *are* justice, A God of truth and without injustice; Righteous and upright *is* He.

Faithfulness

God, having perfect faithfulness, means that He is completely true, trustworthy, loyal, reliable, believable, devoted, dependable, committed, realistic, accurate, dedicated and authentic to His Word and promises. Truth defines His Word and He is Truth. He is always trustworthy and will never be able to lie. So the faithfulness of God is a complete action of the truth and this truth accepted will make one free. The truth shall set you free, God's promise.

Isaiah 25:1 NKJV	[1] O LORD, You *are* my God. I will exalt You, I will praise Your name, For You have done wonderful *things; Your* counsels of old *are* faithfulness *and* truth.
1 John 5:20 NKJV	[20] And we know that the Son of God has come and has given us an understanding, that we may know Him who is true; and we are in Him who is true, in His Son Jesus Christ. This is the true God and eternal life.
Deuteronomy 7:9 NKJV	[9] Therefore know that the LORD your God, He *is* God, the faithful God who keeps covenant and mercy for a thousand generations with those who love Him and keep His commandments;
Hebrews 10:23 NKJV	[23] Let us hold fast the confession of *our* hope without wavering, for He who promised *is* faithful.

The Love of God

The Love of God is God. This is His ultimate nature, a sum of all His other attributes. God is Love, a perfect love which directs all that He does in the universe and with His creations. This is not merely an emotion. But it is an act of God's will in which He gives of Himself. Love is expressed in the Godhead through the Father, Son and Holy Spirit. This love in the Godhead is expressed to mankind, not only in creation, but more wonderfully in redemption. God's holiness and righteousness judged sin in the atoning work of the Cross, while the love of God made available salvation for mankind and extended His Love through the Holy Spirit to guide, help, counsel, direct and empower the believers while they are in this world.

1 John 4:8-11 NKJV	[8] He who does not love does not know God, for God is love. [9] In this the love of God was manifested toward us, that God has sent His only begotten Son into the world, that we might live through Him. [10] In this is love, not that we loved God, but that He loved us and sent His Son *to be* the propitiation for our sins. [1] Beloved, if God so loved us, we also ought to love one another.
2 Corinthians 13:11 NKJV	[11] Finally, brethren, farewell. Become complete. Be of good comfort, be of one mind, live in peace; and the God of love and peace will be with you.

The Goodness of God

In the goodness of God, we see Him providing care for all His creatures. God understands that mankind has needs and He will always meet those needs. If we seek after the Kingdom of God above all things and concerns, putting it as a number one priority in our lives we will not be in need. All of our needs will be met. As the birds of the air are taken care of, God's provision to mankind is even greater because of His love and desire that all come to repentance and seek after God.

Psalm 145:9 KJV	9 The LORD *is* good to all: and his tender mercies *are* over all his works.
Job 38:41 KJV	41 Who provideth for the raven his food? when his young ones cry unto God, they wander for lack of meat.
Matthew 6:26 NKJV	26 Look at the birds of the air, for they neither sow nor reap nor gather into barns; yet your heavenly Father feeds them. Are you not of more value than they?
Acts 14:17 NKJV	17 Nevertheless He did not leave Himself without witness, in that He did good, gave us rain from heaven and fruitful seasons, filling our hearts with food and gladness."
Romans 2:4 NKJV	4 Or do you despise the riches of His goodness, forbearance, and longsuffering, not knowing that the goodness of God leads you to repentance?

The Grace of God

The Greek word for grace is *charis* and is equivalent to the Hebrew word *hesed* which means "loving kindness". Grace is a gift of God and is expressed in God's actions of extending mercy, loving kindness, and salvation to mankind. It is a favor of God to those who participate in His offer of salvation even though it is undeserved, unearned and unmerited. Grace includes the longsuffering and forbearance of God towards sinful mankind.

Romans 3:24 NKJV	24 being justified freely by His grace through the redemption that is in Christ Jesus,
Titus 2:11 NKJV	11 For the grace of God that brings salvation has appeared to all men,
Ephesians 2:5 NKJV	5 even when we were dead in trespasses, made us alive together with Christ (by grace you have been saved),
2 Peter 3:9 NKJV	The Lord is not slack concerning *His* promise, as some count slackness, but is longsuffering toward us,
Exodus 34:6 NKJV	And the LORD passed before him and proclaimed, "The LORD, the LORD God, merciful and gracious, longsuffering, and abounding in goodness and truth,

The Mercy of God

The Lord responds with love towards those who are afflicted or miserable. This is "mercy". This love is especially bestowed upon those who least deserve it. Mercy is the pity of God upon the miserable condition of the sinner because of sin. Scriptures reminds us that the Lord does not deal with us as we fully deserve (Psalms 103:10). The Lord's mercy is rooted in the covenant relationship he has established with mankind. He extends His mercy to us and calls us to receive it but there is an action on our part and that is accepting God's mercy and salvation.

Micah 7:18 NKJV	[18] Who *is* a God like You, Pardoning iniquity And passing over the transgression of the remnant of His heritage? He does not retain His anger forever, Because He delights *in* **mercy.**
Jeremiah 9:24 NKJV	[24] But let him who glories glory in this, That he understands and knows Me, That I *am* the LORD, exercising **loving kindness, judgment**, and **righteousness** in the earth. For in these I delight," says the LORD.
Romans 11: 30-32 NKJV	[30] For as you were once disobedient to God, yet have now obtained **mercy** through their disobedience, [31] even so these also have now been disobedient, that through the **mercy** shown you they also may obtain mercy. [32] For God has committed them all to disobedience, that He might have **mercy** on all.
Ephesians 2:4 HCSB	[4] But God, who is **rich in mercy**, because of His great love that He had for us,
Titus 3:5 HCSB	[5] He saved us — not by works of righteousness that we had done, but according to **His mercy**, through the washing of regeneration and renewal **by the Holy Spirit**.

The Compassion and Kindness of God

God shows His Compassion and Kindness by acting with sorrow and sympathy; by showing pity, mercy, gentle benevolence, goodness and love upon those who are suffering. Jesus exemplified this in His ministry on earth. Now the church which is filled with the Holy Spirit can also exemplify His ministry on earth being led and guided by God's compassion and kindness.

Psalms 145:9 KJV	[9] The LORD *is* good to all: and his tender mercies *are* over all his works.
Matthew 9:36 NKJV	[36] But when He saw the multitudes, He was moved with compassion for them, because they were weary and scattered, like sheep having no shepherd.
Ephesians 2:4-7 NKJV	[4] But God, who is rich in mercy, because of His great love

	with which He loved us, ⁵ even when we were dead in trespasses, made us alive together with Christ (by grace you have been saved), ⁶ and raised *us* up together, and made *us* sit together in the heavenly *places* in Christ Jesus, ⁷ that in the ages to come He might show the exceeding riches of His grace in *His* kindness toward us in Christ Jesus.
Titus 3:4-6 NKJV	But when the kindness and the love of God our Savior toward man appeared, ⁵ not by works of righteousness which we have done, but according to His mercy He saved us, through the washing of regeneration and renewing of the Holy Spirit, ⁶ whom He poured out on us abundantly through Jesus Christ our Savior,
Exodus 34: 7 KJV	⁷ Keeping mercy for thousands, forgiving iniquity and transgression and sin, and that will by no means clear *the guilty*; visiting the iniquity of the fathers upon the children, and upon the children's children, unto the third and to the fourth *generation*.

The Godhead

The Scriptures do not attempt to explain the mystery of the Godhead; they declare it (Colossians 2:2; 1 Timothy 3:16). Much of the misunderstanding relative to the being of God, especially in the area of the distinctions in the Godhead, has come into the Church because of the terminology and theological phraseology that has been developed through the centuries. In the New Testament the term "the Godhead" is used in relation to God. The word refers to that which is Divine, to Deity, involving God's revelation of His own make up of being and that being is ONE God with three different personalities: the Father, the Son and the Holy Spirit.

One way to look at it for an understanding is to compare it to the sun. The sun is a single star, yet it has three major attributes; energy, light, and heat. One sun with three attributes that are not able to be separated and can be considered equal to each other and co-exist. The sun is needed to sustain life on earth, as God is needed to sustain the entire universe.

The very fact that the Father, Son and Holy Spirit are linked together in the baptismal command (Matthew 28:19) shows that there is co-existence, co-equality in nature, power and attributes, as well as co-eternity of being. God is one undivided and indivisible essence, but in the one true God there are three eternal distinctions, the Father, Son and Holy Spirit.

Although the Bible never formally speaks of the Person of God, it does reveal the personality of God as Father, Son and Holy Spirit. So when we speak of the Persons in the Eternal Godhead, it is not used in the ordinary sense as used of human persons. The Scriptures clearly show that the Father, Son and Holy Spirit each have the characteristics and qualities of personality. The word "trinity" was introduced by *Tertullian*, one of the early Church Fathers, to define the teaching concerning the Godhead. It simply means "threefold" or "three in one". Though the word "trinity" is not used in the Scriptures, the words "three" and "one" is used. A consideration of these words reveals that the God of the Bible is triune in nature and being.

Let us consider the truth that God is one God and God is three personalities, as set forth in the Scriptures. In doing so, we find that in the Biblical revelation of God, there are two streams of Scripture concerning His Person, as being – God is one, and God is three.

We must avoid heresies such as Unitarianism who overlook the persons of the Father, Son and Holy Spirit. That can lead someone to believe that God is a numerical number one. We also must avoid the heresy of Tri-theism which teaches God is three different Gods, instead of one God with three persons within. This can be avoided by NOT over-emphasizing either. We must keep a balance of the understanding of God's make up and keep our belief in one God, existing in three persons, distinguishable, but indivisible.

Text Message →	Individual → God is one → Distinguishable → God is three

(2 Corinthians 13-14 HCSB) [13] The grace of the Lord Jesus Christ, and the love of God, and the fellowship of the Holy Spirit be with all of you.

(John 3:34-35 NKJV) [34] For He whom God has sent speaks the words of God, for God does not give the Spirit by measure. [35] The Father loves the Son, and has given all things into His hand.

(Colossians 2:9 KJV) "For in Him (Christ) dwells all the fullness of the Godhead bodily"

(Romans 1:20 KJV) "For since the creation of the world His invisible attributes are clearly seen, being understood by the things that are made, even His eternal power and Godhead, so that they are without excuse"

(Matthew 28:19 NKJV) [19] Go therefore and make disciples of all the nations, baptizing them in the name of the Father and of the Son and of the Holy Spirit,

The Oneness of the Godhead

The Old and New Testaments of the Bible both confirm the fact that God is one God and that there are no other gods. Only the one God should be worshiped and prayed to, we should not attempt to worship or pray to others in place of the one and only God and be careful not to separate who God is and He is all of the Father, Son and Holy Spirit; One God.

Old Testament		New Testament	
Deuteronomy 4:35, 39	The Lord He is God, there is none beside Him.	Mark 12:29	"The Lord our God is one God".
Psalm 86:10;	"Thou art God alone."	1 Corinthians	"There is none other

83:18		8:4	God but one."
Exodus 20:3	"Thou shall have no other gods before Me."	Mark 12:32	"For there is one God and there is none other but He."
1 Samuel 2:2; 2 Samuel 7:22	There is none besides thee.	1 Timothy 2:5; 1:17	"Thou believes there is one God, thou doest well."
Isaiah 44:6 & 8; 43:10; 45:18	"Besides Me there is no God.	Ephesians 4:6	"One God and Father of all."
Deuteronomy 6:4	"Hear O Israel, the Lord our God is one Lord."	Galatians 3:20	"God is one."

The Trinity of God

The Old and New Testaments of the Bible also teach that not only is God one but that God is three in person. This is called the Trinity of God. This means that there is one God manifested in three Persons. There are two kinds of unity spoken of in the Bible, an absolute and a compound. There are two Greek and two Hebrew words that translate the word "one". The Hebrew words are "*yachead*" and "*echad*". *Yachead* means absolute unity, a numerical number. In the Old Testament it is used, but never to describe the unity of God, instead it is used to signify the one way to God, one Son of God, and one hope of salvation.

(Genesis 22:2 KJV) *Abraham offered up "his only (yachead) son, Isaac.*	2 And he said, Take now thy son, thine only *son* Isaac, whom thou lovest, and get thee into the land of Moriah; and offer him there for a burnt offering upon one of the mountains which I will tell thee of.
(Zechariah 12:10 KJV) *They shall mourn for Him, as one mourned for his only (yachead) son.*	10 And I will pour upon the house of David, and upon the inhabitants of Jerusalem, the spirit of grace and of supplications: and they shall look upon me whom they have pierced, and they shall mourn for him, as one mourneth for *his* only *son*, and shall be in bitterness for him, as one that is in bitterness for *his* firstborn.

Echad speaks of a compound or collective unity which comprises more than one person, like one crowd, one people, and one nation.

(Genesis 2:24 KJV) *These two shall be one (echad) flesh.*	24 Therefore shall a man leave his father and his mother, and shall cleave unto his wife: and they shall be one flesh.
(Ezra 3:1 KJV) *"People gathered together as one".*	1 And when the seventh month was come, and the children of Israel *were* in the cities, the people gathered themselves together as one man to Jerusalem.
(1 Chronicles 12:38 KJV)	38 All these men of war, that could keep rank, came with a

All the rest of Israel were of one heart to make David king.	perfect heart to Hebron, to make David king over all Israel: and all the rest also of Israel *were* of one heart to make David king.

In the Old Testament the Hebrew word *"echad"* is used many times and it usually has the thought of a compound unity; the unity of more than one. This word is used in the Old Testament concerning the one God. The two Greek words that have the same usage are *"heis"* and *"monos"*. God is referred to as one but not just referring to a number one but to a compound unity; unity of one with more than one person within. This identifies the plurality of Divine Persons in the one God. This unity is a compound tri-unity, the union of three in one.
The Scripture (Deuteronomy 6:4) uses this and states that "Jehovah Elohim" is a united one, uni-plural in nature and being.

The word *"elohim"* is a uni-plural word implying plurality of divine persons. Yet it was this which preserved Israel from total lapse into heathen polytheistic religions, the worship of many gods. *" In that day, there shall be one (echad) Lord, and His Name one (echad)."* (Zechariah 14:9KJV)

Throughout the Bible God is always identified as one God, undivided and existing with three eternal distinctions. In the Godhead which is represented by the Father, the Son and the Holy Spirit are three persons in one God, distinguishable but indivisible.

Old Testament Scriptures

All of these verses speak of the plurality of divine Persons in the one God, and generally this Hebrew uni-plural word *"Elohim"* is used in the Old Testament to speak of the Eternal Godhead. It is the Old Testament equivalent for the New Testament definition of God as Father, Son and Holy Spirit, or, the Godhead.

(Genesis 1:26 KJV)	26 And God said, Let us make man in our image, after our likeness: and let them have dominion over the fish of the sea, and over the fowl of the air, and over the cattle, and over all the earth, and over every creeping thing that creepeth upon the earth.
(Genesis 3:22 KJV)	22 And the LORD God said, Behold, the man is become as one of us, to know good and evil: and now, lest he put forth his hand, and take also of the tree of life, and eat, and live for ever:
(Isaiah 48:16 NKJV)	16 "Come near to Me, hear this: I have not spoken in secret from the beginning; From the time that it was, I *was* there. And now the Lord GOD and His Spirit Have sent Me."
(Isaiah 61:1 NKJV)	1 "The Spirit of the Lord GOD *is* upon Me, Because the LORD has anointed Me To preach good tidings to the poor;

The Spirit (the Holy Spirit) of the Lord (the Father) is upon Me, because He hath anointed Me (the Son).	He has sent Me to heal the brokenhearted, To proclaim liberty to the captives, And the opening of the prison to *those who are* bound;

The Old Testament speaks of The Father (Isaiah 63:16; Malachi 2:10) The Son (Psalm 45:6-7; 2:6-7,12; Proverbs 30:4; Isaiah 7:14; 9:6) The Holy Spirit (Genesis 1:2; Isaiah 11:1-3; 48:16; Genesis 6:3; 61:1; 63:10).

New Testament Scriptures

Jesus Christ, the Living Word, is the Son person of God. He is one with the Father and Holy Spirit. He is revealed in the New Testament as He spoke the Word of God to mankind.

(Hebrews 1:1-2 NKJV) God, who at various times and in various ways spoke in time past to the fathers by the prophets, has in these last days spoken to us by His Son, whom He has appointed heir of all things, through whom also He made the worlds;

(Matthew 11:27 NKJV) "All things have been delivered to Me by My Father, an no one knows the Son except the Father. Nor does anyone know the Father except the Son, and the one to whom the Son wills to reveal Him."

Distinction in the Godhead	
(Matthew 3:16-17 NKJV) ***Fathers*** *– voice was spoke from heaven;* ***Son*** *– of God in Jordan's waters of baptism;* ***Holy Spirit*** *– descending bodily in the shape of a dove*	[16] When He had been baptized, Jesus came up immediately from the water; and behold, the heavens were opened to Him, and He saw the Spirit of God descending like a dove and alighting upon Him. [17] And suddenly a voice *came* from heaven, saying, "This is My beloved Son, in whom I am well pleased."
(1 John 5:7-8 NKJV) There are three that bear record in heaven: The **Father**, The **Word (Son)**, and the **Holy Spirit** (*NOTE – and these three are one – that is tri-unity, One God who is manifested into three Persons.*)	For there are three that bear witness in heaven: the Father, the Word, and the Holy Spirit; and these three are one. [8] And there are three that bear witness on earth:
(Matthew 28:19 NKJV) *baptizing them in the name of the –* ***Father****, and of the* ***Son*** *and of*	[19] Go therefore and make disciples of all the nations, baptizing them in the name of the Father and of the Son and of the Holy Spirit,

the **Holy Spirit**	
(2 Corinthians 13:14 NKJV) *The grace of our **Lord Jesus Christ** (Son); The Love of **God** (Father); The communion of the **Holy Spirit** (Holy Spirit).*	[14] The grace of the Lord Jesus Christ, and the love of God, and the communion of the Holy Spirit *be* with you all. Amen.

Relationship and Distinction in the Godhead

Although the Father, Son and Holy Spirit maintain common qualities they also remain distinct from each other.

Scriptures recognize three as God.	The Father is God – John 6:27;1 Peter 1:2; Romans 1:7	Christ is God – John 1:1, 18; Titus 2:13; Romans 9:5	The Holy Spirit is God – Acts 5:3,4
Scriptures recognize clear distinctions as Persons.	Son recognizes the Father distinct from Himself – John 5:32, 37	Father and Son are distinguished as the Begetter and Begotten – Psalm 2:7; John 1:14-18; 3:16	Son recognizes that He was sent by the Father and that the Holy Spirit will be sent from the Father through the Son – John 10:36; 14:16, 17; 15:26; Galatians 4:4
Scriptures identify three in creation.	The Father in Creation – Exodus 20:11	The Son in Creation – Colossians 1:16-17; John 1:3; Hebrews 1:2, 10	The Holy Spirit in Creation – Job 26:13; 33:4; Psalm 104:30; Genesis 1:2
Scriptures show the eternity of the Godhead.	Eternity of the Father – Deuteronomy 33:27; Psalm 104:30	Eternity of the Son – Micah 5:2; John 1:1; Philippians 2:6	Eternity of the Holy Spirit – Hebrews 9:14
Omnipresence of the Godhead.	Omnipresence of the Father – Jeremiah 23:23-24	Omnipresence of the Son – Ephesians 1:23; Matthew 18:20	Omnipresence of the Holy Spirit – Hebrews 9:14
Omniscience of the Godhead.	Omniscience of the Father – Proverbs 15:3; Hebrews 4:12; I John 3:20	Omniscience of the Son – John 21:17; Colossians 2:3	Omniscience of the Holy Spirit – 1 Corinthians 2:10
Omnipotence of the Godhead.	Omnipotence of the Father – Matthew 19:26	Omnipotence of the Son – Philippians 3:21; Matthew 28:18; Revelation 1:8	Omnipotence of the Holy Spirit – 1 Corinthians 12:8-11

The Father

The Father is God and is a distinct person in the Godhead. He is invisible, eternal, self-existent, and immortal, residing in the light which is unapproachable by man and who no one has seen, nor can see.

(1 Timothy 6:16 NKJV) ¹⁶ who alone has immortality, dwelling in unapproachable light, whom no man has seen or can see, to whom *be* honor and everlasting power. Amen.

(Malachi 2:10 KJV) ¹⁰ Have we not all one father? hath not one God created us? why do we deal treacherously every man against his brother, by profaning the covenant of our fathers?

The Son

The Son is God and is a distinct person in the Godhead. He is co-equal with the Father and Holy Spirit. He is the Living Word manifested in the flesh. He always existed and is eternal with the Father and Holy Spirit.

(John 1:3 NKJV) ³ All things were made through Him, and without Him nothing was made that was made.

(1 Corinthians 15:47 NKJV) ⁴⁷ The first man *was* of the earth, *made* of dust; the second Man *is* the Lord from heaven.

(Colossians 1:17 NKJV) ¹⁷ And He is before all things, and in Him all things consist. ¹⁸ And He is the head of the body, the church, who is the beginning, the firstborn from the dead, that in all things He may have the preeminence. ¹⁹ For it pleased *the Father that* in Him all the fullness should dwell, ²⁰ and by Him to reconcile all things to Himself, by Him, whether things on earth or things in heaven, having made peace through the blood of His cross.

> Text Message → The Son is to be worshipped as God – this would be blasphemy and idolatry if the Son were not God and co-equal and co-eternal with the Father.

The Holy Spirit

The Holy Spirit is God and a distinct person in the Godhead. He is not merely an influence but a divine Person equal with the Father and Son. He is Who helps the Church and each individual believer with their work of God on this earth. He gives us strength, wisdom, truth, and power to sustain our daily walk with God.

(1 John 5:7-8 NKJV) ⁷ For there are three that bear witness in heaven: the Father, the Word, and the Holy Spirit; and these three are one. ⁸ And there are three that bear witness on earth: the Spirit, the water, and the blood; and these three agree as one.

(2 Timothy 1:14 NKJV) [14] That good thing which was committed to you, keep by the Holy Spirit who dwells in us

(1 Corinthians 2:13 NKJV) [13] These things we also speak, not in words which man's wisdom teaches but which the Holy Spirit teaches, comparing spiritual things with spiritual.

Text Message → Remember, One Holy Bible, One revelation which is the Holy Bible made up of the Scriptures, and One God who is the Father, Son and Holy Spirit leading us to One way to Salvation through Jesus Christ, the One and Only way.

Begin With Prayer

Biblical Teaching/Doctrine of Christ

Biblical Building Block # 5

(John 3:16-18 HCSB)

16 "For God loved the world in this way: He gave His One and Only Son, so that everyone who believes in Him will not perish but have eternal life. 17 For God did not send His Son into the world that He might condemn the world, but that the world might be saved through Him. 18 Anyone who believes in Him is not condemned, but anyone who does not believe is already condemned, because he has not believed in the name of the One and Only Son of God.

(1 John 4:10 HCSB)

10 Love consists in this: not that we loved God, but that He loved us and sent His Son to be the propitiation for our sins.

When someone really, really loves you, they will give all that they have including their life. This is exactly what Jesus Christ did for all of mankind. He came out of paradise to a hostile world who He knew would eventually take His life. Not only did He come out of paradise but He kept at bay all of the power available to Him and clothed Himself in a human body. He experienced all the things that mankind experiences on this earth, hunger, thirst, loneliness, grief, and temptations. The task for Him was greater than any person has been given since Adam and that was to be sinless, without blame and pay the price of death for doing it and He knew all of this in advance. But He still came to our rescue. He became a servant to mankind, being an example of how life should be lived and how we should face death. In all this He gave us hope that by our faith in Him and accepting Him as our Savior we will have eternal life in paradise and He gave us the power through the Holy Spirit to wage a spiritual war in this world for the Kingdom of God. Yes, He gave His life and that is love of no measure, all He asks mankind is to believe and have faith and He will take us the rest of the way.

1. Can you explain what is meant by the incarnation of Christ?

2. Can you explain how Jesus Christ can be God and man?

3. Why was the incarnation something that needed to happen?

4. Make a list of several attributes of Jesus Christ that describe His deity.

5. Make a list of several attributes of Jesus Christ that describe His humanity.

6. What does the term *mediator* mean in relation to Jesus?

7. Why was Jesus sinless while all other men are born with a sin nature?

Introduction

The Bible itself declares that Jesus Christ is God manifested in the flesh. He is the eternal Son of God, who made the perfect sacrifice for sin and made redemption available for fallen mankind. His virgin birth, sinless humanity, death, burial and resurrection are fulfillment of a promise that was identified throughout the Old Testament and was completed in the New Testament. God's plan of salvation was put in motion and revealed by Jesus Christ.

It now becomes critical for all of mankind to face and answer three questions related to the Lord Jesus Christ. The questions were asked of the religious leaders in the time of Jesus and also by Pilate of the many seeking to bring about the death and crucifixion of Jesus. They are saying: "What do you think about the Christ"? "Whose Son is He"? (Matthew 22:42 NKJV) and Pilate said to them, "What then shall I do with Jesus who is called Christ"? (Matthew 27:22 NKJV). How a person answers these questions will dictate their decision of accepting the salvation plan given to mankind by God. The plan of salvation was revealed by God in Jesus Christ and what a person believes about Jesus Christ is the most important decision that they will ever make in this lifetime. This decision also will determine their eternal existence with their creator, God, or an eternal separation apart from God, eternal damnation.

There is no other way, of salvation – there is no other plan – there is no other God – there is only one path to God and that is through Jesus Christ. (John 14:6 NKJ) *⁶ Jesus said to him, "I am the way, the truth, and the life. No one comes to the Father except through Me.*

Heresies Concerning the Person of Christ

Heresies concerning the person of Christ were started during early stages of the church. The Gospels and Epistles of the apostolic writers dealt with these issues as they became known. Today these same basic heresies exist in our culture. Because of these heresies various councils of the Patristic Church (fathers of the early Christian Church) got together and formulated doctrinal statements and creeds to defend the Biblical Christology. Following are the most prominent heresies concerning the person of Christ, which the false cults in Christendom base their teachings upon.

Ebionites	This denied Christ's deity.
Gnostics	This denied Christ's humanity.
Arians	Taught that Christ was a created being (like all men).
Apollinarians	This denied the completeness of Christ's human nature.
Nestorians	This denied the union of the two natures in Christ, reducing Him to a man filled with God.
Eutychians	This denied the distinction of the 2 natures of Christ, making a third or hybrid nature of the two.
Monophysites	This denied the two natures and wills in the one person of Christ.

Orthodox Statement Concerning the Person of Christ

Due to the heresies that fumed over the person of Christ, the different church councils got together periodically to forge out creeds on the anvil of truth in an attempt to defend and safeguard them. (Jude 3 HCSB) *"Dear friends, although I was eager to write you about the salvation we share, I found it necessary to write and exhort you to contend for the faith that was delivered to the saints once for all."*

Such creeds were not done by the apostles but the truth was written within their writings. These truths needed to be pulled together and organized in such a fashion to articulate creeds that would identify and clearly define the truths concerning the person of Christ.

Noted is the Creed from "Council of Chalcedon". This best states the orthodox (adhering to the accepted or traditional and established faith – early church) position concerning Christ's glorious person.

This Creed is that which was formulated by the 'Council of Chalcedon' in 451 A.D.

"Following the holy fathers we all with one consent teach and confess one and the same Son, our Lord Jesus Christ, the same perfect in deity, and the same perfect in humanity, truly God, and the same truly Man, of reasonable soul and body, of the same substance with the Father as to His divinity, of the same substance with us as to His humanity, in all things like to us, except sin, before the ages begotten of the Father as to His deity, but in the latter days for us, and for our redemption, begotten (the same) of the Virgin Mary, the mother of God, as to His humanity, one and the same Christ, Son, Lord. Only-begotten manifested in two natures, without confusion, without conversion, indivisibly, inseparably. The distinction of natures being by no means abolished by the union, but rather the property of each preserved and combined into one person and one hypostasis; not one severed or divided into two." (Robert Clark, in "The Christ of God" pp.41-42)

Prophecies in the Old Testament Concerning the Person of Christ

The Old Testament prophecies pertaining to the coming of the Messiah reveals that there were two types of thought. One type speaks of the deity of Christ, while the other speaks of the humanity of Christ.

The Deity of Christ - the following Scriptures identify the deity of Christ, stating that the Savior/Redeemer would be God incarnated. (Manifested in the flesh – embodied in human form)

(Isaiah 7:14 KJV)	14 Therefore the Lord himself shall give you a sign; Behold, a virgin shall conceive, and bear a son, and shall call his name Immanuel.
(Isaiah 9:6 KJV)	6 For unto us a child is born, unto us a son is given: and the government shall be upon his shoulder: and his name shall be called Wonderful, Counselor, The mighty God, The everlasting Father,

	The Prince of Peace.
(Jeremiah 23:5-6 KJV)	5 Behold, the days come, saith the LORD, that I will raise unto David a righteous Branch, and a King shall reign and prosper, and shall execute judgment and justice in the earth. 6 In his days Judah shall be saved, and Israel shall dwell safely: and this is his name whereby he shall be called, THE LORD OUR RIGHTEOUSNESS.
(Micah 5:2 KJV)	2 But thou, Bethlehem Ephratah, though thou be little among the thousands of Judah, yet out of thee shall he come forth unto me that is to be ruler in Israel; whose goings forth have been from of old, from everlasting.

The Humanity of Christ - The following Scriptures indicated that the Redeemer would be a man, born of a woman. They set forth the humanity of the Messiah, even as the previous Scriptures set forth His deity.

(Genesis 22:18 NKJV) Would Come from the seed of Abraham.	18 In your seed all the nations of the earth shall be blessed, because you have obeyed My voice."
(Numbers 24:17-19 NKJV) The Messiah would come from the nation of Israel.	17 "I see Him, but not now; I behold Him, but not near; A Star shall come out of Jacob; A Scepter shall rise out of Israel, And batter the brow of Moab, And destroy all the sons of tumult. 18 "And Edom shall be a possession; Seir also, his enemies, shall be a possession, While Israel does valiantly. 19 Out of Jacob One shall have dominion, And destroy the remains of the city."
(2 Samuel 7:12-14 KJV) Will be eternal.	12 And when thy days be fulfilled, and thou shalt sleep with thy fathers, I will set up thy seed after thee, which shall proceed out of thy bowels, and I will establish his kingdom. 13 He shall build an house for my name, and I will stablish the throne of his kingdom for ever. 14 I will be his father, and he shall be my son. If he commit iniquity, I will chasten him with the rod of men, and with the stripes of the children of men:
(Isaiah 7:14 HCSB) Came from a virgin. (Isaiah 11:1-5 HCSB)	14 Therefore, the Lord Himself will give you a sign: The virgin will conceive, have a son, and name him Immanuel. 1 Then a shoot will grow from the stump of Jesse, and a branch from his roots will bear fruit. 2 The Spirit of the LORD will rest on Him — a Spirit of wisdom and understanding, a Spirit of counsel and strength, a Spirit of knowledge and of the fear of the LORD. 3 His delight will be in the fear of the LORD. He will not judge by what He sees with His eyes, He will not execute justice by what He hears with His ears, 4 but He will judge the poor righteously and execute justice for the oppressed

	of the land. He will strike the land with discipline from His mouth, and He will kill the wicked with a command from His lips. **5** Righteousness will be a belt around His loins; faithfulness will be a belt around His waist.

These verses link together how God identified and worked through a man, a nation from a man, a tribe of the nation, a house from the tribe, and a virgin woman from the house and then preserved the genealogy of the Messiah as to His humanity.

Foretelling of the Messiah in the Old Testament was done by the prophets. They all agreed that this Messiah would be God and man in one person possessing divine and human natures. Since the creation of Adam and Eve all of mankind was born of an earthly father and mother. The Messiah would be born of a women that is a virgin and His father would not be an earthly human father but of God. The child would be a seed of the woman as stated in (Genesis 3:15), and yet the Son of God by a virgin (Isaiah 7:14). The birth of Jesus Christ was the fulfillment of these prophecies (Matthew 1:18-23 with Luke 1:35).

It is upon this fact of the virgin birth that Biblical doctrine hangs. *If Jesus Christ is not virgin born, He is not sinless, and if He is not sinless, then He Himself needs a Savior. If He Himself needs salvation, then He cannot be our Savior, Lord or King, and the entire redemptive plan falls powerless to the ground. So we need to understand and believe the foundational significance of the incarnation.*

The Incarnation of Christ

All of the New Testament writers bear witness to the truth of the incarnation. It is a historical fact that Jesus Christ was born. Under the inspiration of the Holy Spirit men of God were used to document in detail the facts and truths of this extraordinary event. **The word "incarnation" means "God taking on Himself human flesh".** God became man in Jesus, deity took upon Himself humanity.

To Mary

Mary who was a young Hebrew virgin was visited by the Angel Gabriel announcing the virgin birth of the Messiah. Man would not be the father of this child but the Holy Spirit Himself would overshadow the virgin and place within her womb the seed of the Father God. A miracle would take place and cause this child to be born, sinless. Natural means of mankind cannot account for this miracle. Mary, in total faith, was willing to accept the responsibility and challenge of being the mother of the Christ-child. Becoming obedient to what God had called her to do.

(Luke 1:26-35 NKJV) [26] Now in the sixth month the angel Gabriel was sent by God to a city of Galilee named Nazareth, [27] to a virgin betrothed to a man whose name was Joseph, of the house of David. The virgin's name *was* Mary. [28] And having come in, the angel said to her,

"Rejoice, highly favored *one,* the Lord *is* with you; blessed *are* you among women!" [29] But when she saw *him,* she was troubled at his saying, and considered what manner of greeting this was. [30] Then the angel said to her, "Do not be afraid, Mary, for you have found favor with God. [31] And behold, you will conceive in your womb and bring forth a Son, and shall call His name JESUS. [32] He will be great, and will be called the Son of the Highest; and the Lord God will give Him the throne of His father David. [33] And He will reign over the house of Jacob forever, and of His kingdom there will be no end." [34] Then Mary said to the angel, "How can this be, since I do not know a man?" [35] And the angel answered and said to her, "*The* Holy Spirit will come upon you, and the power of the Highest will overshadow you; therefore, also, that Holy One who is to be born will be called the Son of God.

To Joseph

In the book of Matthew Jesus' birth is introduced after a listing of genealogy breaking the pattern of common decent. The account of this miraculous birth stated that Mary was found with child of the Holy Spirit. The Messianic genealogy was begotten of men, but the Messiah was born outside of men to Mary. So Joseph, after finding out about Mary carrying a child, was ready to have her put away with a bill of divorcement rather than have her stoned to death, which was the Law of Moses at that time, since he knew he was the physical father. Then an Angel of the Lord appeared to him and specifically told him that the child would be a Son whose name was to be called Jesus. This child was the result of the overshadowing of the Holy Spirit and would be Immanuel, "God with us". Joseph, in faith became willing to take the legal custody of the child, accepting the testimony of the Angel concerning the purity of his espoused wife, and accepting the miraculous virgin birth, acting in obedience to God.

(Matthew 1:18-25 NKJV) [18] Now the birth of Jesus Christ was as follows: After His mother Mary was betrothed to Joseph, before they came together, she was found with child of the Holy Spirit. [19] Then Joseph her husband, being a just *man,* and not wanting to make her a public example, was minded to put her away secretly. [20] But while he thought about these things, behold, an angel of the Lord appeared to him in a dream, saying, "Joseph, son of David, do not be afraid to take to you Mary your wife, for that which is conceived in her is of the Holy Spirit. [21] And she will bring forth a Son, and you shall call His name JESUS, for He will save His people from their sins." [22] So all this was done that it might be fulfilled which was spoken by the Lord through the prophet, saying: [23] *"Behold, the virgin shall be with child, and bear a Son, and they shall call His name Immanuel,"* which is translated, "God with us." [24] Then Joseph, being aroused from sleep, did as the angel of the Lord commanded him and took to him his wife, [25] and did not know her till she had brought forth her firstborn Son. And he called His name JESUS.

The Incarnation Personally

Evidence of His own origin, the truth of His miraculous birth was identified by Jesus Himself. Jesus said "I came out from God; I came forth from the Father". He knew that He was David's Lord, as to His deity and David's son, as to His humanity. He claimed God as His Father on numerous occasions, never saying that Joseph was His father. Three times God the Father spoke from heaven bearing witness to the Son's miraculous birth.

(Matthew 3:16-17 KJV) **16** And Jesus, when he was baptized, went up straightway out of the water: and, lo, the heavens were opened unto him, and he saw the Spirit of God descending like a dove, and lighting upon him: **17** And lo a voice from heaven, saying, This is my beloved Son, in whom I am well pleased.

(Matthew 17:1-5 NKJV) **1** Now after six days Jesus took Peter, James, and John his brother, led them up on a high mountain by themselves; **2** and He was transfigured before them. His face shone like the sun, and His clothes became as white as the light. **3** And behold, Moses and Elijah appeared to them, talking with Him. **4** Then Peter answered and said to Jesus, "Lord, it is good for us to be here; if You wish, let us make here three tabernacles: one for You, one for Moses, and one for Elijah." **5** While he was still speaking, behold, a bright cloud overshadowed them; and suddenly a voice came out of the cloud, saying, "This is My beloved Son, in whom I am well pleased. Hear Him!"

(John 16:27-28 NKJV) **27** for the Father Himself loves you, because you have loved Me, and have believed that I came forth from God. **28** I came forth from the Father and have come into the world. Again, I leave the world and go to the Father."

The Incarnation Theologically

There are those who reject the virgin birth and lay claim that the writers of the Epistles never spoke about it. This is not accurate, the writers of the Epistles do speak of both Christ's deity and humanity in a language of theology.

Following are Scriptures from the Apostle Paul, Apostle Peter, and Apostle John confirming the truth of the virgin birth. A consideration of these references all point to the truth of the incarnation; Jesus Christ is God manifest in the flesh. He is the God-Man. The apostles confirmed theologically in the epistles the virgin birth as set forth historically in the Gospels.

Apostle Paul	
(Romans 1:3-4 HCSB)	**3** concerning His Son, Jesus Christ our Lord, who was a descendant of David according to the flesh **4** and who has been declared to be the powerful Son of God by the resurrection from the dead according to the Spirit of holiness.

(Galatians 4:4 HCSB)	**4** When the time came to completion, God sent His Son, born of a woman, born under the law,
(1 Timothy 3:16 HCSB)	**16** And most certainly, the mystery of godliness is great: He was manifested in the flesh, vindicated in the Spirit, seen by angels, preached among the nations, believed on in the world, taken up in glory.
(1 Timothy 2:5 NKJV)	**5** For *there is* one God and one Mediator between God and men, *the* Man Christ Jesus,
(Hebrews 2:14 HCSB)	**14** Now since the children have flesh and blood in common, Jesus also shared in these, so that through His death He might destroy the one holding the power of death—that is, the Devil
(Philippians 2:5-8 NKJV)	**5** Let this mind be in you which was also in Christ Jesus, **6** who, being in the form of God, did not consider it robbery to be equal with God, **7** but made Himself of no reputation, taking the form of a bondservant, *and* coming in the likeness of men. **8** And being found in appearance as a man, He humbled Himself and became obedient to *the point of* death, even the death of the cross.
Apostle Peter	
(Matthew 16:16 HCSB)	**16** Simon Peter answered, "You are the Messiah, the Son of the living God!"
(I Peter 1:18-21 NKJV)	**18** knowing that you were not redeemed with corruptible things, *like* silver or gold, from your aimless conduct *received* by tradition from your fathers, **19** but with the precious blood of Christ, as of a lamb without blemish and without spot. **20** He indeed was foreordained before the foundation of the world, but was manifest in these last times for you **21** who through Him believe in God, who raised Him from the dead and gave Him glory, so that your faith and hope are in God.
Apostle John	
(John 1:14-18 HCSB)	**14** The Word became flesh and took up residence among us. We observed His glory, the glory as the One and Only Son from the Father, full of grace and truth. **15** (John testified concerning Him and exclaimed, "This was the One of whom I said, 'The One coming after me has surpassed me, because He existed before me.'") **16** Indeed, we have all received grace after grace from His fullness, **17** for the law was given through Moses, grace and truth came through Jesus Christ. **18** No one has ever

	seen God. The One and Only Son — the One who is at the Father's side — He has revealed Him.
(1 John 4:9-10 HCSB)	**9** God's love was revealed among us in this way: God sent His One and Only Son into the world so that we might live through Him. **10** Love consists in this: not that we loved God, but that He loved us and sent His Son to be the propitiation for our sins
(1 John 4:2 HCSB)	**2** This is how you know the Spirit of God: Every spirit who confesses that Jesus Christ has come in the flesh is from God.

In Matthew → Jesus is introduced as the Son of David (Isaiah 11:1; Matthew 1:1)
In John → Jesus is introduced as the Son of God (Isaiah 4:2; 7:14; John 3:16)
In Mark → Jesus is introduced as the Son of Man (Zechariah 3:8; Mark 8:38)
In Luke → Jesus is introduced as the Son of Adam (Zechariah 6:12-13; Luke 3:38)

The Necessity of the Incarnation

The Incarnation became necessary when mankind sinned, causing mankind's separation from God and bringing on a death penalty (Genesis 2:16-17 NKJV) *¹⁶ And the LORD God commanded the man, saying, "Of every tree of the garden you may freely eat; ¹⁷ but of the tree of the knowledge of good and evil you shall not eat, for in the day that you eat of it you shall surely die." -* Also read - (Genesis Chapter 3). Mankind then needed someone to redeem them from their sin, death, and restore their relationship with God. However, all those who would be born of Adam's race/seed would be born in sin and need redemption from sin and death for themselves. None of Adam's race/seed could by any means redeem his brother. If mankind is to be redeemed, then someone must shed their blood for mankind, and if no one of Adam's race/seed could do this then only God could redeem mankind. By His own law, God had to become man to accomplish this act. The fall of mankind necessitated God to become a man in order to redeem mankind back to a relationship with Himself/God.

(1 Corinthians 15:21-22 NKJV)	²¹ For since by man *came* death, by Man also *came* the resurrection of the dead. ²² For as in Adam all die, even so in Christ all shall be made alive.
(Romans 5:12-21 NKJV)	¹² Therefore, just as through one man sin entered the world, and death through sin, and thus death spread to all men, because all sinned-- ¹³ (For until the law sin was in the world, but sin is not imputed when there is no law. ¹⁴ Nevertheless death reigned from Adam to Moses, even over those who had not sinned according to the likeness of the transgression of Adam, who is a type of Him who was to come. ¹⁵ But the free gift *is* not like the offense. For if by the one man's offense many died, much more the grace of God and the gift by the grace of the one Man, Jesus Christ, abounded to many. ¹⁶ And the gift *is* not like *that which came* through the one who

	sinned. For the judgment *which came* from one *offense resulted* in condemnation, but the free gift *which came* from many offenses *resulted* in justification. [17] For if by the one man's offense death reigned through the one, much more those who receive abundance of grace and of the gift of righteousness will reign in life through the One, Jesus Christ.) [18] Therefore, as through one man's offense *judgment* came to all men, resulting in condemnation, even so through one Man's righteous act *the free gift came* to all men, resulting in justification of life. [19] For as by one man's disobedience many were made sinners, so also by one Man's obedience many will be made righteous. [20] Moreover the law entered that the offense might abound. But where sin abounded, grace abounded much more, [21] so that as sin reigned in death, even so grace might reign through righteousness to eternal life through Jesus Christ our Lord.
(Galatians 4:4-5 NKJV)	[4] But when the fullness of the time had come, God sent forth His Son, born of a woman, born under the law, [5] to redeem those who were under the law, that we might receive the adoption as sons.
(1 John 3:5 NKJV)	[5] And you know that He was manifested to take away our sins, and in Him there is no sin.
(2 Corinthians 5:21 NKJV)	[21] For He made Him who knew no sin *to be* sin for us, that we might become the righteousness of God in Him.

The Nature of the Incarnation

The nature of the Incarnation is given to us by Paul in the Philippians epistle in the seven-fold humiliation of the Christ of God. The seven steps of humiliation are noted in the following outline of (Philippians 2:6-8 NKJV) *who, being in the form of God, did not consider it robbery to be equal with God,* [7] *but made Himself of no reputation, taking the form of a bondservant,* and *coming in the likeness of men.* [8] *And being found in appearance as a man, He humbled Himself and became obedient to* the point of *death, even the death of the cross.*

The 7-fold humiliation of Christ in summary	
His deity	Who, being in the form of God.
	Thought it not robbery to be equal with God.
His humanity	But made Himself of no reputation.
	And took upon Himself the form of a servant.
	And was made in the likeness of men.
His crucifixion	And being found in fashion as a man, He humbled Himself.
	And became obedient unto death, even the death of the cross.

This statement by Paul about Christ – "made Himself of no reputation"- is saying that Christ emptied Himself by being in "the form of God" and taking upon Himself "the form of man". This was a self-emptying course of action. This is identified as the *Kenosis Theory*. The phrases "emptied Himself" come from a Greek word "kenoo" meaning "to make empty". Theologians in general accept this theory. But there is some misunderstanding concerning it. Some of the common questions asked are: in what way did Christ empty Himself? – What did this self-emptying consist of? And, in be coming man did He cease to be God? All legitimate questions.

False Concepts

He emptied Himself of His Deity.
He emptied Himself of the possession of divine attributes.
He emptied Himself of the use of divine attributes.

Proper Concepts

In becoming man Christ did not cease being God. He did not give up the possession or use of His divine attributes. God was not changed into a man, but assumed the nature of man without ceasing to be God, yes a miracle that only God is capable of performing.

Christ always possessed divine attributes such as omnipresence, omnipotence, omniscience, immutable, self-existence, eternal, holiness, righteousness, love, and faithfulness; these being both essential and moral attributes of God.

In His self-emptying Christ became a man with the same dependencies as all mankind. The glory, majesty and outward expression of the Godhead that He had with the Father and Holy Spirit had been put aside so that He could become the redeemer of mankind. Taking on the status of a servant He still retained the status of God. This was completed in the virgin birth. During this period He did the Father's will in speech and in action and not the will of this human nature. He came into voluntary dependence upon the anointing of the Holy Spirit. This was self-subordination for a redemptive purpose. He never acted for selfish purpose keeping His divine prerogatives under control.

(John 17:5 NKJV) [5] And now, O Father, glorify Me together with Yourself, with the glory which I had with You before the world was.

(Matthew 12:38-39 NKJV) [38] Then some of the scribes and Pharisees answered, saying, "Teacher, we want to see a sign from You." [39] But He answered and said to them, "An evil and adulterous generation seeks after a sign, and no sign will be given to it except the sign of the prophet Jonah.

(John 5:36 NKJV) [36] But I have a greater witness than John's; for the works which the Father has given Me to finish--the very works that I do--bear witness of Me, that the Father has sent Me.

(John 6:38-40 KJV) **38** For I came down from heaven, not to do mine own will, but the will of him that sent me. **39** And this is the Father's will which hath sent me, that of all which he hath given me I should lose nothing, but should raise it up again at the last day. **40** And this is the will of him that sent me, that every one which seeth the Son, and believeth on him, may have everlasting life: and I will raise him up at the last day.

The Basis of the Incarnation

Fulfilling the promises of salvation made to the Patriarchs.	God made covenants of promise with the patriarchs; Adam, Noah, Abraham, Isaac and Jacob. These covenants involved the salvation for both Israel and the Gentiles, the Lord Jesus Christ, through the seed of the woman. Christ came by the incarnation to fulfill these promises made to the fathers.	Matthew 1:1; Isaiah 7:14: 9:6-9; Genesis 3:15; 22:18; Micah 5:1-2
To fulfill the Law, the Psalms and the Prophets.	Jesus came to fulfill the demands of the Law and satisfy the claims of God's holiness. Jesus is the only man who has ever perfectly kept the Law of God. The typical aspects of the law involved the sanctuary services, the priesthood, the offerings and the festival seasons. The Law, Psalms, and Prophets prophesied of His person and work. Jesus specifically stated that He came to fulfill all that was in them.	Matthew 5:17-18; Luke 16:16; 24:27, 44-46; Romans 2:21; Hebrews 10:5-8; Galatians 4:4-5; Psalms 16:8-10; 22:1-18; 41:9-11
Give a complete revelation of the Father God.	Jesus Christ was the fullest and clearest revelation of the Father and Son relationship that God desires the redeemed to come into by the new birth – Only the Son of God could do this.	John 1:14-18; 3:1-5; 14:9; 16:27; Matthew 6:8; 5:45; 11:27; Psalm 103:13; 1 John 3:1-2
To live a perfectly sinless human life.	Jesus alone had no sin, no imperfections in His character. He had not fallen to carnal human nature (worldly desires of the flesh). He therefore was a perfect man.	1 John 2:6; I Peter 2:21; Matthew 11:29

Put away sin by the sacrifice of Himself.	The wages of sin is death and the only way sin could be dealt with was through the death of a sacrifice. Only a perfect sinless man could atone for sin. Christ fulfilled and abolished all animal sacrifices.	Leviticus 16:10-22; Isaiah 53:6; Hebrews 10:1-10; 2:9-14; 2 Corinthians 5:21; Mark 10:45; 1 John 3:5; John 1:29,36
Bring into effect the New Covenant.	The New Covenant is the fulfillment of all previous covenants and brings redeemed mankind into the purposes of the covenant made in the counsels of the Godhead in eternity before sin began.	Jeremiah 31:31-34; Matthew 26:26-28; Hebrews 13:20
Jesus Christ combined in Himself all of these OT offices. As Judge, Christ is God's Savior and Deliverer. As Prophet, He is God's Word. As Priest He is God's Mediator, Advocate and Intercessor. As King He is God's Ruler and authority over us.		
Fulfill Old Testament offices of the Judge.	The Judges were deliverers and saviors of God's people, Israel. This is also Christ's ministry to His people.	Gospel of John; Judges 2:14; Nehemiah 9:27; John 5:19-20; Acts 5:31; 17:31; Isaiah 33:22; Revelation20: 11-15
Fulfill Old Testament offices of the Prophet.	Prophets of Israel were God's spokesmen to the people. Christ is the infallible teacher and prophet of God.	Gospel of Mark; John 1:17-18; Luke 10:16; Hebrews 1:1-2; Acts 2:22-23; 7:37; Exodus 4:14-16; Deuteronomy 18:15-18
Fulfill Old Testament offices of the Priest.	As the prophet represented God to man, the priest represented man to God. This office is vitally connected with the sacrificial system of the offerings for sin. Christ, as High Priest, offering Himself combines both offered and offering in His one person. He is the propitiation, the Advocate, the Intercessor, the High Priest on behalf of the sins of the people. Christ as a priest on earth offered at Calvary's alter his own body and blood as the supreme sacrifice for sin.	Leviticus 8:23-26; 21:16-24; Hebrews 1:9; Zechariah 6:12-13: 1 Samuel 2:27-35; Hebrews 2:10, 17-18; 4:15-16; 5:1-5; 1 Timothy 2:5; Isaiah 53:10-12; John 1:29,36; 2:1-2; Psalm 110:4; Hebrews 7:26-27; Romans 3:25: 8:34
Fulfill Old Testament offices of the King.	As King-Priest Jesus combined in Himself that which was set forth	Psalm 2; 89; 45; 72; 110; John 18:36; 2 Samuel 7:8-

	in the order of Melchisedek – The kings of Israel and Judah, though imperfect in character and deeds, shadowed forth the Lord Jesus Christ who would be King of Kings and Lord of Lords, the Son of David. The incarnation was also for the fulfillment of the Davidic Covenant which promised Messiah the King to be the ultimate ruler of the world.	17; Revelation 15:3; 19:16; 2 Timothy 4:18; Jeremiah 23:5-6; Genesis 14:18-19; Hebrews 7:1-29; Matthew 2:2; John 1:49; 1 Timothy 1:17; 6:5
To consummate the redemptive plan in His second Coming.	The first coming of Christ by the incarnation was but preparatory for the second coming of Christ. The first coming was the inauguration of redemptions' plan, the second coming will be the consummation of it. The second coming completes that which was begun in the first coming; each is incomplete without the other.	Daniel 9:24-27; Romans 8:18-25; Hebrews 9:27-28; Philippians 3:21; 1 Corinthians 15:25-28; 1 Thessalonians 4:15-18
To destroy the works of the devil and his kingdom.	Jesus Christ is King of Kings and Lord of Lords and will ultimately destroy the devils work and kingdom.	1 John 3:5,8; Romans 13:12; Ephesians 5:11; Galatians 5:19; Hebrews 2:14-15; John 12:31; 14:30; Revelation 20:10-15

The Deity of Christ

Jesus Christ completed the work that was His to complete. He became a man, one without sin, and He lived and taught the Living Word to mankind. He led a life of example and put together a team of disciples to carry on the work that He had started. He set up the Church and then gave His life as a ransom, a last sacrifice to cover all of the sins of mankind and opened the door to salvation for mankind to enter. Just by doing a simple task of believing that He, Jesus Christ did die and arose from the dead and now is alive and is the judge of all mankind and accept his invitation of salvation (repent of the world and receive His word and spirit into your heart,) believing that Jesus is God manifest in the flesh, one can experience salvation. He is and was always God. He possesses and continues to have all of the attributes of God, being of eternity, self-existence, all powerful, all knowing, immutable, infallible, perfect in holiness, righteous, faithfulness and most of all perfect in love being Love. Jesus Christ is God.

Attributes Pertaining to Jesus Christ Divinity

Being of eternity	(Revelation 1:8 NKJV) [8] "I am the Alpha and the Omega, *the* Beginning and *the* End,"
Pre-existence of Being	(Revelation 1:17-18 NKJV) [17] And when I saw Him, I fell at His feet as dead. But He laid His right hand on me, saying to me, "Do not be afraid; I am the First and the Last. [18] I *am* He who lives, and was dead, and behold, I am alive forevermore. Amen. And I have the keys of Hades and of Death.
Self-existence	(Hebrews 7:16 NKJV) [16] who has come, not according to the law of a fleshly commandment, but according to the power of an endless life.
Omnipotence - all powerful	(Matthew 28:18 NKJV) [18] And Jesus came and spoke to them, saying, "All authority has been given to Me in heaven and on earth.
Omniscience - all knowing	(Colossians 2:3 NKJV) [3] in whom are hidden all the treasures of wisdom and knowledge
Omnipresence - everywhere present at all times	(Ephesians 1:23 NKJV) [23] which is His body, the fullness of Him who fills all in all.
Immutable - unchanged & unchangeable, the same yesterday, today and forever	(Malachi 3:6 KJV) **6** For I *am* the LORD, I change not; therefore ye sons of Jacob are not consumed.
Infallible - not able to err or to make mistakes	(John 14:6 NKJV) **6** Jesus said to him, "I am the way, the truth, and the life. No one comes to the Father except through Me.
Sovereign - Every knee shall bow to the Son of God	(Philippians 2:9-11 NKJV) [9] Therefore God also has highly exalted Him and given Him the name which is above every name, [10] that at the name of Jesus every knee should bow, of those in heaven, and of those on earth, and of those under the earth, [11] and *that* every tongue should confess that Jesus Christ *is* Lord, to the glory of God the Father.
Perfect Holiness	(1 Peter 2:22 NKJV) [22] *"Who committed no sin, Nor was deceit found in His mouth";*
Perfect Righteousness	(Jeremiah 23:5-6 KJV) **5** Behold, the days come, saith the LORD, that I will raise unto David a righteous Branch, and a King shall reign and prosper, and shall execute judgment and justice in the earth. **6** In his days Judah shall be saved, and Israel shall dwell safely: and this *is* his name whereby he shall be called, THE LORD OUR RIGHTEOUSNESS.

Perfect Love	(John 3:16 NKJV) ¹⁶ For God so loved the world that He gave His only begotten Son, that whoever believes in Him should not perish but have everlasting life.
Perfect Faithfulness	(Revelation 1:5 KJV) ⁵ And from Jesus Christ, *who is* the faithful witness, *and* the first begotten of the dead, and the prince of the kings of the earth. Unto him that loved us, and washed us from our sins in his own blood,

The Testimony of Scriptures Witness to the Deity of Christ

Existed in the beginning and was with God the Father.	(John 1:1-4 NKJV) ¹ In the beginning was the Word, and the Word was with God, and the Word was God. ² He was in the beginning with God. ³ All things were made through Him, and without Him nothing was made that was made. ⁴ In Him was life, and the life was the light of men.
Manifest in the flesh.	(1Timothy 3:16 NKJV) ¹⁶ And without controversy great is the mystery of godliness: God was manifested in the flesh, Justified in the Spirit, Seen by angels, Preached among the Gentiles, Believed on in the world, Received up in glory.
He is Immanuel, God with us.	(Matthew 1:23 NKJV) ²³ *"Behold, the virgin shall be with child, and bear a Son, and they shall call His name Immanuel,"* which is translated, "God with us."
The Word made flesh.	(John 1:14 NKJV) ¹⁴ And the Word became flesh and dwelt among us, and we beheld His glory, the glory as of the only begotten of the Father, full of grace and truth.
He is our God and Savior.	(2 Peter 1:1 NKJV) ¹ Simon Peter, a bondservant and apostle of Jesus Christ, To those who have obtained like precious faith with us by the righteousness of our God and Savior Jesus Christ:

Divine Claims Made by Christ

Claims made by Jesus could only have been made by God. Jesus was either a liar and imposter or self deceived if these claims are not true. But we know that these claims are true. He died but also arose from the dead (the resurrection) and was seen by many in His resurrected body.

No normal person could do this or has done this but only God is able and also able to resurrect the redeemed.

Claimed to be one with God.	(John 5:23 NKJV) ²³ that all should honor the Son just as they honor the Father. He who does not honor the Son does not honor the Father who sent Him.
Claimed God as	(Revelation 3:21 NKJV) ²¹ To him who overcomes I will grant to sit

109

His Father.	with Me on My throne, as I also overcame and sat down with My Father on His throne.
Claimed to be the I AM, denoting eternal existence.	(Revelation 22:13 NKJV) [13] I am the Alpha and the Omega, *the* Beginning and *the* End, the First and the Last."
Claimed divine Son-ship, making Himself God.	(1 John 5:20-21 NKJV) [20] And we know that the Son of God has come and has given us an understanding, that we may know Him who is true; and we are in Him who is true, in His Son Jesus Christ. This is the true God and eternal life. [21] Little children, keep yourselves from idols. Amen.

Divine Works

The Creator of the universe.	(Hebrews 1:10 NKJV) And: *"You, LORD, in the beginning laid the foundation of the earth, And the heavens are the work of Your hands.*
The Creator of angels and man.	(Genesis 1:26 KJV) [26] And God said, Let us make man in our image, after our likeness: and let them have dominion over the fish of the sea, and over the fowl of the air, and over the cattle, and over all the earth, and over every creeping thing that creepeth upon the earth.
Forgave sins.	(Acts 5:31 NKJV) [31] Him God has exalted to His right hand *to be* Prince and Savior, to give repentance to Israel and forgiveness of sins.
Raised the dead and will change the bodies of believers at His coming by reason of who He is.	(John 5:28-29 NKJV) [28] Do not marvel at this; for the hour is coming in which all who are in the graves will hear His voice [29] and come forth--those who have done good, to the resurrection of life, and those who have done evil, to the resurrection of condemnation.
Will judge the living and dead and it is His kingdom.	(2 Timothy 4:1 NKJV) [1] I charge *you* therefore before God and the Lord Jesus Christ, who will judge the living and the dead at His appearing and His kingdom
Giver of eternal life to all who trust the Father through Himself.	(John 10:28 NKJV) [28] And I give them eternal life, and they shall never perish; neither shall anyone snatch them out of My hand.

Divine Worship Given to Jesus Christ

Jesus was bestowed Divine worship in which He received. He never refused such worship. This is very much different then other men of God who absolutely refused worship of or from other people, as did the elect angels. Worshipping Jesus as God, if He is not God, would be blasphemy and idolatry. So, for Jesus to accept worship which belongs only to God His Father would be taking something that was not appropriate, be blasphemy and also be idolatry, but Jesus and the Father are one and it was appropriate because Jesus is God.

(Revelation 22:8-9 NKJV) ⁸ Now I, John, saw and heard these things. And when I heard and saw, I fell down to worship before the feet of the angel who showed me these things. ⁹ Then he said to me, "See *that you do* not *do that.* For I am your fellow servant, and of your brethren the prophets, and of those who keep the words of this book. Worship God."

(Acts 10:25-26 NKJV) ²⁵ As Peter was coming in, Cornelius met him and fell down at his feet and worshiped *him.* ²⁶ But Peter lifted him up, saying, "Stand up; I myself am also a man."

Worshipped by angels.	(Hebrews 1:6 NKJV) ⁶ But when He again brings the firstborn into the world, He says: *"Let all the angels of God worship Him."*
Worshipped by man.	(Matthew 8:2 NKJV) ² And behold, a leper came and worshiped Him, saying, "Lord, if You are willing, You can make me clean."
Worshipped by all creatures.	(Revelation 5:13 KJV) ¹³ And every creature which is in heaven, and on the earth, and under the earth, and such as are in the sea, and all that are in them, heard I saying, Blessing, and honour, and glory, and power, *be* unto him that sitteth upon the throne, and unto the Lamb for ever and ever.
Prayed to as praying to God.	(Acts 1:24 NKJV) ²⁴ And they prayed and said, "You, O Lord, who know the hearts of all, show which of these two You have chosen
Honored equally with the Father God.	(Revelation 1:5-6 KJV) ⁵ And from Jesus Christ, *who is* the faithful witness, *and* the first begotten of the dead, and the prince of the kings of the earth. Unto him that loved us, and washed us from our sins in his own blood, ⁶ And hath made us kings and priests unto God and his Father; to him *be* glory and dominion for ever and ever. Amen.

The Humanity of Christ

Had a Human Birth and Human Ancestry

Jesus was born a man of a woman, Mary, and came from the nation of Israel, of the seed of David. The genealogy of Christ on earth is tracked back to David and Adam in Luke's Gospel through His mother Mary and back to David and Abraham in Matthew's Gospel through, Joseph the husband of Mary. (***The Historical Book of Josephus records Jesus as a real person. (Book XVIII – From the Banishment of Archelaus to the departure of the Jews from Babylon – Chapter III – beginning paragraph 3)***

Born of a woman.	(Matthew 2:11 KJV) [11] And when they had come into the house, they saw the young Child with Mary His mother, and fell down and worshiped Him. And when they had opened their treasures, they presented gifts to Him: gold, frankincense, and myrrh.
Spoken of as being the seed of David.	(Romans 1:3 KJV) [3] Concerning his Son Jesus Christ our Lord, which was made of the seed of David according to the flesh;
Promised seed of the women.	(Isaiah 7:14 KJV) [14] Therefore the Lord himself shall give you a sign; Behold, a virgin shall conceive, and bear a son, and shall call his name Immanuel.
The Word made and manifest in the flesh.	(John 1:14 KJV) [14] And the Word was made flesh, and dwelt among us, (and we beheld his glory, the glory as of the only begotten of the Father,) full of grace and truth.

Had Human Names and Titles Applied to Him

He was called Jesus.	(Matthew 1:21-23 NKJV) [21] And she will bring forth a Son, and you shall call His name JESUS, for He will save His people from their sins." [22] So all this was done that it might be fulfilled which was spoken by the Lord through the prophet, saying: [23] *"Behold, the virgin shall be with child, and bear a Son, and they shall call His name Immanuel,"* which is translated, "God with us."
Called the Son of David & Abraham.	(Matthew 1:1 KJV) [1] The book of the generation of Jesus Christ, the son of David, the son of Abraham.
Called a Jew.	(John 4:9 NKJV) [9] Then the woman of Samaria said to Him, "How is it that You, being a Jew, ask a drink from me, a Samaritan woman?" For Jews have no dealings with Samaritans.
Called the second Man after Adam and the heavenly Man.	(1 Corinthians 15:47-49 NKJV) [47] The first man *was* of the earth, made of dust; the second Man *is* the Lord from heaven. [48] As *was* the man of dust, so also *are* those *who are made* of dust; and as *is* the heavenly *Man,* so also *are* those *who are* heavenly. [49] And as we have borne the image of the *man* of dust, we shall also bear the image of the heavenly *Man.*
Called a man of Nazareth.	(Acts 2:22 NKJV) [22] "Men of Israel, hear these words: Jesus of Nazareth, a Man attested by God to you by miracles, wonders, and signs which God did through Him in your midst, as you yourselves also know

Had Complete Human Nature

Had a human spirit.	(Luke 23:46 NKJV) [46] And when Jesus had cried out with a loud voice, He said, "Father, *'into Your hands I commit My spirit.'* "
Had a soul.	(Matthew 14:34 NKJV) [34] Then He said to them, "My soul is

	exceedingly sorrowful, *even* to death. Stay here and watch."
Had a human body, of flesh, bones and blood.	(Hebrews 2:14 NKJV) ¹⁴ Inasmuch then as the children have partaken of flesh and blood, He Himself likewise shared in the same, that through death He might destroy him who had the power of death, that is, the devil,

Experienced Human Development

Grew as a child.	(Luke 2:40 NKJV) ⁴⁰ And the Child grew and became strong in spirit, filled with wisdom; and the grace of God was upon Him.
Learned obedience by the things He suffered.	(Hebrews 5:8 NKJV) ⁸ though He was a Son, *yet* He learned obedience by the things which He suffered.
Worked as a carpenter.	(Mark 6:3 NKJV) ³ Is this not the carpenter, the Son of Mary, and brother of James, Joses, Judas, and Simon? And are not His sisters here with us?" And they were offended at Him.
Experienced human temptations.	(Hebrews 4:15 NKJV) ¹⁵ For we do not have a High Priest who cannot sympathize with our weaknesses, but was in all *points* tempted as *we are, yet* without sin.
Learned to live in dependence upon the Father by continual prayer.	(Hebrews 5:7-8 NKJV) ⁷ who, in the days of His flesh, when He had offered up prayers and supplications, with vehement cries and tears to Him who was able to save Him from death, and was heard because of His godly fear, ⁸ though He was a Son, *yet* He learned obedience by the things which He suffered.
Desired human sympathy in the Garden.	(Matthew 26:39 NKJV) ³⁹ He went a little farther and fell on His face, and prayed, saying, "O My Father, if it is possible, let this cup pass from Me; nevertheless, not as I will, but as You *will.*"

Had Sinless Infirmities of Human Nature

As a man Christ suffered the limitations and infirmities of human nature, which are NOT sinful in themselves, but are part of mankind's lot since the fall. The glorified human body will not have these sinless infirmities (Philippians 3:20-21).

(Philippians 3:20-21 NKJV) ²⁰ For our citizenship is in heaven, from which we also eagerly wait for the Savior, the Lord Jesus Christ, ²¹ who will transform our lowly body that it may be conformed to His glorious body, according to the working by which He is able even to subdue all things to Himself.

Jesus grew weary.	(John 4:6 NKJV) ⁶ Now Jacob's well was there. Jesus therefore, being wearied from *His* journey, sat thus by the well. It was about the sixth hour.
Had normal appetites and was hungry.	(Matthew 4:2 NKJV) ² And when He had fasted forty days and forty nights, afterward He was hungry.
Was thirsty.	(John 4:7 NKJV) ⁷ A woman of Samaria came to draw water. Jesus said to her, "Give Me a drink."
Enjoyed natural sleep.	(Matthew 8:24 NKJV) ²⁴ And suddenly a great tempest arose on the sea, so that the boat was covered with the waves. But He was asleep.
Groaned to Himself.	(John 11:33 KJV) ³³ When Jesus therefore saw her weeping, and the Jews also weeping which came with her, he groaned in the spirit, and was troubled,
Wept over people.	(John 11:35 KJV) ³⁵ Jesus wept
Experienced agony.	(Luke 22:44 NKJV) ⁴⁴ And being in agony, He prayed more earnestly. Then His sweat became like great drops of blood falling down to the ground.

Suffered Human Death and Experienced Human Resurrection

When Jesus took our sin upon Himself, in His own body on the cross, He suffered the wages of sin, which is death. His earthly body did die but was resurrected because it was sinless. Jesus Christ is alive now in His resurrected body.

(1 Peter 2:24 HCSB) **24** He Himself bore our sins in His body on the tree, so that, having died to sins, we might live for righteousness; you have been healed by His wounds.

(Hebrews 9:27 NKJV) **27** And as it is appointed for men to die once, but after this the judgment,

Jesus still possesses His glorified body, after being raised from the dead. This body is sinless, immortal and incorruptible. As the Father commanded Him, He (Jesus) laid down His life for all of mankind. This was *OBEDIECE ACTED OUT*.

Jesus, in His ascension has taken manhood to the Godhead. This resurrection serves as a sample of all other human resurrections. He is at the throne on high glorified as the man Christ Jesus.

Jesus' humanity is a fact. He was born and lived upon earth. He is the eternal son of God and became the Son of Mankind. Being one person both deity and humanity united as one. He experienced a complete human life. Birth, genealogy, names, titles, sufferings, limitations, death and resurrection all confirm the reality of His existence as a human being. He is now glorified and when He comes again, in the second coming it will be the same Jesus coming from heaven.

The Old and New Testament Scriptures testify that Jesus was incorruptible and sinless in His humanity. His sinless nature was a must for Jesus Christ to be the Savior of the world. This sinless nature is total obedience and submission to the will of God in deed and action.

(Luke 23:39 NKJV) [39] Then one of the criminals who were hanged blasphemed Him, saying, "If You are the Christ, save Yourself and us."

(Acts 1:11 NKJV) [11] who also said, "Men of Galilee, why do you stand gazing up into heaven? This *same* Jesus, who was taken up from you into heaven, will so come in like manner as you saw Him go into heaven."

(John 20:27-28 NKJV) [27] Then He said to Thomas, "Reach your finger here, and look at My hands; and reach your hand *here,* and put *it* into My side. Do not be unbelieving, but believing." [28] And Thomas answered and said to Him, "My Lord and my God!"

(1 Timothy 2:5 NKJV) [5] For *there is* one God and one Mediator between God and men, *the* Man Christ Jesus,

Temptations of Adam, Jesus and Mankind

Scriptures identify two temptations that were unique. In a distinctive sense Adam and Jesus both were Sons of God. Being created of God, Adam and being begotten of God, Jesus. They both had a sinless human nature; the corruption of sin was not within their being. The devil tempted both of them from without and Adam responded to this temptation but Jesus did not. Adam and Jesus are the representative men of the old creation race and the new creation race. God sees all mankind either "in Adam" or "in Christ Jesus." The temptations that mankind will experience is different because they will face temptation in a sinful body/nature making Adam and Jesus' temptations unique.

(Luke 3:38 NKJV) [38] *the son* of Enos, *the son* of Seth, *the son* of Adam, *the son* of God.

(1 Corinthians 15:46-49 NKJV) [46] However, the spiritual is not first, but the natural, and afterward the spiritual. [47] The first man *was* of the earth, *made* of dust; the second Man *is* the Lord from heaven. [48] As *was* the *man* of dust, so also *are* those *who are made* of dust; and as *is* the heavenly *Man,* so also *are* those *who are* heavenly. [49] And as we have borne the image of the *man* of dust, we shall also bear the image of the heavenly *Man.*

Sin Was a Violation Into Adam's Humanity.

There is an assertion in Romans 8:3 that states Christ was "made in the likeness of sinful flesh".

This needs clarification so that it is not misunderstood. It does not say that Christ had "sinful flesh" but that He was "made in the likeness of sinful flesh". Here "likeness" is the sinless infirmities of human nature. Christ was sinless in His flesh born of no original sin or sin-principle. ***Sin is not essential to human nature, but a violation.***

The Greek word *peirazo* has been translated two ways in English Bibles. It is often rendered "test" in the sense of meaning "to try" or "to make proof of". When ascribed to God in His dealings with people, it means, and can mean, no more than this. But for the most part in Scripture, *peirazo* is used in a negative sense and means "to entice," or "provoke to sin," "to tempt." Hence, the name given to Satan is "the tempter".

(Matthew 4:3 NKJV) ³ Now when the tempter came to Him, he said, "If You are the Son of God, command that these stones become bread."

When Jesus was led by the Spirit out into the wilderness for forty days, He was both "tested" and "tempted." His faith was "tested" by the "temptations" of the wicked one, whose object was to seduce Jesus from His allegiance as God. Both Matthew and Luke record the details of the temptations to which Jesus was subjected by the devil. All these temptations presented short-cuts which, if pursued would have deflected Jesus from His calling. The record leaves us in no doubt that Jesus gained the victory. Both Gospels show that He accomplished this by appealing to Scripture. Jesus is also seen in this event as a genuine man who, like all other men, was subject to temptation. Yet Jesus did not give in to "temptation"; He passed the "test."

The writer of the letter to the Hebrews notes that all of Jesus' trials qualified Him to become our High Priest who intercedes on our behalf. Jesus came to earth as a human being to experience our trials; therefore, He understands our weaknesses and shows mercy to us. Because he was fully human, Jesus "himself was tested by what He suffered."

(2 Corinthians 5:21 NKJV) ²¹ For He made Him who knew no sin *to be* sin for us, that we might become the righteousness of God in Him.

(Hebrews 2:18 NKJV)¹⁸ For in that He Himself has suffered, being tempted, He is able to aid those who are tempted.

(Hebrews 4:15 NKJV) ¹⁵ For we do not have a High Priest who cannot sympathize with our weaknesses, but was in all *points* tempted as *we are, yet* without sin.

Comparison & Contrast of the Temptations of Adam and Jesus	
ADAM	JESUS
The First Adam	The Last Adam
The first man, created	The second man, Lord from Heaven
No evil tendency originally	No evil tendency within Him

Liability to sin	No liability to sin
One nature, human nature	Two natures, divine and human
Tempted from without in spirit, soul & body	Tempted from without in spirit, soul & body
Response to sin	No response to sin
Now fallen human nature	No fallen sinless human nature
A creation of God	The incarnation of God
A created Son of God	The Begotten Son of God
A human being	A divine-human being

Comparison & Contrast of the Unbelievers and Believers

Unbelievers	Believers
"In Adam" sons of men	"In Christ" sons of God
The natural birth	The natural and now spiritual birth
Fallen human nature	Fallen human nature (now) partakers of divine nature
Sinful tendencies	Sinful tendencies (now) to be over comers
Tempted from within and without	Tempted from within and without (now) strengthened to over come by the Holy Spirit
Born in sin	Born in sin (now) born again with sin being covered by Christ Jesus
Sin will destroy unto death	Sin to be overcome unto life

Testimony of Jesus Christ's being Sinless

Gabriel spoke of Jesus as being "that Holy thing".	(Luke 1:35 NKJV) [35] And the angel answered and said to her, "*The Holy Spirit will come upon you, and the power of the Highest will overshadow you; therefore, also, that Holy One who is to be born will be called the Son of God.*
Demons recognized Jesus as being "the Holy one.	(Mark 1:23-24 NKJV) [23] Now there was a man in their synagogue with an unclean spirit. And he cried out, [24] saying, "Let *us* alone! What have we to do with You, Jesus of Nazareth? Did You come to destroy us? I know who You are--the Holy One of God!"
Testimony of Men – called the Holy child.	(Acts 4:27-30 NKJV) [27] "For truly against Your holy Servant Jesus, whom You anointed, both Herod and Pontius Pilate, with the Gentiles and the people of Israel, were gathered together [28] to do whatever Your hand and Your purpose determined before to be done. [29] Now, Lord, look on their threats, and grant to Your servants that with all boldness they may speak Your word, [30] by stretching out Your hand to heal, and that signs and wonders may be done through the name of Your holy Servant Jesus."
Pilate found no	(John 18:38 NKJV) [38] Pilate said to Him, "What is truth?" And

fault in him.	when he had said this, he went out again to the Jews, and said to them, "I find no fault in Him at all.
Pilate's wife testified that he was a just man.	(Matthew 27:19 NKJV) ¹⁹ While he was sitting on the judgment seat, his wife sent to him, saying, "Have nothing to do with that just Man, for I have suffered many things today in a dream because of Him."
The dying thief recognized Jesus as not worthy to die.	(Luke 23:41 NKJV) ⁴¹ And we indeed justly, for we receive the due reward of our deeds; but this Man has done nothing wrong."
Centurion recognized Jesus as "the Son of God.	(Luke 23: 47 NKJV) ⁴⁷ So when the centurion saw what had happened, he glorified God, saying, "Certainly this was a righteous Man!"
Apostle Paul said "He knows no sin.	(2 Corinthians 5:21 NKJV) ²¹ For He made Him who knew no sin *to be* sin for us, that we might become the righteousness of God in Him.

Jesus Christ -The Example for Humanity

Christ as a perfect man was totally dependent upon the Father for all He was, said and did, obeying the Fathers will. He was the example of what God intended mankind to be like. Being the perfect example for all believers to follow. Peter declared that Christ left "us an example, that ye should follow in His steps".

(1 Peter 2:21 NKJV) ²¹ For to this you were called, because Christ also suffered for us, leaving us an example, that you should follow His steps:

The Greek word "*hupogrammos*" translated "example" means "an under-writing, i.e. copy for imitation". It comes from the custom of tracing letters for scholars to copy.

Text Message → So, the believer is to follow Jesus Christ, and exemplify Jesus Christ, no other.

The believer is to seek after the following in his/her life:

- Holiness (sinless, pleasing the Father)
- Love (this is the very nature of God)
- Faith (trusting the Father in all things)
- Meekness (humility, not pride, being ready to serve not be served)
- In Word (teaching and preaching)

- In Actions (devotion, prayer life, self-abnegation, service, patience, gentleness, anger, courage, compassion, obedience, optimism and worship)

Christ as Mediator

The Greek word '*mesites*' is comprised of the words '*mesos*', meaning "middle," and *eimi*, meaning "to go." So, *mesites* means "a go-between", a "mediator" between two parties. Jesus Christ is the mediator for mankind within and to the Godhead. This is a fulfillment and the end of all mediation. His mediation supersedes all others and He is the only go between for mankind to their creator. The Old Testament shadowed forth this truth in the priesthood of Melchizededk and the New Testament shows its fulfillment in the Lord Jesus Christ.

Old Testament

The patriarch Job in his distress under Satan's attack expressed the heart cry of all mankind for a mediator between God and mankind.

(Job 16:21 KJV) "Oh, that one might plead for a man with God, As a man pleads for his neighbor!"

Moses first acted as a mediator of the law covenant when God spoke to him for Israel. The Book of Hebrews sets forth Christ as being the one greater than Moses and Aaron in His mediator work.

(Hebrews 3:1-5 NKJV) [1] Therefore, holy brethren, partakers of the heavenly calling, consider the Apostle and High Priest of our confession, Christ Jesus, [2] who was faithful to Him who appointed Him, as Moses also *was faithful* in all His house. [3] For this One has been counted worthy of more glory than Moses, inasmuch as He who built the house has more honor than the house. [4] For every house is built by someone, but He who built all things *is* God. [5] And Moses indeed *was* faithful in all His house as a servant, for a testimony of those things which would be spoken *afterward,*

New Testament

The New Testament declares that people's knowledge of God, path to salvation, and hope comes through Christ alone. (No other, not Mary, not Moses, not any of the Saints—only Jesus Christ). No one knows the Father except the Son and those to whom the Son reveals Him. No one comes to the Father but through Jesus – neither is there salvation in any other person or god. This is made explicit by Paul in the following verse.

(1 Timothy 2:5 NKJV) [5] For *there is* one God and one Mediator between God and men, *the* Man Christ Jesus,

Christ's mediation is the fulfillment and end of all mediation. The book of Hebrews opens with the assertion that Christ surpasses all other mediators – angels, Moses, and the priest of the Aaronic priesthood. Christ's priesthood is a timeless priesthood, like Melchizedek's. The new covenant He established between the Godhead and believers offers better promises, the last sacrifice, a better sanctuary, and a better hope. Christ's mediation excels all others and can never be superseded. He is the only way to God; there is no other way – no other "go-between."

(Hebrews 7:19 NKJV) ¹⁹ for the law made nothing perfect; on the other hand, *there is the* bringing in of a better hope, through which we draw near to God
(Hebrews 8:6 NKJV) ⁶ But now He has obtained a more excellent ministry, inasmuch as He is also Mediator of a better covenant, which was established on better promises.

(Hebrews 9:11-15 NKJV) ¹¹ But Christ came *as* High Priest of the good things to come, with the greater and more perfect tabernacle not made with hands, that is, not of this creation. ¹² Not with the blood of goats and calves, but with His own blood He entered the Most Holy Place once for all, having obtained eternal redemption. ¹³ For if the blood of bulls and goats and the ashes of a heifer, sprinkling the unclean, sanctifies for the purifying of the flesh, ¹⁴ how much more shall the blood of Christ, who through the eternal Spirit offered Himself without spot to God, cleanse your conscience from dead works to serve the living God? ¹⁵ And for this reason He is the Mediator of the new covenant, by means of death, for the redemption of the transgressions under the first covenant, that those who are called may receive the promise of the eternal inheritance.

Conclusion

Keeping a Balance of understanding between the divine and human natures of Christ is critical to avoid heretical imbalance. The great mystery of Godliness is that "God was manifested in the flesh".

(1 Timothy 3:15-16 NKJV) ¹⁵ but if I am delayed, *I write* so that you may know how you ought to conduct yourself in the house of God, which is the church of the living God, the pillar and ground of the truth. ¹⁶ And without controversy great is the mystery of godliness: God was manifested in the flesh, Justified in the Spirit, Seen by angels, Preached among the Gentiles, Believed on in the world, Received up in glory.

(Colossians 2:2-3 NKJV) ² that their hearts may be encouraged, being knit together in love, and *attaining* to all riches of the full assurance of understanding, to the knowledge of the mystery of God, both of the Father and of Christ, ³ in whom are hidden all the treasures of wisdom and knowledge.

Christ is fully God and fully man. He is NOT two, but one person having both divine and human natures. Jesus always spoke as a single person and the New Testament does also. So the attributes of both deity and humanity are assigned to this one person.

Christ is called a Theanthropic Person (Theos God: Anthropos Man). He does not possess a Theanthroic nature. His person is Theanthropic, not His nature. His person is one; His natures are two. He is eternally the God-Man. He is truly God, perfect Man, one person, having two unconfused natures. He was not a humanized God or a deified Man. He was and is the God-Man.

The New Testament writer under the inspiration of the Holy Spirit set forth the delicate balance between the deity and humanity of Christ in their writings. Some of the references as examples of this balance are:

(1 Corinthians 2:8 NKJV) [8] which none of the rulers of this age knew; for had they known, they would not have crucified the Lord of glory. [9] But as it is written: *"Eye has not seen, nor ear heard, Nor have entered into the heart of man The things which God has prepared for those who love Him."* [10] But God has revealed *them* to us through His Spirit. For the Spirit searches all things, yes, the deep things of God.

(Matthew 1:21 HCSB) [21] She will give birth to a son, and you are to name Him Jesus, because He will save His people from their sins."

(Romans 9:5 NKJV) [5] of whom *are* the fathers and from whom, according to the flesh, Christ *came,* who is over all, *the* eternally blessed God. Amen.

(Acts 17:31 NKJV) [31] because He has appointed a day on which He will judge the world in righteousness by the Man whom He has ordained. He has given assurance of this to all by raising Him from the dead."

Begin With Prayer

Biblical Teaching/Doctrine of The Holy Spirit

Biblical Building Block # 6

(1 John 4:12 HCSB)

If we love one another, God remains in us and His love is perfected in us.

God's love is perfected in us through the Holy Spirit Who has been sent to live within the hearts of all believers. The Holy Spirit gives us the fruit of love, joy, peace, longsuffering, kindness, goodness, faithfulness, gentleness and self-control. This fruit is what all of mankind is seeking and longing for. God has made it available to all mankind if they only trust and obey God by putting faith in and believing that Jesus Christ is the one and only Savior. There is no other way and no philosophy of mankind that can provide true love, agape love (spiritual love). This kind of love comes only from God and he desires so much that we accept all that He has for us, perfecting His love within us.

1. Explain what the Holy Spirit is, pertaining to the Bible.

2. Explain the relationship of the Holy Spirit to the Godhead.

3. Can you identify some qualities and characteristics of the Holy Spirit?

4. How does one become acquainted with the Holy Spirit?

5. Can you identify some divine attributes of the Holy Spirit?

6. Explain the workings of the Holy Spirit in the Old Testament and currently in the New Testament times.

7. How is the Holy Spirit involved in the work of the Church?

8. Why is the Holy Spirit important in the life of the believer?

Why the Doctrine of the Holy Spirit is Significant

One of the most significant doctrines is the Doctrine of the Holy Spirit. All believers need to seek after the understanding of truths concerning the person, ministry, power and work pertaining to the Holy Spirit. The Holy Spirit has been observed in action and operation from the book of Genesis through the book of Revelation. During a time when the earth was formless, dark and empty, as spoken of in Genesis 1:1-2, the Holy Spirit was active. And the Spirit of God moved upon the face of the waters. In Revelation 22:17 there is a final reference "… the Spirit and the bride say, come". The Bible gives us a wealth of understanding and revelation of the Holy Spirit's activities, nature, characteristics and purpose, from beginning to fulfillment.

During the Old Testament times, the Holy Spirit was only available to a select few, yet these Ancient Scriptures foretold of a time when, in the last days, the Spirit would be poured out on all flesh. This present age (the church) has been given over to the ministry of the Holy Spirit according to God's plan.

The Holy Spirit is mentioned in both the Old Testament and the New Testament numerous times. Many titles and names have been used to identify the Holy Spirit. Only 2 John and 3 John do not have a reference of the Holy Spirit.

Text Message → In the KJV the Holy Spirit is also called the Holy Ghost

---

It is significant that the believer come to know, understand, seek after and experience the Person, work and ministry of the Holy Spirit in their life. Through the Holy Spirit the believer will experience the truths and the revelation of God in a new way, God working from within the heart. A personal relationship with God will truly be known. The following verses identify the Holy Spirit being promised to the believer to give truth, to help, and teach.

(John 14:15-26 NKJV) "If you love Me, keep my commandments. And I will pray the Father, and he will give you another Helper, that He may abide with you forever – "the Spirit of Truth, whom the world cannot receive, because it neither sees Him nor knows Him; but you know Him, for He dwells with you and will be in you. " I will not leave you orphans: I will come to you. "A little while longer and the world will see Me no more, but you will see Me. Because I live, you will live also. "At that day you will know that I am in My Father, and you in Me, and I in you. "He who has My commandments and keeps them, it is he who loves Me. And he who loves Me will be loved by My Father and I will love him and manifest myself to him." Judas (not Iscariot) said to Him, "Lord how is it that You will manifest Yourself to us, and not to the world?" Jesus answered and said to him, "If anyone loves Me, he will keep My word: and My Father will love him, and We will come to him and make Our home with him. "He who does not keep My words; and the word which you hear is not Mine but the Father's who sent Me. "These things I have spoken to you while being present with you. "But the Helper, the Holy Spirit whom the Father will send in My name, he will teach you all things, and bring to your remembrance all things that I said to you.

Because of ignorance, fear, misunderstanding and formalism in the churches the teaching of the Holy Spirit is being overlooked or not given equal adherence. This is causing believers to be without the guidance, power and teaching of the truth that only the Holy Spirit can provide to each person individually and to the churches corporately.

Personality of the Holy Spirit

The Holy Spirit is Not an Influence

The Holy Spirit should not be thought of or viewed as just some kind of influence. Yes the Holy Spirit does influence a believer's life in a personal way. His guidance, wisdom, power, enlightenment of the truths of God, and a desire for a personal relationship must be sought after. It is sad that there are many believers missing out on this experience of the Holy Spirit because of their misunderstanding of what is available to them. They need only to open their hearts and allow His love and power to work within them in order to have a true personal relationship with God.

Some of the Misunderstandings

The Greek word "*pneuma*" means "breath" or "wind" and implies the notion of an unseen force. The Holy Spirit is spoken of as being "The Spirit (*pneuma*) of God".

(John 3:5-8 NKJV) Jesus answered, "Most assuredly, I say to you, unless one is born of water and the Spirit, he cannot enter the kingdom of God. ⁶ That which is born of the flesh is flesh, and that which is born of the Spirit is spirit. ⁷ Do not marvel that I said to you, 'You must be born again.' ⁸ The wind blows where it wishes, and you hear the sound of it, but cannot tell where it comes from and where it goes. So is everyone who is born of the Spirit."

Objects such as wind, oil, fire, water, a seal and other impersonal objects have symbolized the Holy Spirit. These symbols should not deny that the Holy Spirit is a Divine Person with a personality of His own. *An example* would be that the Son (Jesus Christ) is symbolized with impersonal objects such as a lamb, a rock, and a lion. Although the Holy Spirit seems somewhat mystical, invisible, and secret, He still possesses a personality and is a real person with a Divine nature. He is God and God is spirit.

(John 4:24 KJV) ²⁴ God *is* a Spirit: and they that worship him must worship *him* in spirit and in truth.

Believers seem to have a harder time relating to the Holy Spirit as a Divine title compared to the Father and the Son. This is most likely due to the fact that these titles have a more human feeling about them than the Holy Spirit. So, one must be carful not to deny the personality of the Holy Spirit remembering that the Godhead is the Father, the Son and the Holy Spirit.

Although He is invisible and not having a physical existence, He is a real person. Mankind is also a spirit being with a soul, a body and personality.

(Matthew 28:19 NKJV) [19] Go therefore and make disciples of all the nations, baptizing them in the name of the Father and of the Son and of the Holy Spirit,

(1 Timothy 4:1 NKJV) [1] Now the Spirit expressly says that in latter times some will depart from the faith, giving heed to deceiving spirits and doctrines of demons.

Here are some reasons why the Believer should not consider the Holy Spirit as a mere influence or impersonal force:
- It is contrary to Scripture. The Bible teaches that the Holy Spirit is a divine person.
- It will hinder worship. The Holy Spirit teaches us how to worship.
- It will hinder our prayers. We sometimes do not know how or what we should pray for. This is where the Holy Spirit can assist us.
- It can hinder our understanding of the Scriptures. The Holy Spirit is able to guide us to an understanding of the Word of God so that it will be effective in our lives.
- The avoidance of the Holy Spirit will hinder our relationship with God. God desires a personal relationship with us. God Himself comes and lives within us through the Person of the Holy Spirit. It would be impossible to have a relationship with an impersonal force. We must know the Holy Spirit as our friend, helper, comforter, and indweller. In this way, we can honor Him.

And most of all, avoidance of the Holy Spirit will hinder our relationship with God. God desires a personal relationship with us. God Himself comes and lives within us through the person of the Holy Spirit. It would be impossible to have a relationship with an impersonal force. We must know the Holy Spirit as our friend, helper, comforter, and indweller. In this way we can honor Him.

(Jude 1:20 NKJV) [20] But you, beloved, building yourselves up on your most holy faith, praying in the Holy Spirit,

(2 Peter 1:21 NKJV) [21] for prophecy never came by the will of man, but holy men of God spoke *as they were* moved by the Holy Spirit.

(2 Timothy 1:14 NKJV) That good thing which was committed to you, keep by the Holy Spirit who dwells in us.

(1 Corinthians 2:13 NKJV) [13] These things we also speak, not in words which man's wisdom teaches but which the Holy Spirit teaches, comparing spiritual things with spiritual.

The Holy Spirit Revealed as a Person

Throughout the Scriptures the third Person of the Godhead is identified as the Holy Spirit. This identification is repeatedly associated with the person of the Father and the person of the

Son, making Him a Divine Person by association. The fulfillment of God's will can be worked by the believer who is redeemed and filled with the spirit, that being the Spirit of God the Holy Spirit. To have the knowledge of the Holy Spirit within one's heart is a blessed and glorious privilege, available to all believers in Jesus Christ.

(2 Corinthians 13:14 NKJV) [14] The grace of the Lord Jesus Christ, and the love of God, and the communion of the Holy Spirit *be* with you all. Amen.

(1 John 5:7-8 NKV) [7] For there are three that bear witness in heaven: the Father, the Word, and the Holy Spirit; and these three are one. [8] And there are three that bear witness on earth:

(John 15:26-27 NKJV) [26] "But when the Helper comes, whom I shall send to you from the Father, the Spirit of truth who proceeds from the Father, He will testify of Me. [27] And you also will bear witness, because you have been with Me from the beginning.

Spoken of as Having Personal Qualities

The Holy Spirit is spoken of as having a mind, will and emotions which are personal qualities. Not just a force but a real person with actions of a person.

Mind

(Romans 8:27 NKJV) [27] Now He who searches the hearts knows what the mind of the Spirit *is,* because He makes intercession for the saints according to *the will of* God.

Will

(1 Corinthians 12:11 NKJV) [11] But one and the same Spirit works all these things, distributing to each one individually as He wills.

Emotions

(Colossians 1:8 NKJV) [8] who also declared to us your love in the Spirit.

Spoken of Under Personal Titles

The Holy Spirit is called "the Comforter/helper/counselor" which also means "the Advocate". In John 14:16 Jesus speaks of the Holy Spirit as "another Comforter/helper/counselor". This same title is used of Jesus as a person, meaning "one who stands alongside/defender".

(John 14:16 NKJV) [16] And I will pray the Father, and He will give you another Helper, that He may abide with you forever - (*NOTE- the KJV uses "comforter" the HCSB uses "counselor"*)

(John 14:26 HCSB) **26** But the Counselor, the Holy Spirit —the Father will send Him in My name—will teach you all things and remind you of everything I have told you

(John 15:26 KJV) **26** But when the Comforter is come, whom I will send unto you from the Father, *even* the Spirit of truth, which proceedeth from the Father, he shall testify of me:

The Spirit Performs Personal Acts

Works	(1 Corinthians 12:11)
Searches	(1 Corinthians 2:10)
Speaks	(Acts 13:2; Revelation 2:7; 2 Samuel 23:2; Matthew 10:20; (1 Timothy 4:1)
Testifies	(John 15:26)
Bears witness	(1 John 5:6)
Teaches	(John 14:26)
Instructs	(Nehemiah 9:20)
Reproves	(John 16:8-11)
Prays and makes intercession	(Romans 8:26)
Leads	(Matthew 4:1)
Guides the believer to all truths	(John 16:13)
Glorifies the Lord Jesus Christ	(John 16:14)
Brings about regeneration	(John 3:5, 6)
Strives with mankind	(Genesis 6:3)
Convicts men	(John 16:8)
Imparts spiritual gifts to believers	(1 Corinthians 12:7-11)

Spoken of as Having Personal Feelings

Can be grieved	(Ephesians 4:30)
Can be insulted	(Hebrews 10:29)
Can be lied to	(Acts 5:3)
Can be blasphemed	(Matthew 12:31-32)
Can be resisted	(Acts 7:51)
Can be tempted	(Acts 6:9)
Can be vexed	(Isaiah 63:10)
Can be quenched	(1 Thessalonians 5:19)

Deity of the Holy Spirit

The Bible is quite clear and declares that the Holy Spirit is God, a peer (equal) with the Father and the Son, and an individual person within the Godhead.

Divine Association With the Father and the Son

In the baptismal command of Jesus, the Father, Son and Holy Spirit are associated together as one. This shows that the Holy Spirit is co-eternal in the Godhead. They are all linked in the triune name. Jesus' teaching's plainly relates that the Holy Spirit is one with the Father and Himself. We see all three (Father, Son and Holy Spirit) in baptism, administration of the Church and involved in apostolic benediction.

(Matthew 28:19 NKJV) [19] Go therefore and make disciples of all the nations, baptizing them in the name of the Father and of the Son and of the Holy Spirit,

(1 John 5:7 NKJV) For there are three that bear witness in heaven: the Father, the Word, and the Holy Spirit; and these three are one.

(Acts 2:33 NKJV) [33] Therefore being exalted to the right hand of God, and having received from the Father the promise of the Holy Spirit, He poured out this which you now see and hear.

Divine Distinction from the Father and the Son

The Holy Spirit is one with the Father and Son but also has distinctions of His own.

The Son is sent by the Father and Holy Spirit.	(Isaiah 48:12-16 NKJV) [12] "Listen to Me, O Jacob, And Israel, My called: I *am* He, I *am* the First, I *am* also the Last. [13] Indeed My hand has laid the foundation of the earth, And My right hand has stretched out the heavens; *When* I call to them, They stand up together. [14] "All of you, assemble yourselves, and hear! Who among them has declared these *things?* The LORD loves him; He shall do His pleasure on Babylon, And His arm *shall be against* the Chaldeans. [15] I, *even* I, have spoken; Yes, I have called him, I have brought him, and his way will prosper. [16] "Come near to Me, hear this: I have not spoken in secret from the beginning; From the time that it was, I *was* there. And now the Lord GOD and His Spirit Have sent Me."
The Holy Spirit is partaker of the triune name, the name of the Godhead to be used in administering baptism.	(Luke 3:21-22 NKJV) [21] When all the people were baptized, it came to pass that Jesus also was baptized; and while He prayed, the heaven was opened. [22] And the Holy Spirit descended in bodily form like a dove upon Him, and a voice came from heaven which said, "You are My beloved Son; in You I am well pleased."
The Son prays to the Father, to send the Holy Spirit who is the Comforter in KJV.	(John 16:7-13 KJV) Nevertheless I tell you the truth; It is expedient for you that I go away: for if I go not away, the Comforter will not come unto you; but if I depart, I will send him unto you. 8 And when he is come, he will reprove the

Counselor in HCSB *Helper in NKJV*	world of sin, and of righteousness, and of judgment: **9** Of sin, because they believe not on me; **10** Of righteousness, because I go to my Father, and ye see me no more; **11** Of judgment, because the prince of this world is judged. **12** I have yet many things to say unto you, but ye cannot bear them now. **13** Howbeit when he, the Spirit of truth, is come, he will guide you into all truth: for he shall not speak of himself; but whatsoever he shall hear, *that* shall he speak: and he will shew you things to come
The believer has access to the Father, the Son by the Holy Spirit.	(Ephesians 2:18 NKJV) **18** For through Him we both have access by one Spirit to the Father.
The Holy Spirit proceeds from the Father through the Son.	(John 14:26 NKJV) **26** But the Helper, the Holy Spirit, whom the Father will send in My name, He will teach you all things, and bring to your remembrance all things that I said to you.

Divine Attributes

Called God	(Acts 5:3-4 HCSB) **3** Then Peter said, "Ananias, why has Satan filled your heart to lie to the Holy Spirit and keep back part of the proceeds from the field? **4** Wasn't it yours while you possessed it? And after it was sold, wasn't it at your disposal? Why is it that you planned this thing in your heart? You have not lied to men but to God!"
Is eternal	(Hebrews 9:14 NKJV) **14** how much more shall the blood of Christ, who through the eternal Spirit offered Himself without spot to God, cleanse your conscience from dead works to serve the living God?
Is omnipotent 'all powerful'	(Luke 1:35 HCSB) **35** The angel replied to her: "The Holy Spirit will come upon you, and the power of the Most High will overshadow you. Therefore, the holy One to be born will be called the Son of God.
Is omniscient 'all knowing'	(Romans 8:26-27 NKJV) **26** Likewise the Spirit also helps in our weaknesses. For we do not know what we should pray for as we ought, but the Spirit Himself makes intercession for us with groanings which cannot be uttered. **27** Now He who searches the hearts knows what the mind of the Spirit *is,* because He makes intercession for the saints according to *the will of* God.
Is omnipresent 'everywhere-present'	(Psalms 139:7-10 KJV) **7** Whither shall I go from thy spirit? or whither shall I flee from thy presence? **8** If I ascend up into heaven, thou *art* there: if I make my bed in hell, behold, thou *art there.* **9** *If* I take the wings of the morning, *and* dwell in the

	uttermost parts of the sea; 10 Even there shall thy hand lead me, and thy right hand shall hold me.
Is the life source	(Romans 8:2 NKJV) 2 For the law of the Spirit of life in Christ Jesus has made me free from the law of sin and death.
Spirit of Truth	(John 16:13 HCSB) 13 When the Spirit of truth comes, He will guide you into all the truth. For He will not speak on His own, but He will speak whatever He hears. He will also declare to you what is to come.
Spirit has/is Love	(Romans 15:30 HCSB) 30 Now I appeal to you, brothers, through our Lord Jesus Christ and through the love of the Spirit, to join with me in fervent prayers to God on my behalf.
Spirit of Holiness	(Romans 1:4 NKJV) 4 *and* declared *to be* the Son of God with power according to the Spirit of holiness, by the resurrection from the dead.

Divine Works Attributed to Him

Active in the creation of the world/s, man and beasts.	(Genesis 1:1-2 KJV) 1 In the beginning God created the heaven and the earth. 2 And the earth was without form, and void; and darkness *was* upon the face of the deep. And the Spirit of God moved upon the face of the waters.
Active in the inspiration of the Sacred Scriptures.	(2 Timothy 3:16 NKJV) 16 All Scripture *is* given by inspiration of God, and *is* profitable for doctrine, for reproof, for correction, for instruction in righteousness,
Active in the regeneration of fallen man, in making man a new creation.	(John 3:3-5 NKJV) 3 Jesus answered and said to him, "Most assuredly, I say to you, unless one is born again, he cannot see the kingdom of God." 4 Nicodemus said to Him, "How can a man be born when he is old? Can he enter a second time into his mother's womb and be born?" 5 Jesus answered, "Most assuredly, I say to you, unless one is born of water and the Spirit, he cannot enter the kingdom of God.
Active in the resurrection of the body, which involves a creative act.	(Romans 8:11 NKJV) 11 But if the Spirit of Him who raised Jesus from the dead dwells in you, He who raised Christ from the dead will also give life to your mortal bodies through His Spirit who dwells in you.

The Work of the Holy Spirit in the Old Testament

The involvement of the Holy Spirit is mentioned many times in the Old Testament, but was not available to all mankind in this period. He was seen working with selected men and the chosen nation of Israel.

Work of the Holy Spirit in Redemption

The Spirit of God strove with man in the days of Noah.	(Genesis 6:3 KJV) **3** And the LORD said, My spirit shall not always strive with man, for that he also *is* flesh: yet his days shall be an hundred and twenty years.
The Spirit of God spoke to Noah while the ark was being prepared.	(1 Peter 3:18-20 NKJV) [18] For Christ also suffered once for sins, the just for the unjust, that He might bring us to God, being put to death in the flesh but made alive by the Spirit, [19] by whom also He went and preached to the spirits in prison, [20] who formerly were disobedient, when once the Divine longsuffering waited in the days of Noah, while *the* ark was being prepared, in which a few, that is, eight souls, were saved through water.
The nation of Israel often resisted the Spirit of God who spoke through the various prophets in their history.	(Acts 7:51 NKJV) [51] "*You* stiffnecked and uncircumcised in heart and ears! You always resist the Holy Spirit; as your fathers *did,* so *do* you.

Work of the Holy Spirit in Inspiration

In both the Old and New Testaments the prophets experienced the Holy Spirit moving upon them and giving revelation, inspiration and causing them to write the sacred Scriptures. The prophets foretold as they were inspired by the Holy Spirit about the suffering of Christ and the glory that would follow in the Church.

(Acts 1:16 NKJV) [16] "Men *and* brethren, this Scripture had to be fulfilled, which the Holy Spirit spoke before by the mouth of David concerning Judas, who became a guide to those who arrested Jesus;

(2 Peter 1:21 NKJV) [21] for prophecy never came by the will of man, but holy men of God spoke *as they were* moved by the Holy Spirit.

(2 Samuel 23:2 KJV) **2** The Spirit of the LORD spake by me, and his word *was* in my tongue

Work of the Spirit in Israel

There was only one nation that the Holy Spirit was active and operating in during the Old Testament and that was the chosen nation of Israel. The Holy Spirit can be seen equipping, inspiring, energizing and indwelling men with Himself. In contrast to the New Testament times the Holy Spirit only came upon a select few men but today is available for all believers. Those who experienced the indwelling, power and operations of the Holy Spirit upon them could testify that it was indeed "not by might, not by power, but by My Spirit says the Lord of Hosts".

(Zechariah 4:6 NKJV) **6** So he answered and said to me: "This *is* the word of the LORD to Zerubbabel: 'Not by might nor by power, but by My Spirit,' Says the LORD of hosts.

The Holy Spirit Upon Chosen Ones in Israel

The Spirit of God enabled Joseph to interpret the dreams of Pharaoh.	(Genesis 41:38 KJV) **38** And Pharaoh said unto his servants, Can we find *such a one* as this *is*, a man in whom the Spirit of God *is*?
It was the Holy Spirit who gave wisdom for the building of the Tabernacle of Moses according to the Divine pattern.	(Exodus 28:3 KJV) **3** And thou shalt speak unto all *that are* wise hearted, whom I have filled with the spirit of wisdom, that they may make Aaron's garments to consecrate him, that he may minister unto me in the priest's office.
The Holy Spirit quickened the 70. elders to prophesy in the camp of Israel.	(Numbers 11:16-29)
The Judges as deliverers in Israel were equipped by the Holy Spirit for their ministry.	(Judges 3:9-10) for Othniel; (Judges 6:34) for Gideon; (Judges 11:29) for Jephthah; and (Judges 14:6; 15:14) for Samson.
King Saul came under the prophetic Holy Spirit after his anointing.	(1 Samuel 10:6,10; 11:6; 19:23)
The priests of the Lord had the Holy Spirit upon them.	(2 Chronicles 20:14,17; 24:20; Luke 1:5,67)
Judges, kings, priests and prophets in Israel experienced the Holy Spirit upon them and were known as the Lord's anointed.	Balaam (Numbers 24:2) Azariah (2 Chronicles 15:1-2) Elijah (1 Kings 18:12; 2 Kings 2:16) Elisha (2 Kings 2:1-18) Amasai (1 Chronicles 12:18) Zechariah (2 Chronicles 24:20) Micah (Mican 3:8) Ezekiel (Ezekiel 3:12-14; 8:3; 11:1-5,24) Daniel (Daniel 4:8-9,18; 5:11,14) Isaiah (Acts 28:25) Jeremiah (Jeremiah 1:9; 30:1-2) Joel (Joel 2:28; Acts 2:16-17)

Work of the Holy Spirit in the New Testament

The Holy Spirit was made available to all mankind during the New Testament following Our Lord Jesus' birth, ministry, death on the cross, resurrection, ascension and glorification. The Old Testament prophets clearly foretold a coming day when the Holy Spirit would be poured out upon all flesh, both Israel and Gentiles nations together.

(Joel 2:28-29 NKJV) ²⁸ "And it shall come to pass afterward That I will pour out My Spirit on all flesh; Your sons and your daughters shall prophesy, Your old men shall dream dreams, Your young men shall see visions. ²⁹ And also on *My* menservants and on *My* maidservants I will pour out My Spirit in those days.

(Ezekiel 11:19 KJV) ¹⁹ And I will give them one heart, and I will put a new spirit within you; and I will take the stony heart out of their flesh, and will give them an heart of flesh:

(Isaiah 43:3 KJV) ³ For I *am* the LORD thy God, the Holy One of Israel, thy Saviour: I gave Egypt *for* thy ransom, Ethiopia and Seba for thee.

The believer who accepts the finished work of the cross will find available to them the gift of the Holy Spirit coming under His gracious ministrations of regeneration to glorification.

(Matthew 3:11 NKJV) ¹¹ I indeed baptize you with water unto repentance, but He who is coming after me is mightier than I, whose sandals I am not worthy to carry. He will baptize you with the Holy Spirit and fire.

Jesus Christ the son of God is our pattern. He sets the example of the workings of the Holy Spirit in humanity in full operation. The believer now becomes a son of God and part of God's church. He/she needs to follow Christ's example and to invite and allow the Holy Spirit to work in their lives.

(1 Peter 2:21 NKJV) ²¹ For to this you were called, because Christ also suffered for us, leaving us an example, that you should follow His steps:

Holy Spirit in the Life of the Lord Jesus, and His Church

The whole life of Jesus as the perfect Man was governed by the Holy Spirit. If Jesus depended upon the Holy Spirit in such a manner, how much more should the believer constantly depend upon the Holy Spirit? All that God has for us and wants to do in us will only be done by the operation of the Holy Spirit in our lives. Then the need for believers individually and the Church corporately must open their hearts to seek the fullness of the Holy Spirit and allow His working to be done in their actions and lives.

Text Message → Seek after and allow the Holy Spirit to work within your life.

Holy Spirit in the life of the Lord Jesus & the Church	
Born of the Spirit.	(Luke 1:35 NJKV) ³⁵ And the angel answered and said to her, "*The* Holy Spirit will come upon you, and the power of the Highest will overshadow you; therefore, also, that Holy One who is to be born will be called the Son of God.
Filled with the fullness of the Spirit.	(John 3:34 NKJV) ³⁴ For He whom God has sent speaks the words of God, for God does not give the Spirit by measure.
Led by the Spirit.	(Matthew 4:1 NKJV) ¹ Then Jesus was led up by the Spirit into

	the wilderness to be tempted by the devil
Empowered by the Spirit.	(Luke 4:14 NKJV) 14 Then Jesus returned in the power of the Spirit to Galilee, and news of Him went out through all the surrounding region.
Anointed by the Spirit.	(Luke 4:18 NKJV) 18 *"The Spirit of the LORD is upon Me, Because He has anointed Me To preach the gospel to the poor; He has sent Me to heal the brokenhearted, To proclaim liberty to the captives And recovery of sight to the blind, To set at liberty those who are oppressed;*
Spoke and Taught by the Spirit.	
Healed the sick by the Spirit.	
Cast out devils by the power of the Spirit.	(Matthew 12:28 NKJV) 28 But if I cast out demons by the Spirit of God, surely the kingdom of God has come upon you.
Justified (vindicated) by the Spirit.	(1Timothy 3:16 NKJV) 16 And without controversy great is the mystery of godliness: God was manifested in the flesh, Justified in the Spirit, Seen by angels, Preached among the Gentiles, Believed on in the world, Received up in glory.
Offered up on Calvary by the eternal Spirit.	(Hebrews 9:14 KJV) 14 How much more shall the blood of Christ, who through the eternal Spirit offered himself without spot to God, purge your conscience from dead works to serve the living God?
Resurrected by the Spirit.	(1 Peter 3:18 NKJV) 18 For Christ also suffered once for sins, the just for the unjust, that He might bring us to God, being put to death in the flesh but made alive by the Spirit,
Gave commandments to the disciples by the Spirit.	(Acts 1:2 NKJV) until the day in which He was taken up, after He through the Holy Spirit had given commandments to the apostles whom He had chosen,
Baptized and empowered the Church by the Spirit.	(Acts 1:5 NKJV) 5 for John truly baptized with water, but you shall be baptized with the Holy Spirit not many days from now." (Acts 1:8 NKJV) 8 But you shall receive power when the Holy Spirit has come upon you; and you shall be witnesses to Me in Jerusalem, and in all Judea and Samaria, and to the end of the earth."
Directs and governs the Church by the Spirit.	(Revelation 2:7 KJV) 7 He that hath an ear, let him hear what the Spirit saith unto the churches; To him that overcometh will I give to eat of the tree of life, which is in the midst of the paradise of God. (Revelation 2:11 KJV) 11 He that hath an ear, let him hear what the Spirit saith unto the churches; He that overcometh shall not be hurt of the second death.

Holy Spirit in the Life of the Believer

The expression "baptism in or with the Holy Spirit" is a Scriptural expression and experience.
Being filled with the spirit – according to Acts is associated with the Baptism of the Holy Spirit. At the beginning of Acts, Jesus repeated John the Baptist's prediction that the Messiah would baptize people in the Holy Spirit. This prophecy was fulfilled on the day of Pentecost, when all the assembled believers were baptized in the Holy Spirit and thereby "filled" with the Holy Spirit.

Once saturated with the Holy Spirit, this Spirit-effusion gave them the boldness to speak out for Jesus. Acts 4:8 says that Peter, when full of the Holy Spirit, spoke boldly to the rulers and elders. At the end of the same chapter, it says that all the church was filled with the Holy Spirit and thereby "spoke the word of God with all boldness". In nearly every case, the effusion of the Holy Spirit enables the person to speak or preach for God. The filling/baptism of the Holy Spirit is related to the prophetic ministry given as a revelation of this truth and today the fulfillment of God's Word. The Holy Spirit is the gift Jesus gave us to lead us, to guide us in truth, and understand God's Word.

(Acts 1:5 NKJV) ⁵ for John truly baptized with water, but you shall be baptized with the Holy Spirit not many days from now."

(Acts 4:31 NKJV) ³¹ And when they had prayed, the place where they were assembled together was shaken; and they were all filled with the Holy Spirit, and they spoke the word of God with boldness.

The Holy Spirit indwells the believer's spirit.	(Romans 8:9 NKJV) ⁹ But you are not in the flesh but in the Spirit, if indeed the Spirit of God dwells in you. Now if anyone does not have the Spirit of Christ, he is not His.
The Holy Spirit gives assurance of salvation.	(Romans 8:16 NKJV) ¹⁶ The Spirit Himself bears witness with our spirit that we are children of God,
The Holy Spirit fills the believer with Himself.	(Acts 2:4 HCSB) Then they were all filled with the Holy Spirit and began to speak in different languages, as the Spirit gave them ability for speech.
The Holy Spirit speaks to the believer.	(Acts 8:29 NKJV) ²⁹ Then the Spirit said to Philip, "Go near and overtake this chariot."
The Spirit open the believer understands to the things of God.	(1 Corinthians 2:12 KJV) ¹² Now we have received, not the spirit of the world, but the spirit which is of God; that we might know the things that are freely given to us of God.
Teaches the believer, and guides him into all truth.	(John 16:13 NKJV) ¹³ However, when He, the Spirit of truth, has come, He will guide you into all truth; for He will not speak on His own *authority,* but whatever He hears He will

	speak; and He will tell you things to come.
Strengthens the believer's inner being.	(Ephesians 3:16 KJV) [16] That he would grant you, according to the riches of his glory, to be strengthened with might by his Spirit in the inner man;
Enables the believer to pray.	(Jude 1:20 NKJV) [20] But you, beloved, building yourselves up on your most holy faith, praying in the Holy Spirit,
Enables the believer to put fleshly deeds to death & leads the believer.	(Romans 8:13-14 NKJV) [13] For if you live according to the flesh you will die; but if by the Spirit you put to death the deeds of the body, you will live. [14] For as many as are led by the Spirit of God, these are sons of God.
Produces Christ likeness in character and fruit in the believer's life.	(Galatians 5:22-25 KJV) [22] But the fruit of the Spirit is love, joy, peace, longsuffering, gentleness, goodness, faith, [23] Meekness, temperance: against such there is no law. [24] And they that are Christ's have crucified the flesh with the affections and lusts. [25] If we live in the Spirit, let us also walk in the Spirit.
Gives a calling to the believer for special service.	(Acts 13:4 NKJV) [4] So, being sent out by the Holy Spirit, they went down to Seleucia, and from there they sailed to Cyprus.
Imparts spiritual gifts to the believer as the Holy Spirit wills.	(1 Corinthians 12:7-11 NKJV) [7] But the manifestation of the Spirit is given to each one for the profit *of all:* [8] for to one is given the word of wisdom through the Spirit, to another the word of knowledge through the same Spirit, [9] to another faith by the same Spirit, to another gifts of healings by the same Spirit, [10] to another the working of miracles, to another prophecy, to another discerning of spirits, to another *different* kinds of tongues, to another the interpretation of tongues. [11] But one and the same Spirit works all these things, distributing to each one individually as He wills.
Will bring about the resurrection &immortality to the believers' bodies in the last day.	(Romans 8:11 KJV) [11] But if the Spirit of him that raised up Jesus from the dead dwell in you, he that raised up Christ from the dead shall also quicken your mortal bodies by his Spirit that dwelleth in you.

Tongues (Greek expression → glossa – Pronounced → GLOHSS sah

The Greek term *glossa* means "languages". When the early believers were empowered with the Holy Spirit on the Day of Pentecost, they were given the ability to speak in many different "languages," so that those visiting from all around the Greco-Roman world could hear the glories of God being uttered in their native tongue (Acts 2:4-11). The household of Cornelius also spoke in different languages when they were baptized in the Holy Spirit (Acts 10:46). The same phenomenon happened with the new disciples from Ephesus (Acts 19:6).

Not all spoke in "tongues" when they received the Holy Spirit (Acts 8:15-17). It wasn't the unique sign for having received the Holy Spirit. The Scriptures teach that all believers are baptized by the Spirit as they become integrated into the body of Christ (1 Corinthians 12:13). The genuine evidence of the work of the Holy Spirit is the "fruit of the Spirit" as defined in Galatians 5:22-23. In any event, some members of the early church regularly spoke in different languages as a way of praying to God, and others who spoke in private did not need interpretation. When they were spoken in the meetings, Paul required interpretation so that the others could understand and be edified (1 Corinthians 14:2-27).

In order to establish firmly the public practice of tongue-speaking as a ministry to the church and to prevent its abuse as a quest for personal fulfillment, Paul put forth a set of rules designed to control its corporate exercise. These are explained in (1 Corinthians 14:27-33). Those people speaking in tongues must always have their utterances interpreted for the benefit of others. Persons participating in worship should be in control of their conduct at all times. They may not appeal to ecstatic states to excuse disorderly conduct or infractions to the rules of worship. Finally, Paul taught that the gift of tongues is not to be sought after. Only the "higher gifts" involving communication through directly intelligible speech are to be earnestly desired
(1 Corinthians 12:31; 14:1&5).

Holy Spirit in the Life of the Church

The work of the Holy Spirit is seen not only in the life of an individual but greatly in the Church corporately. The Lord Jesus Christ stated that one would come (the Holy Spirit) after Him and be upon the believers who are the church, building it, strengthening it, guiding it, and empowering it. Before the Holy Spirit was able to come, Jesus Christ needed to complete His work, His death, burial, resurrection, ascension and glorification.

(John 7:38-39 NKJV) [38] He who believes in Me, as the Scripture has said, out of his heart will flow rivers of living water." [39] But this He spoke concerning the Spirit, whom those believing in Him would receive; for the Holy Spirit was not yet *given,* because Jesus was not yet glorified.

The difference between the Old Testament and New Testament times is the indwelling of the Holy Spirit within the believer. During the Old Testament this was not a common thing available to all believers but was only experienced by a select few men of God. Today all believers have the availability of the Holy Spirit as seen in the baptismal sign which was given to John the Baptist, concerning the Messiah, John 1:33 says "… Upon whom you see the Spirit descending and remaining on Him, this is He who baptizes with the Holy Spirit". This qualified Jesus to be the Baptizer in the Holy Spirit.

On the day of Pentecost the Holy Spirit formed the Church into a corporate unit, the Body of Christ, baptizing them into a living structure. This day, the day of Pentecost is called the birthday of the Church. Forming the Church, the Holy Spirit made it to be a living temple of

God. The believers became the living stones in this New Covenant temple. As the New Covenant Priestly Body, the Holy Spirit produces anointing, illumination, guidance, teaching and direction to the church. As to the membership of the Church the Holy Spirit makes available gifts of the Spirit which prove His divinity and equal place in the Godhead. Evidence of His nature and character are seen in the fruits of the Church and in each believer, producing the fruits of the Spirit.

The Lord Jesus is the head of the Church in heaven and He directs His affairs in His Body by means of the Holy Spirit. The Church is directed and governed by the Holy Spirit who calls, quickens, energizes and equips the various ministries in the Church and every member of the Body of Christ according to their particular place.

The Work of the Holy Spirit is summarized clearly in John 16:9-11. The Holy Spirit has come in relation to the world; to reprove the world of sin, righteousness and judgment – using the Church to minister this.

(John 16:9-13 NKJV) [9] of sin, because they do not believe in Me; [10] of righteousness, because I go to My Father and you see Me no more; [11] of judgment, because the ruler of this world is judged. [12] I still have many things to say to you, but you cannot bear *them* now. [13] However, when He, the Spirit of truth, has come, He will guide you into all truth; for He will not speak on His own *authority,* but whatever He hears He will speak; and He will tell you things to come.

The work of the Holy Spirit in relation to the unconverted is to convince, convict and convert. This is a major responsibility of the Church. The church is to take the Word of God, the Gospel of Jesus Christ and let the world know of it. We are to live a life of holiness, and righteous so that we can be examples to others and live in the Truth. By this the world will truly say they are (believers in Jesus Christ) a peculiar people, standing apart from the worldly things and ideas of disbelief that will eventually destroy the physical life and worst of all their eternal life.

(Acts 2:1-4 NKJV) [1] When the Day of Pentecost had fully come, they were all with one accord in one place. [2] And suddenly there came a sound from heaven, as of a rushing mighty wind, and it filled the whole house where they were sitting. [3] Then there appeared to them divided tongues, as of fire, and *one* sat upon each of them. [4] And they were all filled with the Holy Spirit and began to speak with other tongues, as the Spirit gave them utterance.

(1 Corinthians 3:16 NKJV) [16] Do you not know that you are the temple of God and *that* the Spirit of God dwells in you?

(Ephesians 2:20-22 NKJV) [20] having been built on the foundation of the apostles and prophets, Jesus Christ Himself being the chief corner *stone,* [21] in whom the whole building, being joined together, grows into a holy temple in the Lord, [22] in whom you also are being built together for a dwelling place of God in the Spirit.

(2 Corinthians 1:21 NKJV) [21] Now He who establishes us with you in Christ and has anointed us *is* God,

(Ephesians 1:17 NKJV) [17] that the God of our Lord Jesus Christ, the Father of glory, may give to you the spirit of wisdom and revelation in the knowledge of Him,

(1 Corinthians 12:4-11 NKJV) [4] There are diversities of gifts, but the same Spirit. [5] There are differences of ministries, but the same Lord. [6] And there are diversities of activities, but it is the same God who works all in all. [7] But the manifestation of the Spirit is given to each one for the profit *of all:* [8] for to one is given the word of wisdom through the Spirit, to another the word of knowledge through the same Spirit, [9] to another faith by the same Spirit, to another gifts of healings by the same Spirit, [10] to another the working of miracles, to another prophecy, to another discerning of spirits, to another *different* kinds of tongues, to another the interpretation of tongues. [11] But one and the same Spirit works all these things, distributing to each one individually as He wills.

(Galatians 5:22-23 NKJV) [22] But the fruit of the Spirit is love, joy, peace, longsuffering, kindness, goodness, faithfulness, [23] gentleness, self-control. Against such there is no law.

Symbols of the Holy Spirit

Fire	*Symbolizes the holiness of God where by the Holy Spirit is sent forth in judgment to purge, purify, and enliven with zeal.*	Matthew 3:11; Acts 2:3; Isaiah 4:4; Exodus 19:18; Malachi 3:2,3; Hebrews 13:29
Water	*As water speaks of the life-giving flow which refreshes and satisfies. It also speaks of washing, cleansing, and fruitfulness.*	John 7:38,39; Psalm 72:6; Isaiah 44:3; Exodus 17:6 with 1 Corinthians 10:4
Dew	*Dew only comes in the stillness of the night, bringing refreshing to the mown grass. So it is with the refreshing work of the Spirit in the Believer/Church.*	Psalm 133:1-3; Hosea 14:5
Wind or Breath	*Symbolize the life-giving breath of God in its regeneration power. It underscores the fact that the Holy Spirit is invisible as a person, yet the effect of His work can be seen.*	Acts 2:2; John 3:8; Ezekiel 37: 9-10; Isaiah 40:7
Oil	*Oil was distinctly involved in the anointing of the prophets priests and kings to their offices. It speaks of his consecration and supernatural enablement of the Spirit's anointing grace, the illumination of His teaching, the soothing and healing balm of*	Luke 4:18; Acts 10:38; 1 John 2:20 ,27; Psalm 23:5

	His presence. It is the Spirit who anoints the members of the Church to their priestly functions.	
The Dove	*The symbol of the dove is used to represent purity, beauty, gentleness and peace, the nature and character of the Holy Spirit.*	Matthew 3:16; Luke 3:22; Genesis 1:2; Matthew 10:16
The Seal	*A seal is significant of ownership, genuineness and security. This emphasizes the Spirit's activity confirming to us God's ownership of us, His authority over us and our security in Him.*	Ephesians 1:13; 2 Corinthians 1:22; Ephesians 4:30; 2 Timothy 2:19
The Still Small Voice	*The Spirit is the voice of God within man bringing a revelation of God's will to him.*	Genesis 3:8; 1 Kings 19:11-13
Finger of God	*The Spirit is the one who points the accusing finger at the sinner, to bring about conviction with a view to the accused accepting Jesus Christ as his advocate.*	Luke 11:20; Matthew 12:28
The First Fruits	*The first fruits were always symbolic of the full harvest to come, so the Spirit's initial work of regeneration points to the full salvation and glorification of the believer before God.*	Romans 8:23
The Earnest	*The earnest was always a down payment, a pledge of more to come. So the Spirit's work in salvation is simply the pledge of full and total redemption to come. This is similar to the first fruits symbol.*	2 Corinthians 1:22; Ephesians 1:13-14
Endued	*Is the symbol meaning the clothing of the Spirit upon the believers. The baptism of the Holy Spirit is this divine clothing from God. It is the believers garment for ministry before the Lord*	Luke 24:49; Isaiah 61:10

Titles of the Holy Spirit

The Holy Spirit has many names and titles stated in Scripture just as the Father and Son does. These titles identify different aspects of the Spirit's character, functions or ministrations. Other titles identify more particularly the essential and moral attributes of the Holy Spirit. Each of these attributes is related to some special need of mankind.

Text Message → It is the Holy Spirit who brings to us the wisdom, faith and power of God. All that is necessary is brought to us by the Holy Spirit. He is within each believer.

Titles of His Deity, Ministry, & Attributes

The Spirit	(John 3:6-8)
The Holy Spirit	(Luke 11:13; Isaiah 63:11)
The Spirit of God	(1 Corinthians 3:16)
The Spirit of the Lord God	(Isaiah 61:1)
The Spirit of the Living God	(2 Corinthians 3:3)
The Spirit of Jesus	(Acts 16:6-6)
The Holy Spirit of God	(Ephesians 4:30)
The Spirit of Christ	(Romans 8:9; 1 Peter 1:11)
The Spirit of Jesus Christ	(Philippians 1:19)
The Spirit which is of God	(1 Corinthians 2:12)
The Spirit of Wisdom	(Isaiah 11:2; Ephesians 1:17)
The Spirit of Knowledge	(Isaiah 11:2)
The Spirit of Counsel and Might	(Isaiah 11:2)
The Spirit of Judgment	(Isaiah 4:4)
The Spirit of the Almighty	(Job 32:8; 33:4)
The Spirit of Him who raised Jesus from the dead	(Romans 8:11)
The power of the Highest	(Luke 1:35)
The Eternal Spirit	(Hebrews 9:14)
The Spirit of Holiness	(Romans 1:4)
The Comforter	(John 14:16, 26; 15:26; 16:7)
The Spirit of Love	(2 Timothy 1:7)
The Spirit of Truth	(John 14:17; 16:13; 15:26; 1 John 4:6)
The Spirit of Life	(Romans 8:2; Revelation 11:11)
The Spirit of Adoption	(Romans 8:15)
The Spirit of Faith	(2 Corinthians 4:13)
The Spirit of Promise	(Ephesians 1:13-14)
The Spirit of Grace	(Zechariah 12:10; Hebrews 10:29)
The Spirit of Glory	(1 Peter 4:14)
The Spirit of Power	(2 Timothy 1:7)
The Spirit of Wisdom and revelation	(Ephesians 1:17)
The Spirit of Prophecy	(Revelation 19:10)
The anointing which teaches us	(1 John 2:27)

In the New Testament the work of the Holy Spirit is what it was in the Old Testament but now the Spirit is available for all believers and all nations, not only Israel.

The Holy Spirit now is within the believer, to remain and abide forever within their heart. This is the fulfilled promise of the Father to the Son, and the fulfilled promise of the Son

to the believer. The Holy Spirit as the Spirit of promise brings all the promises and Truths of God to mankind, and to the church perfecting His love in us.

Text Message → Remember, Jesus Christ first came to the world, the Living Word, and after His resurrection the Comforter, Helper, Counselor (Holy Spirit) came upon mankind as they repented and believed in the Living Word empowering them to walk the faith.

Begin With Prayer

Biblical Teaching/Doctrine of Atonement

Biblical Building Block # 7

(John 13:34-35 HCSB)

34 "I give you a new command: Love one another. Just as I have loved you, you must also love one another. **35** By this all people will know that you are My disciples, if you have love for one another."

A new commandment was given to the believers from Jesus Christ, "to love one another just as I have loved you." Jesus proved His love to mankind by becoming the atonement for mankind's sin. He became the last sin offering. By laying down His life He became the example of what love is all about. No, not just dying for a cause but by living for a cause. Jesus' life was a life full of love giving all that He had to others and helping others and caring for others. He now has given the command to each believer to do the same become a giver of love, act in love and most of all become a lover of God. Love does cover all things. This is why the Scriptures state that God is love. He is all things and all that we will ever need.

1. What is the meaning of atonement?

2. Why did mankind need atonement?

3. Can you explain the nature of the atonement?

4. What was the work of the atonement?

5. Explain the resurrection of Jesus Christ?

6. What is meant by the phrase "the ascension of Jesus Christ"?

7. Do you understand what the final Judgment is and who will be judged?

Atonement - The Work of Christ

The atoning work of Christ includes His crucifixion, resurrection, ascension, glorification, exaltation, intercession and His second advent. It includes the Living Word of God given to the world and the setting up of the Church. So, the results of His death are called the atonement. *Kaphar,* a Hebrew word used in the Old Testament (Leviticus 16:6) meant "to cover." The blood of bulls and goats could not take away sin. It just covered sin until the blood of Christ was shed to cleanse the sinner from sin's defilement, (the work of the atonement).

The foundation scripture for blood atonement is found in Leviticus 17:11. Thousands of animal sacrifices were offered in the Old Testament times but Jesus offered one perfect, sinless, human sacrifice, once for all. The atonement was this one time sin offering that could only come from a sinless nature, a perfect being, Jesus Christ.

However, modern use of the word "atonement" has a broad sense, including substitution, redemption, propitiation, and reconciliation. Jesus was conscious of a particular work His Father sent Him to do. His work was to fulfill the will of the Father.

(Leviticus 17:11 KJV) ¹¹ For the life of the flesh *is* in the blood: and I have given it to you upon the altar to make an atonement for your souls: for it *is* the blood *that* maketh an atonement for the soul.

(Exodus 12:12-12 KJV) ¹² For I will pass through the land of Egypt this night, and will smite all the firstborn in the land of Egypt, both man and beast; and against all the gods of Egypt I will execute judgment: I *am* the LORD. ¹³ And the blood shall be to you for a token upon the houses where ye *are*: and when I see the blood, I will pass over you, and the plague shall not be upon you to destroy *you*, when I smite the land of Egypt.

(Hebrews 10:4 NKJV) For *it is* not possible that the blood of bulls and goats could take away sins.

(Hebrews 10:11-14 NKJV) ¹¹ And every priest stands ministering daily and offering repeatedly the same sacrifices, which can never take away sins. ¹² But this Man, after He had offered one sacrifice for sins forever, sat down at the right hand of God, ¹³ from that time waiting till His enemies are made His footstool. ¹⁴ For by one offering He has perfected forever those who are being sanctified.

(Romans 3:25 NKJV) ²⁵ whom God set forth *as* a propitiation by His blood, through faith, to demonstrate His righteousness, because in His forbearance God had passed over the sins that were previously committed,

(John 17:4-5 NKJV) ⁴ I have glorified You on the earth. I have finished the work which You have given Me to do. ⁵ And now, O Father, glorify Me together with Yourself, with the glory which I had with You before the world was.

Text Message → also read (John 17:14-27)

Necessity of the Atonement

To understand the necessity or need of the atonement, the relationship between the holiness of God, the sinfulness of mankind, and God's divine law and divine wrath should be realized. God's holiness demands that mankind's sinfulness be dealt with and that wrath be executed upon it. But divine grace restrains immediate wrath waiting for God to provide a means for mankind to escape the wrath. These are the things that necessitate the atonement.

Holiness of God

Holiness is a moral attribute of God. It describes God's inward character, His very essence. God is perfectly holy in all He says and does because He is holiness personified. Because God is absolutely holy, He expects no less than holiness from His creatures. God cannot tolerate sin which is unholy and demands that sin be exposed, judged, and punished.

In the New Testament the word *Hagasmos* means "holiness" and denotes "separation from everything ceremonially impure". Note (Revelation 4: 8 NKJV*) ⁸ The *four living creatures, each having six wings, were full of eyes around and within. And they do not rest day or night, saying: "Holy, holy, holy, Lord God Almighty, Who was and is and is to come!"* This verse identifies that God is to be worshiped daily because of His holiness, the very essence of God.

(Leviticus 19:2 KJV) ² Speak unto all the congregation of the children of Israel, and say unto them, Ye shall be holy: for I the LORD your God *am* holy.

(Isaiah 57:15 KJV) ¹⁵ For thus saith the high and lofty One that inhabiteth eternity, whose name *is* Holy; I dwell in the high and holy *place*, with him also *that is* of a contrite and humble spirit, to revive the spirit of the humble, and to revive the heart of the contrite ones.

Divine Law of God

God's creation must live within the boundaries of God's will. He created angelic and human beings with a free will that must be obedient to God's divine law which is a standard of righteousness. Without law there would be no order, and all would be chaos. God's will was His law and His law was His will. The laws governing God's own being were to be the laws which would govern all created beings. God gave Adam and Eve the law of obedience. To transgress this law was sin.

(Genesis 2:17 KJV) **17** But of the tree of the knowledge of good and evil, thou shalt not eat of it: for in the day that thou eatest thereof thou shalt surely die.

Sinfulness of Man

Adam and Eve violated the one law God had given them and sin entered the world impacting all mankind through this act of disobedience. (1 John 3:4 NKJV) *4 Whoever commits sin also commits lawlessness, and sin is lawlessness.* Sin separated mankind from God creating a gap between mankind and God, which is not a natural state. Mankind now possesses a sinful nature and this nature will continue to sin in this world until that gap between mankind and God can be bridged. The atonement bridged this gap.

Wrath of God

When the holiness of God comes into conflict with the sinfulness of mankind divine wrath is manifested. The wrath of God is simply the righteous anger of a Holy God against sin. Sin cannot be tolerated in the presences of God and it must be dealt with and come under divine judgment. If it goes without judgment then God's law, holiness, righteousness, and justice are violated.

(Romans 1:18 NKJV) **18** For the wrath of God is revealed from heaven against all ungodliness and unrighteousness of men, who suppress the truth in unrighteousness,

(Romans 4:15 NKJV) **15** because the law brings about wrath; for where there is no law *there is* no transgression.

Nature of the Atonement

As we have seen, the Hebrew word "*Kaphar*" means "to cover"; figuratively "to expiate or condone, to placate or conceal". It is translated by these words: "appease, make atonement, cleanse, disannul, forgive, be merciful, pacify, purge, reconcile". The Old English word "atonement" means "to be made at one", "to reconcile, to bring about agreement or concord".

So, "atonement" is spoken of as the covering, the expiation, the satisfaction, the appeasement of the reconciliation. Mankind broke God's Holy law, violating the principles of righteousness by their disobedience. This brought mankind under the power of sin. With the violation of the divine law also came the divine penalty of death (Genesis 2:17; Romans 6:23). The atonement was then necessary to appease the divine law of God and through Jesus Christ the work of the atonement was fulfilled.

(Exodus 29:33-37 KJV) **33** And they shall eat those things wherewith the atonement was made, to consecrate *and* to sanctify them: but a stranger shall not eat *thereof*, because they *are* holy. **34** And if ought of the flesh of the consecrations, or of the bread, remain unto the morning, then thou shalt burn the remainder with fire: it shall not be eaten, because it *is* holy. **35** And thus shalt thou do unto Aaron, and to his sons, according to all *things* which I have commanded thee: seven days shalt thou consecrate them. **36** And thou shalt offer every day a bullock *for* a sin offering for atonement: and thou shalt cleanse the altar, when thou hast made an atonement for it, and thou shalt anoint it, to sanctify it. ³⁷ Seven days thou shalt make an atonement for the altar, and sanctify it; and it shall be an altar most holy: whatsoever toucheth the altar shall be holy.

Work of the Atonement

The work of the Atonement can be seen as the acts of Jesus Christ from His death, burial, resurrection, ascension, glorification, exaltation, second coming and Final Judgment. Results of the Atonement can be seen as God's grace, redemption, ransom, substitution, propitiation, reconciliation, atonement, and salvation for mankind.

Results of the Atonement	Factors of the Atonement
Grace	Jesus Christ Death
Redemption	Burial
Ransom	Resurrection
Substitution	Ascension
Propitiation	Glorification
Reconciliation	Exaltation
Atonement	Second coming
Salvation	Final Judgment

Jesus Christ Death, Burial, and Resurrection

The death of Jesus Christ and His resurrection is what Christianity is structured upon. Some will accept Jesus Christ as a great man, teacher, or prophet, but deny the atonement. They deny His death as being a sacrifice for all mankind in which He covered the sins of the world with His blood, and provided a way of salvation for all of mankind. One must simply believe by faith that Jesus Christ is the only path of salvation and by believing you shall be saved (salvation). Note that Jesus Christ died for our "sins" is the doctrinal interpretation of the atonement. His soul was made an offering for the sin of mankind and He was resurrected, being seen by many.

(1 Corinthians 15:3-8 NKJV) ³ For I delivered to you first of all that which I also received: that Christ died for our sins according to the Scriptures, ⁴ and that He was buried, and that He rose again the third day according to the Scriptures, ⁵ and that He was seen by Cephas, then by the twelve. ⁶ After that He was seen by over five hundred brethren at once, of whom the greater part remain to the present, but some have fallen asleep. ⁷ After that He was seen by James, then by all the apostles. ⁸ Then last of all He was seen by me also, as by one born out of due time.

(John 3:16-18 NKJV) ¹⁶ For God so loved the world that He gave His only begotten Son, that whoever believes in Him should not perish but have everlasting life. ¹⁷ For God did not send His Son into the world to condemn the world, but that the world through Him might be saved. [18] He who believes in Him is not condemned; but he who does not believe is condemned already, because he has not believed in the name of the only begotten Son of God.

Jesus Christ's death and resurrection was not just by chance but by a plan of God	
God's eternal Plan for the world.	(Revelation 13:8 NKJV) [8] All who dwell on the earth will worship him, whose names have not been written in the Book of Life of the Lamb slain from the foundation of the world. (1 Peter 1:18-20; Acts 2:22-23)
Scriptures foretold under the Law, Psalms, Prophets.	(Luke 24:27 NKJV) [27] And beginning at Moses and all the Prophets, He expounded to them in all the Scriptures the things concerning Himself. (Luke 24:44-45; Matthew 5:17-18; 11:13)
Main purpose of the Incarnation - a ransom for many.	(Matthew 20:28 NKJV) [28] just as the Son of Man did not come to be served, but to serve, and to give His life a ransom for many." (Mark 10:45; Hebrews 2:9,14; 9:26; 1 John 3:5)
Essential to Salvation for mankind.	(John 3:14-16 NKJV) [14] And as Moses lifted up the serpent in the wilderness, even so must the Son of Man be lifted up, [15] that whoever believes in Him should not perish but have eternal life. [16] For God so loved the world that He gave His only begotten Son, that whoever believes in Him should not perish but have everlasting life. (John 3:12:24; Romans 3:25-26; Matthew 16:21; Mark 8:31; Luke 9:22; 17:25; Acts 17:3; 1 Peter 3:18; 1 John 3:5; Hebrews 8:28 ; 2 Corinthians 5:14)
Takes away the sins of the world.	(John 1:29 NKJV) [29] The next day John saw Jesus coming toward him, and said, "Behold! The Lamb of God who takes away the sin of the world! (John 3:16; 1 John 3:16; Romans 5:8; Psalm 85:10)
To destroy the power of Satan over mankind.	(Hebrews 2:14-15 NKJV) [14] Inasmuch then as the children have partaken of flesh and blood, He Himself likewise shared in the same, that through death He might destroy him who had the power of death, that is, the devil, [15] and release those who through fear of death were all their lifetime subject to bondage.

Jesus Christ Resurrection and Ascension

The Resurrection of Jesus Christ took place after 3 days and 3 nights. Jesus said that He would be in the heart of the earth for a period of 3 days and 3 nights, fulfilling the sign of the prophet Jonah when he was 3 days and 3 nights in the heart of the great fish.

NOTE – There are three views about what occurred with the spirit of Jesus during these 3 days and nights.

Descent to Hades - Teaches that Christ descended to Hell (Greek: Hades) or *Sheol* (Hebrew) and preached to the spirits in prison during the 3 days. At either the beginning or end of these 3 days He stripped Satan of the keys of death and Hades and led the host of captive saints up to heaven. Those that hold this view base it on a misunderstanding of *1 Peter 3:18-22; 4:6* and *Ephesians 4:8-10*. NOTE – these Scriptures show that it was the Spirit of Christ preaching through Noah while the Ark was in preparation, not a preaching going on during the 3 days and 3 nights of Calvary's period. The time element is the key to a proper understanding of these passages.

Ascent to Heaven - Teaches that Christ ascended to His Father and was with the Father during the 3 days and nights. At the end of the 3 days His spirit returned to earth and He experienced the resurrection of His incorruptible body. Then after 40 days with His disciples, he ascended bodily to heaven to begin His High Priestly intercessory ministry. (Based upon *Luke 23:46; 2 Corinthians 12:1-4; John 13:36; 14:1-6*). It holds that the Old Testament saints went to heaven at death; not a righteous section of Hell or Hades. When interpreting Christ leading "captivity captive" (Ephesians 4:8-10) it is said that this refers to sin, sickness and death, which are the things which held the human race captive to Satan. It was this captivity that Christ led captive. This view seems to be much nearer the teaching of Scripture then the 'descent to Hades' thought.

Ascent and Decent - This third view teaches Christ did go to heaven/paradise and was with the Father during a period of time of the 3 days. It rejects the teaching that Christ preached during this time to the spirits in prison. But it holds that the spirits of the Old Testament righteous were in a division of Hades and were released by Christ either at the beginning or close of the 3 day period and taken to the third heaven, Paradise. After this, Christ descended to the tomb and His physical resurrection took place. The following Scriptures are in support of this theory.

(Matthew 12:39-41 NKJV) [39] But He answered and said to them, "An evil and adulterous generation seeks after a sign, and no sign will be given to it except the sign of the prophet Jonah. [40] For as Jonah was three days and three nights in the belly of the great fish, so will the Son of Man be three days and three nights in the heart of the earth. [41] The men of Nineveh will rise up in the judgment with this generation and condemn it, because they repented at the preaching of Jonah; and indeed a greater than Jonah *is* here.

(Luke 23:39-43) → Jesus promised the repentant thief that he would be with Him in Paradise that day.

(John 13:1,36; 14:1-6,28; 16:5,16-22; 17:11,13) → Jesus, before His death, clearly told the disciples that he was going "to the Father" not to Hades.

(Ephesians 4:8-10)→ Scriptures say that Christ descended into the lower parts or the lower down divisions of the earth and then led captivity captive.

Scriptures then show that the Lord Jesus Christ, at His death, ascended in spirit to the Father and was with the Father during the 3 days and nights while His physical body lay in the tomb. The Old Testament saints who died in faith, and were waiting in *Sheol*, were taken to heaven to be with the Father. This was the triumphant entry of the king of Glory into the gates of the heavenly Jerusalem with a host of captives (Psalm 24). At the close of the 3 days and nights Jesus returned to earth and re-entered His incorruptible body. From this point we see the Lord Jesus appearing to His disciples for 40 days.

Resurrection

This is one of the great fundamental doctrines of the Christian Faith. In the New Testament there are about 104 references to the resurrection of Christ. The resurrection took place after 3 days and 3 nights after the death of Jesus Christ. The resurrection was the foundation of the apostolic preaching and almost every sermon in the Book of Acts refers to it. The resurrection was God's seal and sign of an acceptable atonement. Jesus also knew and stated his death and resurrection.

(Acts 5:30-32 NKJV) [30] The God of our fathers raised up Jesus whom you murdered by hanging on a tree. [31] Him God has exalted to His right hand *to be* Prince and Savior, to give repentance to Israel and forgiveness of sins. [32] And we are His witnesses to these things, and *so* also *is* the Holy Spirit whom God has given to those who obey Him."

(Romans 1:4 NKJV) [4] *and* declared *to be* the Son of God with power according to the Spirit of holiness, by the resurrection from the dead.

(John 2:18-22 NKJV) [18] So the Jews answered and said to Him, "What sign do You show to us, since You do these things?" [19] Jesus answered and said to them, "Destroy this temple, and in three days I will raise it up." [20] Then the Jews said, "It has taken forty-six years to build this temple, and will You raise it up in three days?" [21] But He was speaking of the temple of His body. [22] Therefore, when He had risen from the dead, His disciples remembered that He had said this to them;

Other Scriptures → Acts 1:21-22; 2,24,32; 3:15; 4:10,33; 5:30; 13:30,34; 17:31; Philippians 3:21; 1 Corinthians 15; Romans 1:4; Acts 3:13-15; Mark 16:16; 1 Corinthians 15:3-4

Although the resurrection was not seen, the resurrected Christ did appear.	
To	Scriptures
Two messengers in the tomb.	(Mark 16:6 NKJV) 6 But he said to them, "Do not be alarmed. You seek Jesus of Nazareth, who was crucified. He is risen! He is not here. See the place where they laid Him.
Mary Magdalene.	(Mark 16:9 NKJV) Now when *He* rose early on the first *day* of the week, He appeared first to Mary Magdalene, out of whom He had cast seven demons.
Other women who told the disciples.	(Matthew 28:9 NKJV) 9 And as they went to tell His disciples, behold, Jesus met them, saying, "Rejoice!" So they came and held Him by the feet and worshiped Him.
To Peter, James & 500 brethren.	(1 Corinthians 15:5-8 NKJV) 5 and that He was seen by Cephas, then by the twelve. 6 After that He was seen by over five hundred brethren at once, of whom the greater part remain to the present, but some have fallen asleep. 7 After that He was seen by James, then by all the apostles. 8 Then last of all He was seen by me also, as by one born out of due time.
Disciples at Bethany at the Mount of Ascension.	(Acts 1:3-5 NKJV) 3 to whom He also presented Himself alive after His suffering by many infallible proofs, being seen by them during forty days and speaking of the things pertaining to the kingdom of God. 4 And being assembled together with *them,* He commanded them not to depart from Jerusalem, but to wait for the Promise of the Father, "which," *He said,* "you have heard from Me; 5 for John truly baptized with water, but you shall be baptized with the Holy Spirit not many days from now."

The Ascension

The ascension of Jesus Christ means His going back to heaven to the Father, with His resurrected and glorified body. There were 40 days between the resurrection and ascension. During the 40 days before the ascension to heaven Jesus taught and instructed His disciples concerning the Kingdom of God, and the Great Commission was given to the disciple which is the final charge before His ascension. This ascension was a necessary event which was the closing act of His earthly ministry. The earthly church currently is ministered to by the Holy Spirit (empowered from on high).

(Acts 1:3 NKJV) ³ to whom He also presented Himself alive after His suffering by many infallible proofs, being seen by them during forty days and speaking of the things pertaining to the kingdom of God.

(Mark 16:14-15 NKJV) ¹⁴ Later He appeared to the eleven as they sat at the table; and He rebuked their unbelief and hardness of heart, because they did not believe those who had seen Him after He had risen. ¹⁵ And He said to them, "Go into all the world and preach the gospel to every creature.

(Acts 1:7-8 NKJV) ⁷ And He said to them, "It is not for you to know times or seasons which the Father has put in His own authority. ⁸ But you shall receive power when the Holy Spirit has come upon you; and you shall be witnesses to Me in Jerusalem, and in all Judea and Samaria, and to the end of the earth."

Notation → The translation of Enoch (Genesis 5:24; Hebrews 11:5), Moses (Deuteronomy 34:5-6; Jude 9; Matthew 17:1-9), and Elijah (Matthew 17:1-9 with 2 Kings 2:11-18) translates to shadowing forth of the resurrection and the translation of the saints at the coming of Christ (1 Thessalonians 2:1; 1 Corinthians 15:51-57; Revelation 12:5). The ascension of Jesus stands unique among all men. In contrast to these OT saints, and the translation of the saints at Christ's second coming, Jesus ascended to heaven by His own right, because of who He is and what he had done. These OT saints were translated by the power of God, not their own power or right. Jesus ascended by His own right and power as the God-Man (John 3:13; Psalm 24:1-4; 68:18; 110:1-4).

Glorification

Scriptures laid claim of the coming glory of Jesus Christ. Christ Himself spoke of it. The disciple wrote about it. Glory has the meaning of great honor, praise, distinction, adoration, majestic beauty and splendor. In glorification Jesus Christ received all that glory can mean. The Son of God laid aside the glory that He had and humbled Himself in the incarnation, becoming man. After the fulfillment of His ministry Jesus was entitled to receive this glory back. This glorification was the same eternal glory that now pertained to His humanity, Jesus now being glorified as the perfect God-Man. His glorified body is the sample of that glory which the saints will experience at His second coming and for all eternity.

Scriptures on Glorification	
Prophets foretold of the suffering and glory.	(Luke 24:26-27 NKJV) ²⁶ Ought not the Christ to have suffered these things and to enter into His glory?" ²⁷ And beginning at Moses and all the Prophets, He expounded to them in all the Scriptures the things concerning Himself.
Jesus laid aside His glory.	(Philippians 2:5-8 NKJV) ⁵ Let this mind be in you which

	was also in Christ Jesus, ⁶ who, being in the form of God, did not consider it robbery to be equal with God, ⁷ but made Himself of no reputation, taking the form of a bondservant, *and* coming in the likeness of men. ⁸ And being found in appearance as a man, He humbled Himself and became obedient to *the point of* death, even the death of the cross.
Jesus prayed about His glory.	(John 17:4-5 NKJV) ⁴ I have glorified You on the earth. I have finished the work which You have given Me to do. ⁵ And now, O Father, glorify Me together with Yourself, with the glory which I had with You before the world was.
Told the disciples He must be glorified before the Holy Spirit could be given.	(John 7:39 NKJV) ³⁹ But this He spoke concerning the Spirit, whom those believing in Him would receive; for the Holy Spirit was not yet *given,* because Jesus was not yet glorified.
In His ascension Jesus was received in glory.	(1 Timothy 3:16 NKJV) ¹⁶ And without controversy great is the mystery of godliness: God was manifested in the flesh, Justified in the Spirit, Seen by angels, Preached among the Gentiles, Believed on in the world, Received up in glory.
Now upon him as man.	(1 Peter 1:21 NKJV) ²¹ who through Him believe in God, who raised Him from the dead and gave Him glory, so that your faith and hope are in God.

Exaltation

With the glorification came exaltation, which included praise, honor and joy. This involved Jesus Christ's enthronement, a placement of glory and the reception of His exalted Name. Christ was exalted by the Father to sit at the throne with Him. This act of exaltation was the Father's bestowal of His name upon His Son making Him the Lord Jesus Christ. He was raised from the dead to be "Lord both of the dead and the living". Paul said in (Philippians 2:9-11 KJV), *"God also has highly exalted Him, and given Him a name which is above every name… that every tongue should confess that Jesus Christ is the Lord to the glory of God the Father"…* Confession of the Lordship of Jesus is necessary for salvation.

(Psalm 110:1 NKJV) ¹ A Psalm of David. The LORD said to my Lord, "Sit at My right hand, Till I make Your enemies Your footstool."

(Romans 14:9 NKJV) ⁹ For to this end Christ died and rose and lived again, that He might be Lord of both the dead and the living.

(Romans 10:9-13 NKJV) ⁹ that if you confess with your mouth the Lord Jesus and believe in your heart that God has raised Him from the dead, you will be saved. ¹⁰ For with the heart one believes unto righteousness, and with the mouth confession is made unto salvation. ¹¹ For the Scripture says, *"Whoever believes on Him will not be put to shame."* ¹² For there is no distinction between Jew and Greek, for the same Lord over all is rich to all who call upon Him. [13] For *"whoever calls on the name of the LORD shall be saved."*

Seated as Prophet - Jesus is the true Word of God who speaks to mankind in behalf of God and speaks the truth of God, also predicting the events of the future.

> John 14:6; 7:40; 9:17; 10:24; Acts 3:22; 7:37; Matthew 24-25; Luke 21; Mark 13; John 16:9-16; Jeremiah 26:12; John 12:49-50; 6:26-51; Deuteronomy 18:12-19

Seated as Priest - Jesus is the mediator, advocate, reconciler and intercessor for mankind. As priest He speaks to God on behalf of mankind. Chosen from among mankind He is appointed and anointed as priest and makes intersession as the Mediator between mankind and God.

> Hebrews 5:1-10; 8:1; 4:15; 7:25; 9:11-28; 10:19-22; 1 Timothy 2:5-6; Zachariah 6:12-13; 1 John 2:1,9

Seated as King - Jesus is the ruler and governor of the universe. Jesus Christ as King-Priest has been given all power and authority. He is a King-Priest which constitutes Him in the Order of Melchisedek. The Kings of Judah sat upon the throne of David. Christ as the greater Son of David was to sit on the throne forever. There will be no end to his kingdom. The right hand is symbolic of a place of honor, power and authority. The Father gave this place to Jesus.
He is the king of the saints and He is King of Kings and Lord of Lords– He is the King of Glory.

> Zechariah 3:1; Psalm 110:1; Genesis 48:13-19; Psalm 110:5; Revelation 12:10; 15:3;19:16 Matthew 26:64; Psalm 24:7-10

Seated as Judge - Jesus will judge mankind and all creation. As judge the Father has committed all things to His Son. To judge all mankind at an appointed day, judging and rewarding all the saints and judging the sinners/unbelievers. The judgment of rewards for the saints will take place at His second coming and the ungodly will be judged at the Great White Throne judgment.

> John 5:19-30; 1 Corinthians 3:10-15; 2 Corinthians 5:10; Romans 14:10; Revelation 20:11-15; Acts 17:31

Second Coming (His Advent)

The second coming is mentioned about 318 times in the New Testament. There are more references to the coming of Christ than any other New Testament doctrine. The reason for this is evident in that His coming consummates all other doctrine. The coming of Christ is foretold in both Old and New Testaments. The Old Testament identified particularly the first coming and the New Testament the second coming. Jesus Himself foretold of His coming again. Apostle Peter, Apostle Paul, Apostle James spoke of it and Apostle John wrote extensively about it.

(Matthew 16:27 NKJV) [27] For the Son of Man will come in the glory of His Father with His angels, and then He will reward each according to his works.

(James 5:7-8 NKJV) [7] Therefore be patient, brethren, until the coming of the Lord. See *how* the farmer waits for the precious fruit of the earth, waiting patiently for it until it receives the early and latter rain. [8] You also be patient. Establish your hearts, for the coming of the Lord is at hand.

(Titus 2:13 NKJV) [13] looking for the blessed hope and glorious appearing of our great God and Savior Jesus Christ,

(1 John 2:28 NKJV) [28] And now, little children, abide in Him, that when He appears, we may have confidence and not be ashamed before Him at His coming.

Final Judgment

Judgment is the final phase of the redemptive work of Christ. The very fact that God is just, righteous, and holy in His being, demands that He judge all unrighteousness and sin in His creatures. The purpose of Christ's resurrection was inclusive of the judgment of mankind. This will come after the period of probation for all mankind.

At the coming of Christ there is a judgment for all believers. This judgment is not pertaining to their salvation, but to their works and service. Satan will be judged at Christ's coming and will be cast into the bottomless pit for 1,000 years. Then after a short release, he will be eternally judged by being cast into the Lake of Fire. Fallen angels and demon spirits will also be judged. There will also be a judgment on all ungodly mankind.

(Acts 17:30-31 NKJV) [30] Truly, these times of ignorance God overlooked, but now commands all men everywhere to repent, [31] because He has appointed a day on which He will judge the world in righteousness by the Man whom He has ordained. He has given assurance of this to all by raising Him from the dead."

(2 Corinthians 5:10-11 NKJV) [10] For we must all appear before the judgment seat of Christ, that each one may receive the things *done* in the body, according to what he has done, whether good or bad. [11] Knowing, therefore, the terror of the Lord, we persuade men; but we are well known to God, and I also trust are well known in your consciences.

(Revelation 20:1-3 NKJV) [1] Then I saw an angel coming down from heaven, having the key to the bottomless pit and a great chain in his hand. [2] He laid hold of the dragon, that serpent of old, who is *the* Devil and Satan, and bound him for a thousand years; [3] and he cast him into the bottomless pit, and shut him up, and set a seal on him, so that he should deceive the nations no more till the thousand years were finished. But after these things he must be released for a little while.

(Jude 1:14-15 NKJV) [14] Now Enoch, the seventh from Adam, prophesied about these men also, saying, "Behold, the Lord comes with ten thousands of His saints, [15] to execute judgment on all, to convict all who are ungodly among them of all their ungodly deeds which they have committed in an ungodly way, and of all the harsh things which ungodly sinners have spoken against Him."

Begin With Prayer

Biblical Teaching/Doctrine of Salvation

Biblical Building Block # 8

(John 14:21 HCSB)

21 The one who has My commands and keeps them is the one who loves Me. And the one who loves Me will be loved by My Father. I also will love him and will reveal Myself to him."

God has revealed Himself to mankind through the Holy Scriptures, the Holy Bible. His love for mankind can be found in these Scriptures from the beginning to the end. Love is not just a feel good thing but acts of righteousness. God is righteous, holy, truthful, steadfast, forgiving, caring, which all sums up to true love. He is not a fake resemblance of love such as telling us what we want to hear, but truths that we need to hear, not allowing us to continue doing wrong, but directing our paths to doing what is the best for us, and always being there for us. He never leaves us alone. We are the ones who leave Him. All of this adds up to true love. He has made a provision for mankind for eternal life and full forgiveness of sins, a forgiveness of anything that we have done, if we would only repent (change) and believe in Jesus Christ as our Savior. Remember Jesus Christ gave all He could. He gave you and me and all mankind His life so that we would be able to have eternal life in paradise. That is love.

1. What is the meaning of salvation?

2. Why is there a need for salvation?

3. Can you identify several aspects of salvation?

4. With regard to salvation through Jesus Christ, explain the following terms;

    A. Regeneration

    B. Justification

    C. Adoption

    D. Sanctification

    E. Glorification

5. Can you explain the one and only way of salvation for mankind?

Doctrine of Salvation

In the Gospels, "salvation" is clearly connected with the Old Testament concept of "bringing deliverance, ease, soundness." It is applied to the coming of Christ in Zechariah's prophecy and in Simeon's hymn of praise. While the Greek noun *soteria* does not occur frequently in the Gospels, the concept of salvation is implied in Jesus' statement about entrance into the kingdom of God.

(Matthew 19:24-26 KJV) 24 And again I say unto you, It is easier for a camel to go through the eye of a needle, than for a rich man to enter into the kingdom of God. 25 When his disciples heard *it*, they were exceedingly amazed, saying, Who then can be saved? 26 But Jesus beheld *them*, and said unto them, With men this is impossible; but with God all things are possible.

The Old Testament refers to various forms of deliverance, both temporal and spiritual. God delivers His people from their enemies and from the snares of the wicked, granting forgiveness of sins, answers to prayer, joy and peace.

(Psalms 79:9 KJV) 9 Help us, O God of our salvation, for the glory of thy name: and deliver us, and purge away our sins, for thy name's sake.

(Psalms 69:13 KJV) 13 But as for me, my prayer *is* unto thee, O LORD, *in* an acceptable time: O God, in the multitude of thy mercy hear me, in the truth of thy salvation.

(Psalms 59:2 KJV) 2 Deliver me from the workers of iniquity, and save me from bloody men

The New Testament teaches that salvation has its source in Jesus Christ who is the author and mediator of salvation. Salvation is God's work and is offered by His grace. The message of salvation is contained in the Scriptures and is carried by those who proclaim the work of truth. The appropriate response to salvation is repentance and faith. This was the preaching of the early church as it proclaimed the Savior Jesus and Paul especially proclaimed the universality of salvation. New Testament salvation is regarded almost exclusively from the power and dominion of sin, Jesus Christ being the only way for mankind.

Within the Scripture, there are other terms associated with the concept of "salvation". They are ***redemption, justification, reconciliation, regeneration, adoption, sanctification, and glorification.*** These terms share some common ground with the Biblical concept of salvation, but they all point to the person and work of Jesus Christ the Savior. He has saved us from our sin and will rescue us all in the future from the finite, sin-filled world.

(Romans 1:16 KJV) 16 For I am not ashamed of the gospel of Christ: for it is the power of God unto salvation to every one that believeth; to the Jew first, and also to the Greek

(2 Timothy 2:10 KJV) 10 Therefore I endure all things for the elect's sakes, that they may also obtain the salvation which is in Christ Jesus with eternal glory.

(1 Thessalonians 5:9 NKJV) ⁹ But concerning brotherly love you have no need that I should write to you, for you yourselves are taught by God to love one another;

(Ephesians 2:8-9 KJV) ⁸ For by grace are ye saved through faith; and that not of yourselves: *it is* the gift of God: ⁹ Not of works, lest any man should boast.

The Need for Salvation

Mankind's sin

According to the Book of Genesis when God created mankind He entered into a covenant with them. Adam and Eve were to be obedient to His command, not to eat from one tree, the tree of knowledge of good and evil and to work and watch over the Garden of Eden. By following this command they would be in a state of holiness presentable to God. Obedience would lead to eternal life in communion with God. Disobedience would bring death (Genesis 1 and 2).

According to Genesis chapter 3 mankind chose to disobey their Creator. When confronted by the serpent, Eve submitted to the challenge to assert her independency from God. She ventured into deifying herself and dethroning God. Pride and self-will overcame her and she ate the forbidden fruit from the tree of knowledge of good and evil. She also convinced Adam to eat of it. They both became disobedient to God delivering mankind into a sinful nature.

All are considered sinners by the actions of Adam and Eve. The Apostle Paul, in the book of Romans, establishes the universal condemnation of all mankind because of their sin. Everyone whether Gentile or Jew, has sinned and is failing to reflect the glory of God.

(Romans 5:12 KJV) ¹² Wherefore, as by one man sin entered into the world, and death by sin; and so death passed upon all men, for that all have sinned:

(Romans 3:23 KJV) ²³ For all have sinned, and come short of the glory of God;

Consider Mankind's Condition

Mankind is seeking a reason and a meaning for life and without God as the center of their life falls into anxiety, dread, despair, frustration, alienation, absurdity, meaninglessness, estrangement and emptiness. Only through the saving grace of Jesus Christ can mankind find the true meaning of life and receive eternal life. There is no other option available for salvation with God, but through Jesus Christ.

Nature of Salvation

In the Old Testament the Hebrew word 'Yash' and its equivalents mean "to be wide," "roomy", "to be well off" or "prosperous", and to "be free", "to save". To understand what is implied in Matthew's statement concerning Jesus as "Savior" (Matthew 1:21) the usage of *yasha* and its equivalents disclose the following important concepts as to the meaning of salvation. Salvation is the rescue of fallen mankind through Jesus Christ from all that would ruin his soul (sin) in this life and in the life to come.

Work of a sovereign God.	(Isaiah 43:11 KJV) **11** I, *even* I, *am* the LORD; and beside me *there is* no saviour.
Accomplished in History – Israel's deliverance from Egypt. This deliverance of Israel from Egypt is the supreme OT sign of Yahweh's saving grace. It pointed beyond itself, to that central saving event of history, the coming of Jesus Christ.	(Exodus 14:30 KJV) **30** Thus the LORD saved Israel that day out of the hand of the Egyptians; and Israel saw the Egyptians dead upon the sea shore.
Deliverance from enemies – In the OT God was conceived to be the Savior from all foes, both spiritual and physical. Salvation is deliverance from the enemies of death and fear, the lion's mouth, the battlefield, the wicked, sickness, troubles and sin.	(Deuteronomy 20:4 KJV) **4** For the LORD your God *is* he that goeth with you, to fight for you against your enemies, to save you.
Deliverance to the Lord God – Salvation not only meant saving from what would destroy a person but God wanted to bring Mankind to Himself. A purpose to save mankind so that those rescued should worship, praise and glorify Him through lives dedicated to obedience to God.	(1 Chronicles 16:23 KJV) **23** Sing unto the LORD, all the earth; shew forth from day to day his salvation.
Solely by faith – Mankind can not do any thing but have faith in God and be obedient. No effort of good, no gain of merits, and no deeds done by mankind is appropriate to God but only unconditional faith in God can accomplish God's salvation.	(Psalms 55:16 KJV) **16** As for me, I will call upon God; and the LORD shall save me

In the New Testament the classical Greek verb *sozo* "to save" and the noun *soteria* "salvation" are used for the concept of "deliverance", rescue, or "salvation" and even well being or health. In the Gospels "salvation" is connected with the Old Testament concept of "bringing deliverance."

Salvation resides with God – The whole initiative of salvation is with God.	(John 3:16-17 KJV) 16 For God so loved the world, that he gave his only begotten Son, that whosoever believeth in him should not perish, but have everlasting life. 17 For God sent not his Son into the world to condemn the world; but that the world through him might be saved.
Jesus Christ is the Center- Jesus Christ is the center of God's salvation to mankind and there is no other way.	(Acts 4:12 KJV) 12 Neither is there salvation in any other: for there is none other name under heaven given among men, whereby we must be saved.
Means a total salvation – In the NT this spiritual deliverance means a total salvation of mankind's body and soul (from being lost, from sin, and from wrath.	(Matthew 9:21-22 KJV) 21 For she said within herself, If I may but touch his garment, I shall be whole. 22 But Jesus turned him about, and when he saw her, he said, Daughter, be of good comfort; thy faith hath made thee whole. And the woman was made whole from that hour.
Salvation is eternal – Salvation will be realized in it's fullness after the second coming of Jesus Christ.	(Revelation 12:10 KJV) 10 And I heard a loud voice saying in heaven, Now is come salvation, and strength, and the kingdom of our God, and the power of his Christ: for the accuser of our brethren is cast down, which accused them before our God day and night.

Application of Salvation

In the Scriptures there are other terms associated with the concept of salvation. These terms share some common ground with the Biblical concept of salvation, but they all point to the person and work of Jesus Christ the Savior. He is the only way, there is no other.

Regeneration

Regeneration means a renewal on a higher level. It is a "radically new beginning". This renewal is twofold: it occurs within people's spirits and it will occur when God recreates a new heaven and a new earth. (Titus 3:5 HCSB) *He saved us — not by works of righteousness that we had done, but according to His mercy, through the washing of regeneration and renewal by the Holy Spirit.* Quite simply, the text states that "regeneration" is characterized by, or accompanied by the action of washing.

The regenerative activity of the Holy Spirit is characterized elsewhere in Scripture as "cleansing and purifying". The Greek term for regeneration, *pailiggenesia,* literally means "birth again" – indicating a new birth affected by the Holy Spirit. Regeneration is a necessity for salvation and will affect both mankind and the entire universe.

(Ephesians 1:13-14 NKJV) [13] In Him you also *trusted,* after you heard the word of truth, the gospel of your salvation; in whom also, having believed, you were sealed with the Holy Spirit of promise, [14] who is the guarantee of our inheritance until the redemption of the purchased possession, to the praise of His glory.

(John 3:5-7 NKJV) [5] Jesus answered, "Most assuredly, I say to you, unless one is born of water and the Spirit, he cannot enter the kingdom of God. [6] That which is born of the flesh is flesh, and that which is born of the Spirit is spirit. [7] Do not marvel that I said to you, 'You must be born again.'

Justification

The Greek noun for justification is *dikaiosis.* It is derived from the Greek verb *dikaioo,* meaning "to acquit" or "to declare righteous. Almost all discussion of "justification" in the New Testament is found in the letters of Paul, primarily in Galatians and Romans. Paul makes it clear that no one can withstand God's judgment. The law was not given to "justify" sinners, but to expose their sin. To remedy this situation, God sent His Son to die for mankind's sins in our place. When we believe in Jesus, He credits His righteousness to us, and we are declared righteous or "not guilty" before God. Justification is the restoration of mankind to his original relation to God through the work of Christ.

(Romans 3:26 NKJV) [26] to demonstrate at the present time His righteousness, that He might be just and the justifier of the one who has faith in Jesus.

(Romans 4:2-3 NKJV) [2] For if Abraham was justified by works, he has *something* to boast about, but not before God. [3] For what does the Scripture say? *"Abraham believed God, and it was accounted to him for righteousness."*

(Romans 8:33 KJV) [33] Who shall lay any thing to the charge of God's elect? *It is* God that justifieth.

(Romans 3:28 HCSB) **28** For we conclude that a man is justified by faith apart from the works of the law.

Adoption

The Greek word for "adoption" comes from two words put together, *huios,* meaning "son" and *thesis,* meaning "a placing". So, the word means "placement into son ship" or "children". According to the New Testament, all of mankind are sinners by nature and therefore are called "children of wrath". Believers in Jesus can become adopted into God's family and are called "sons of God". Believers' in Jesus Christ, although "adopted" as God's sons, are not equals with the uncreated, divine Son. Through the work of Jesus Christ, sinners who believe are considered adopted into the family of God.

(Ephesians 2:2 KJV) **2** Wherein in time past ye walked according to the course of this world, according to the prince of the power of the air, the spirit that now worketh in the children of disobedience:

(Ephesians 1:4-6 KJV) **4** According as he hath chosen us in him before the foundation of the world, that we should be holy and without blame before him in love: **5** Having predestinated us unto the adoption of children by Jesus Christ to himself, according to the good pleasure of his will, **6** To the praise of the glory of his grace, wherein he hath made us accepted in the beloved.

(Matthew 5:9 KJV) **9** Blessed *are* the peacemakers: for they shall be called the children of God.

Sanctification

The Greek term for sanctify, *hagiazo*, means to "set apart" for Gods special use or "to make distinct from what is common". So sanctification, is to be made for God's special use and to be distinct from all else and therefore holy. Sanctification has to do with the progressive outworking of the new life implanted by the Holy Spirit in regeneration (new spiritual birth).

The basic meaning of holy is "separated" or "set apart". In addition to God being holy as separate from His creatures, He is also separate from sin. It is this latter ethical aspect of God's holiness that provides the basis for our understanding of the doctrine of sanctification and yet sanctification is not only a separation from that which is sinful but also a separation unto a reflection of the image of God. Sanctification is the progressive refashioning of our natures by the Holy Spirit into the image of God, through Jesus Christ. Since God is holy we (the believers) are to be holy and set apart from the world.

(2 Corinthians 5:17 KJV) **17** Therefore if any man *be* in Christ, *he is* a new creature: old things are passed away; behold, all things are become new

(2 Thessalonians 2:13 KJV) **13** But we are bound to give thanks always to God for you, brethren beloved of the Lord, because God hath from the beginning chosen you to salvation through sanctification of the Spirit and belief of the truth:

Glorification

Glorification is the final climactic act in God's redeeming work. The New Testament represents glorification as a complete juridical pardon, also viewing it as a moral perfecting. It also means full participation in eternal life. Glorification will bring a full realization of freedom from sin and death. Then the believer will be what they truly are. While in this life they strive through the Holy Spirit to be like our Lord; then their souls shall be perfectly conformed to His image. Glorification is the transformation of our mankind-hood into the perfect mankind-hood of the God-Man Jesus Christ.

(Romans 8:30 KJV) **30** Moreover whom he did predestinate, them he also called: and whom he called, them he also justified: and whom he justified, them he also glorified.

(Ephesians 5:27 NKJV) **27** that He might present her to Himself a glorious church, not having spot or wrinkle or any such thing, but that she should be holy and without blemish

Glorification also includes the perfecting of the body. Scriptures attribute a dignity to the human body. Genesis teaches that mankind is not a soul merely inhabiting a body. It is the total person who is said to have been created in the image of God and it was the total mankind affected by sin.

Glorification is the climax of God's saving work, a work which extends to eternity. It involves the total man, soul/spirit, together with the body. In that day all will be complete; death will be no more and God will be everything to everyone.

(1 John 3:2 NKJV) **2** Beloved, now we are children of God; and it has not yet been revealed what we shall be, but we know that when He is revealed, we shall be like Him, for we shall see Him as He is

(Philippians 3:20-21 NKJV) **20** For our citizenship is in heaven, from which we also eagerly wait for the Savior, the Lord Jesus Christ, **21** who will transform our lowly body that it may be conformed to His glorious body, according to the working by which He is able even to subdue all things to Himself.

(Hebrews 10:10 NKJV) **10** By that will we have been sanctified through the offering of the body of Jesus Christ once *for all.*

> Text Message → Salvation is only through Jesus Christ – there is NO other way

(John 3:16 HCSB) **16** *"For God loved the world in this way: He gave His One and Only Son, so that everyone who believes in Him will not perish but have eternal life.*

(Acts 4:12 HCSB) **12** *There is salvation in no one else, for there is no other name under heaven given to people, and we must be saved by it."*

Begin With Prayer

Biblical Teaching/Doctrine of Mankind

Biblical Building Block # 9

(1 John 5:2-5 HCSB)

This is how we know that we love God's children when we love God and obey His commands. ³ For this is what love for God is: to keep His commands. Now His commands are not a burden, ⁴ because whatever has been born of God conquers the world. This is the victory that has conquered the world: our faith. ⁵ And who is the one who conquers the world but the one who believes that Jesus is the Son of God?

God created mankind out of the dust of the earth and breathed life into their being. He is our Father and He loved us and always will love us from the time we are created. Our obedience is all that He requires and the obedience is to love God first and love all of His creation next. Mankind has been equipped with the most awesome variety of abilities. We have intelligence, ability to love, ability to see, feel, touch and experience Gods universe, and most of all an eternal soul. But with all of this we must choose God, Who has given mankind the option of choice. The decision of believing in Jesus Christ as your Savior and calling upon Him is dependent on each person. No one else can make that decision for you. What ever choice you make will determine your destiny into eternity. Life is easier lived by loving God but yet so many choose to live a life without God. Mankind was created to love God and when they do they will find a life of fullness and hope of an eternal existence with God.

1. Biblically, how did mankind begin their existence?

2. List several attributes of mankind?

3. Of what distinct elements is mankind comprised?

4. What is the soul?

5. What is the spirit?

6. What is God's purpose/s for mankind?

Theories Concerning the Origin of Mankind

Anthropology is the study of the Doctrine of Man/Mankind. The Greek words *antropos*, meaning man and *logos* meaning word or discourse are the origin of this word Anthropology. People universally have a need to know the answer to where they came from and what is in store for them in the future and after this life. We all want to know the truth of our own existence. There are three thoughts concerning mankind's origin; Atheistic Evolution, Theistic Evolution, and Theistic Creation.

Atheistic Evolution Theory

This is a belief in the theory that all forms of life evolved from a more primitive life form. The thought on this is that cell matter evolved into a life form/s and then formed into fish, birds, animals, and mankind. Trying to prove this has identified many gaps, missing links and unknowns and as yet the theory has not been proven. What arrived first cannot be accounted for and is based on the survival of the fittest. The theory rejects God and fails to adequately account for the origin of life, holding on to weak assumptions.

Theistic Evolution Theory

Like the previously mentioned theory, Theistic Evolution holds to the theory that higher forms of life evolved from lower forms. It further states that the lower forms of life were created by God. There is a sliver of truth in this and that is the acknowledgement of God as the creator of part of creation. However, it becomes false and a total untruth when compared to what the Bible teaches. Scriptures teach that there was a creation of each species, not an evolution. Fish, birds, animals and mankind were created in their order to reproduce, after their own kind, not to evolve to some higher form.

Theistic Creation

This belief is not considered a theory, the Bible declares that it is the truth. This states the fact that God is the life-source, the originator and maintainer of all forms of life. Also, He is the one who created all to reproduce after their kind. The universe, earth, the heavens, angels, fish, birds, all animals, and all other living things were created by God. Mankind was the last and highest form of life created by God on earth and who has been given dominion of the animals by God.

(Genesis 1:26-31 KJV) 26 And God said, Let us make man in our image, after our likeness: and let them have dominion over the fish of the sea, and over the fowl of the air, and over the cattle, and over all the earth, and over every creeping thing that creepeth upon the earth. 27 So God created man in his *own* image, in the image of God created he him; male and female created he them. 28 And God blessed them, and God said unto them, Be fruitful, and multiply, and replenish the earth, and subdue it: and have dominion over the fish of the sea, and over the fowl of the air, and over every living thing that moveth upon the earth. 29 And God said, Behold, I have given you every herb bearing seed, which *is* upon the face of all the earth, and every tree, in the which *is* the fruit of a tree yielding seed; to you it shall be for meat. [30] And to every beast of the earth, and to every fowl of the air, and to every thing that creepeth upon the earth, wherein *there is* life, *I have given* every green herb for meat: and it was so. [31] And God saw every thing that he had made, and, behold, *it was* very good. And the evening and the morning were the sixth day.

God created the original man (Adam) and woman (Eve). This makes mankind a divinely created being, God's glory and masterpiece. Man and Woman, the original couple, created by God is a direct link to the unity of the entire human race. This link to the Adam and Eve of all nations, are of one blood leading back to the original couple that God created. This leaves only one answer to the question of origin and that is mankind was created by the one and only God as stated in the Bible/Scriptures as the only secure truth.

(Genesis 1:1 KJV) [1] In the beginning God created the heaven and the earth.

(Colossians 1:16-17 KJV) [16] For by him were all things created, that are in heaven, and that are in earth, visible and invisible, whether *they be* thrones, or dominions, or principalities, or powers: all things were created by him, and for him: [17] And he is before all things, and by him all things consist.

(Genesis 1:21-25 KJV) [21] And God created great whales, and every living creature that moveth, which the waters brought forth abundantly, after their kind, and every winged fowl after his kind: and God saw that *it was* good. [22] And God blessed them, saying, Be fruitful, and multiply, and fill the waters in the seas, and let fowl multiply in the earth. [23] And the evening and the morning were the fifth day. [24] And God said, Let the earth bring forth the living creature after his kind, cattle, and creeping thing, and beast of the earth after his kind: and it was so. [25] And God made the beast of the earth after his kind, and cattle after their kind, and every thing that creepeth upon the earth after his kind: and God saw that *it was* good.

(Acts 17:26 NKJV) [26] And He has made from one blood every nation of men to dwell on all the face of the earth, and has determined their preappointed times and the boundaries of their dwellings,

(1 Corinthians 15:21-22 KJV) [21] For since by man *came* death, by man *came* also the resurrection of the dead. [22] For as in Adam all die, even so in Christ shall all be made alive.

What is Man?

Created by God

Genesis 1:26-27 God said "Let us **make Man** in our image, after our likeness..." In the Genesis account two of the words used are significant. The words are create and make (Genesis 1:26; 2:1-3). The word "create" means "to make something out of nothing, to bring into existence". The other word, "make" means "to cause to exist, to bring into existence by forming or modifying materials". The creation of mankind was done by God who formed them from the dust of the earth creating their bodies, spirit, and soul by breathing life into them.

(Zechariah 12:1 NKJV) ¹ The burden of the word of the LORD against Israel. Thus says the LORD, who stretches out the heavens, lays the foundation of the earth, and forms the spirit of man within him:

(Genesis 2:7 KJV) ⁷ And the LORD God formed man *of* the dust of the ground, and breathed into his nostrils the breath of life; and man became a living soul.

(Isaiah 45:12 KJV) ¹² I have made the earth, and created man upon it: I, *even* my hands, have stretched out the heavens, and all their host have I commanded.

(1 Corinthians 11;12 NKJV) ¹² For as woman *came* from man, even so man also *comes* through woman; but all things are from God.

Dependent on God

Mankind was created by God and owes their existence to their creator and has a dependency upon Him. Therefore they cannot be independent of God because of this dependency. If it were not for God we would not exist. Each breath we take is a gift from God. Because of God we live and have our being. He provides all that we need to exist, the air we breathe, the sun for light, and heat, the rain to provide life fuel for plants, trees, people and animals, and He keeps planet earth securely in place, a planet like none other.

(Acts 17:23-31 KJV) ²³ For as I passed by, and beheld your devotions, I found an altar with this inscription, TO THE UNKNOWN GOD. Whom therefore ye ignorantly worship, him declare I unto you. ²⁴ God that made the world and all things therein, seeing that he is Lord of heaven and earth, dwelleth not in temples made with hands; ²⁵ Neither is worshipped with men's hands, as though he needed any thing, seeing he giveth to all life, and breath, and all things; ²⁶ And hath made of one blood all nations of men for to dwell on all the face of the earth, and hath determined the times before appointed, and the bounds of their habitation; ²⁷ That they should seek the Lord, if haply they might feel after him, and find him, though he be not far from every one of us: ²⁸ For in him we live, and move, and have our being; as certain also of your own poets have said, For we are also his offspring. ²⁹ Forasmuch then as we are the offspring of God, we ought not to think that the Godhead is like unto gold, or silver, or stone, graven by art and man's device. ³⁰ And the times of this ignorance God winked at; but now commandeth all men every where to repent: ³¹ Because he hath appointed a day, in the which he will judge the world in righteousness by *that* man whom he hath ordained; *whereof* he hath given assurance unto all *men*, in that he hath raised him from the dead.

Intelligent

Having intelligence, reason, feelings, imagination, and the capability to express our thoughts using languages puts mankind above all other created animals that have instincts and habits. The intelligence that mankind possesses has been distorted by sin and has imagined things that separate them from God their creator. So, this intelligence must be plugged into the wisdom and truths of God or it will continue to go astray.

(Genesis 2:19-20 KJV) **19** And out of the ground the LORD God formed every beast of the field, and every fowl of the air; and brought *them* unto Adam to see what he would call them: and whatsoever Adam called every living creature, that *was* the name thereof. **20** And Adam gave names to all cattle, and to the fowl of the air, and to every beast of the field; but for Adam there was not found an help meet for him.

(Romans 1:21-23 HCSB) **21** For though they knew God, they did not glorify Him as God or show gratitude. Instead, their thinking became nonsense, and their senseless minds were darkened. **22** Claiming to be wise, they became fools **23** and exchanged the glory of the immortal God for images resembling mortal man, birds, four-footed animals, and reptiles.

Moral

Mankind was created as a moral and responsible creature with a free-will and the ability of choice. This capability of choice was also given to the angels by God. The creation of mankind was not to create something like a machine that could not think, have feelings or react in love. But mankind was given a free-will, with emotions and all the capacity to love. God wanted His creation to respond in love with their free will.

Placing a conscience within mankind is what enables the moral sense, distinguishing right from wrong. Conscience means "to have knowledge of self in relation to a known law of right and wrong". When first created they were not aware of evil. They lived in a condition of innocence, purity and uprightness. When they sinned their conscience began to work, and their thoughts began to accuse and excuse themselves.

This conscience is indestructible and will never be destroyed. This is what composes mankind's torment as "the worm that never dies" in Gehenna in eternity. Choices that are made in this life pertaining to God will determine ones destiny in eternity. *NOTE – Gehenna, this is a Greek word, that is translated "Hell" in the KJV. This is considered the final and eternal hell.*

(Mark 9:46-47 NKJV) **46** where *'Their worm does not die, And the fire is not quenched.'* **47** And if your eye causes you to sin, pluck it out. It is better for you to enter the kingdom of God with one eye, rather than having two eyes, to be cast into hell fire--

Mankind's conscience has been corrupted and perverted because of the entry of sin and is not always able to made sound judgment. Conscience in itself then is not a perfect moral standard. The true standard for mankind's conscience is the Bible, the Word of God and the Holy Spirit's guidance and teaching. The Holy Spirit has to bring this conscience under the influence with God's infallible Word.

(Romans 9:1 NKJV) I tell the truth in Christ, I am not lying, my conscience also bearing me witness in the Holy Spirit,

(1 Timothy 4:2 KJV) 2 Speaking lies in hypocrisy; having their conscience seared with a hot iron;

(Hebrews 9:14 KJV) 14 How much more shall the blood of Christ, who through the eternal Spirit offered himself without spot to God, purge your conscience from dead works to serve the living God?

Capable of Love

The capacity to love is the very purpose and reason for the creation of mankind. God, desiring to be loved, created mankind with the ability to love and be loved. Although the universe is awesome in its makeup it cannot respond to the love of God and so the creation of mankind filled Gods desire to be loved. Mankind is equipped with intelligence, a will, a conscience, a soul, a spirit, which are the ingredients needed to respond to love. And without the act of love mankind's being remains empty and as void as the universe.

(1 John 4:16-19 NKJV) 16 And we have known and believed the love that God has for us. God is love, and he who abides in love abides in God, and God in him. 17 Love has been perfected among us in this: that we may have boldness in the day of judgment; because as He is, so are we in this world. 18 There is no fear in love; but perfect love casts out fear, because fear involves torment. But he who fears has not been made perfect in love. 19 We love Him because He first loved us.

Triune Being

There are two theories concerning mankind's being.

Dichotomous Theory - Means that mankind is a dual or bi-partite being, consisting of a spirit/soul (two terms which are synonymous and interchangeable) and a body.

Trichotomous Theory - This is the thought that mankind is a tri-partite being, consisting of spirit, soul and body. The body is the place where the spirit and soul reside and are both distinguishable and indivisible. This seems to be the more consistent with the whole of Scriptures.

There are three different words both in Hebrew and Greek pertaining to mankind's tri-partite being.

Hebrew		Greek	
Ruach	spirit	Pneuma	spirit
Nephesh	soul	Psueche	soul
Beten or heshem	body	Soma	body

Spirit

Spirit is the **God-conscious** part of mankind, capable of knowing God is the Spirit. When God created mankind, He formed the spirit of mankind within them (Zechariah 12:1). God is the God of all spirits (Hebrews 12:9). The spirit is the eternal part of mankind that is able to worship God who is Spirit. It is referred to as the lamp of the Lord (Proverbs 20:27 NKJV) *27 The spirit of a man is the lamp of the LORD, Searching all the inner depths of his heart.* The faculties of the spirit are intuition, conscience and communion. When mankind fell, his spirit (God-conscious) lost its contact with God. This can only be restored through regeneration. In the new birth, it is mankind's spirit that is born again, or renewed. (John 3:6 HCSB) *6 Whatever is born of the flesh is flesh, and whatever is born of the Spirit is spirit. 7 Do not be amazed that I told you that you must be born again.*

(Zechariah 12:1 KJV) 1 The burden of the word of the LORD for Israel, saith the LORD, which stretcheth forth the heavens, and layeth the foundation of the earth, and formeth the spirit of man within him.

(Hebrews 12:9 KJV) Furthermore we have had fathers of our flesh which corrected *us*, and we gave *them* reverence: shall we not much rather be in subjection unto the Father of spirits, and live?

(John 4:24 KJV) 24 God *is* a Spirit: and they that worship him must worship *him* in spirit and in truth.

(Romans 8:16 KJV) 16 The Spirit itself beareth witness with our spirit, that we are the children of God:

Soul

The capability of knowing one's self is the soul in which the self-conscience part of mankind exists in. Moses, in the account of creation tells how God formed man's body out of the dust of the earth, and then breathed into man "the breath of life". (Genesis 2:7 NKJV) *And the LORD God formed man of the dust of the ground, and breathed into his nostrils the breath of life; and man became a living being.*
Mankind, created by God from the earth, received their spirit and soul as God breathed into their body. This breath of life is inclusive of both spirit and soul life. The first man then became a living soul. The soul being the intermediary or middle part of mankind connects the body and spirit together in harmony. Because of its position it can influence the body and spirit.

(Matthew 10:28 KJV) **28** And fear not them which kill the body, but are not able to kill the soul: but rather fear him which is able to destroy both soul and body in hell.

There are Three Theories About the Origin of the Soul

Theory of Pre-existence	States that all souls have previously existed and then enter the human body at some point after conception.	*This has no foundation in Scripture.*
Theory of Creation	States that every soul is created by God some time after conception. It teaches that the person only receives their body form the parents, but the soul from God.	*However, Bible revelation and human experience shows that the sinful nature of Adam and character traits and likenesses of the parents are seen in every child born.*
Theory of Traducianists	States that the human race was created "in Adam" as pertaining to soul and body and that both are the result of natural reproduction.	**This theory seems to be the most consistent with the Word or God.**

Soul is used of persons in general - There is a general use of the word "soul" with reference to persons. When we say "there are 70 souls present", we mean that there are 70 people present.

(Revelations 20:4 NKJV) **4** And I saw thrones, and they sat on them, and judgment was committed to them. Then *I saw* the souls of those who had been beheaded for their witness to Jesus and for the word of God, who had not worshiped the beast or his image, and had not received *his* mark on their foreheads or on their hands. And they lived and reigned with Christ for a thousand years. NOTE→ other Bible versions have used the word persons in place of souls in this verse, example is HCSB.

(1 Peter 3:20 NKJV) **20** who formerly were disobedient, when once the Divine longsuffering waited in the days of Noah, while *the* ark was being prepared, in which a few, that is, eight souls, were saved through water. NOTE→ other Bible versions have used the word persons in place of souls in this verse, example is HCSB.

(Acts 2:41 NKJV) **41** Then those who gladly received his word were baptized; and that day about three thousand souls were added *to them* - NOTE→ other Bible versions have used the word persons in place of souls in this verse, example is HCSB.

Soul is sometimes used interchangeably for spirit - Sometimes the words "soul" and "spirit" are used interchangeable or synonymously. It is for this reason that some expositors hold to the dual being of mankind.

In the bodily resurrection of the child under Elijah's ministry, the Scripture says that the child's soul came again (1 Kings 17:17-23). In the bodily resurrection of the child under Christ's ministry, the Scriptures say that "her spirit came again" (Luke 8:49-56). Hebrews speaks of the dead believers as being "the spirits of just men made perfect" (Hebrews 12:23). Revelation speaks of "souls under the alter" in heaven appealing to God for vengeance (Revelation 6:9-11).

Understanding that the soul and the spirit are discernable but inseparable will relieve any conflict about the interchangeable of synonymous use. The following Scriptures will illustrate this statement. In the bodily resurrection, the child's soul could not come again without the spirit, or the spirit without the soul. The spirits in heaven are souls and the souls are redeemed spirits.

Soul is used to denote soul-faculties -The faculties of the soul are basically – mind, will and emotions –

God has a soul - Though God is a spirit, He is spoken of as having a soul and His soul is grieved over mankind. Spirit and soul are associated with God; distinguishable but indivisible.

(Leviticus 26:11 KJV) 11 And I will set my tabernacle among you: and my soul shall not abhor you.

(Isaiah 1:14 KJV) 14 Your new moons and your appointed feasts my soul hateth: they are a trouble unto me; I am weary to bear *them*.

(Hebrews 10:38 NKJV) 38 Now the just shall live by faith; But if anyone draws back, My soul has no pleasure in him."

Christ has a soul - Several times Scriptures speak of the soul of Christ. As perfect and complete Man, He has a spirit, soul and body. Christ's mind, will and emotions were absolutely one with God the Father and Holy Spirit.

(Psalms 16:10 KJV) 10 For thou wilt not leave my soul in hell; neither wilt thou suffer thine Holy One to see corruption.

(ACTS 2:27-31 NKJV) 27 For You will not leave my soul in Hades, Nor will You allow Your Holy One to see corruption. 28 You have made known to me the ways of life; You will make me full of joy in Your presence.' 29 "Men and brethren, let me speak freely to you of the patriarch David, that he is both dead and buried, and his tomb is with us to this day. 30 Therefore, being a prophet, and knowing that God had sworn with an oath to him that of the fruit of his body, according to the flesh, He would raise up the Christ to sit on his throne, [31] he, foreseeing this, spoke concerning the resurrection of the Christ, that His soul was not left in Hades, nor did His flesh see corruption.

Man has a soul - Mankind not only has a soul but Scriptures show that it is a living soul, one of three parts that make up all human beings, body, soul and spirit. The soul is inclusive of a mind with intelligence, a will for choice, and emotions to express them selves. The usage of the word 'soul' is used about 400 times in the Bible.

(1 Thessalonians 5:23 KJV) **23** And the very God of peace sanctify you wholly; and *I pray God* your whole spirit and soul and body be preserved blameless unto the coming of our Lord Jesus Christ.

(Hebrews 4:12 KJV) **12** For the word of God *is* quick, and powerful, and sharper than any two edged sword, piercing even to the dividing asunder of soul and spirit, and of the joints and marrow, and *is* a discerner of the thoughts and intents of the heart.

Animals have a soul - The Hebrew word "*nephesh*" for "soul" is also translated "living creature" and is used to refer to "animal soul". In the Bible it is used several times for beasts. But there is a very definite distinction between the soul of an animal and that of a human being. The soul of mankind has far superior intelligence of mind, will, the ability to choose and emotions, being able to express feelings. Animals have limited intelligence, instinct instead of will and emotions linked to their instinct. They are not able to commune or have a personal relationship with God. Not having a conscience they are not able to sin and cannot be accountable to God for their actions, but mankind has full accountability of their actions.

Animals were not created in the image and likeness of God but mankind was. Mankind is able to know God and is responsible and accountable before God whereas animals are not. Also mankind has been given dominion over all animals to exercise control. Note, that this control and dominion is also a responsibility given to mankind and is not to be taken lightly and not to be abused.

(Genesis 1:21-24 KJV) **21** And God created great whales, and every living creature that moveth, which the waters brought forth abundantly, after their kind, and every winged fowl after his kind: and God saw that *it was* good. **22** And God blessed them, saying, Be fruitful, and multiply, and fill the waters in the seas, and let fowl multiply in the earth. **23** And the evening and the morning were the fifth day. **24** And God said, Let the earth bring forth the living creature after his kind, cattle, and creeping thing, and beast of the earth after his kind: and it was so.

(Genesis 1:26 KJV) **26** And God said, Let us make man in our image, after our likeness: and let them have dominion over the fish of the sea, and over the fowl of the air, and over the cattle, and over all the earth, and over every creeping thing that creepeth upon the earth.

(Leviticus 11:1-3 KJV) **1** And the LORD spake unto Moses and to Aaron, saying unto them, **2** Speak unto the children of Israel, saying, These *are* the beasts which ye shall eat among all the beasts that *are* on the earth. **3** Whatsoever parteth the hoof, and is clovenfooted, *and* cheweth the cud, among the beasts, that shall ye eat.

Mind

The mind includes the thoughts, imaginations, understanding, memory, reason and intellect. Heart and mind are connected in Scripture. *"As a man think in his heart, so is he"*.

(Proverbs 23:7 KJV). It is out of the heart that thoughts proceed forward. This is not referring to the physical heart but that part of the soul.

(Mark 7:20-23 NKJV) **20** And He said, "What comes out of a man, that defiles a man. **21** For from within, out of the heart of men, proceed evil thoughts, adulteries, fornications, murders, **22** thefts, covetousness, wickedness, deceit, lewdness, an evil eye, blasphemy, pride, foolishness. **23** All these evil things come from within and defile a man."

Will

This is the ability to choose and to make decisions. The heart and will are also connected in Scripture. The will is our choosing grounds where we exercise a freedom born within man to make choices. The choices we make will determine our life, and our eternity, our peace of mind or our conflict with fear, our relationship with God or our loneliness with this empty world.

(1 Chronicles 29:9 NKJV) Then the people rejoiced, for they had offered willingly, because with a loyal heart they had offered willingly to the LORD; and King David also rejoiced greatly.

(Exodus 35:5 KJV) **5** Take ye from among you an offering unto the LORD: whosoever *is* of a willing heart, let him bring it, an offering of the LORD; gold, and silver, and brass,

Emotions

This involves the feelings, good or bad, which are the result of behavior and/or attitudes. All emotions such as joy, exultation, pain, sorrow, anger and fear are all centered in the soul.

(Acts 2:46 HCSB) **46** Every day they devoted themselves ⌊to meeting⌋ together in the temple complex, and broke bread from house to house. They ate their food with a joyful and humble attitude,

(Jeremiah 32:40 KJV) **40** And I will make an everlasting covenant with them, that I will not turn away from them, to do them good; but I will put my fear in their hearts, that they shall not depart from me.

Body

This is the world-conscious part of mankind which is capable of knowing and receiving things from the physical world around them. God made the physical body out of the dust of the earth and formed mankind.

(Genesis 2:7 NKJV) And the LORD God formed man *of* the dust of the ground, and breathed into his nostrils the breath of life; and man became a living being.

Mankind is Like a House

Mankind was built to be indwelt by the Spirit of God just as a house is built to be indwelt by someone. Scripture identifies unclean spirits that desire to live in man's body, as a house.

(2 Corinthians 5:1 NKJV) ¹ For we know that if our earthly house, *this* tent, is destroyed, we have a building from God, a house not made with hands, eternal in the heavens.

(Matthew 12:43-45 KJV) **43** When the unclean spirit is gone out of a man, he walketh through dry places, seeking rest, and findeth none. **44** Then he saith, I will return into my house from whence I came out; and when he is come, he findeth *it* empty, swept, and garnished. **45** Then goeth he, and taketh with himself seven other spirits more wicked than himself, and they enter in and dwell there: and the last *state* of that man is worse than the first. Even so shall it be also unto this wicked generation.

Mankind is Like a Tent

Our bodies are likened as a tent. It is significant of the fact that we are pilgrims on earth. At physical death the tent is taken down and dissolved, as the spirit and soul depart.

(2 Peter 1:13-14 NKJV) ¹³ Yes, I think it is right, as long as I am in this tent, to stir you up by reminding *you,* ¹⁴ knowing that shortly I *must* put off my tent, just as our Lord Jesus Christ showed me.

Mankind is Like a Temple

Once the Holy Spirit is invited through the acceptance of Jesus as our Savior we become a living temple of God. (John 2:21 NKJV) ²¹ But He was speaking of the temple of His body.

(1 Corinthians 3:16-17 NKJV) ¹⁶ Do you not know that you are the temple of God and *that* the Spirit of God dwells in you? ¹⁷ If anyone defiles the temple of God, God will destroy him. For the temple of God is holy, which *temple* you are.

Mankind is the Dust of the Earth

It is from the dust of the earth and upon death it will return to the earth as dust.

(1 Corinthians 15:47-49 NKJV) [47] The first man *was* of the earth, *made* of dust; the second Man *is* the Lord from heaven. [48] As *was* the *man* of dust, so also *are* those *who are made* of dust; and as *is* the heavenly *Man,* so also *are* those *who are* heavenly. [49] And as we have borne the image of the *man* of dust, we shall also bear the image of the heavenly *Man.*

Is a Body of Humiliation

Sin has subjected mankind's body to sickness, disease, infirmity, corruption, bad habits and death. Mankind groans in this mortal or death-doomed body. It is indeed the body of our humiliation and because of this God gave Israel very strict laws for the governing and cleanliness of bodily life, as seen especially in Leviticus (Chapters 11-15).

(Philippians 3:21 NKJV) [21] who will transform our lowly body that it may be conformed to His glorious body, according to the working by which He is able even to subdue all things to Himself.

(1 Corinthians 15:33 NKJV) [33] Do not be deceived: "Evil company corrupts good habits."

(2 Corinthians 5:2-8 NKJV) For we know that if our earthly house, *this* tent, is destroyed, we have a building from God, a house not made with hands, eternal in the heavens. [2] For in this we groan, earnestly desiring to be clothed with our habitation which is from heaven, [3] if indeed, having been clothed, we shall not be found naked. [4] For we who are in *this* tent groan, being burdened, not because we want to be unclothed, but further clothed, that mortality may be swallowed up by life. [5] Now He who has prepared us for this very thing *is* God, who also has given us the Spirit as a guarantee. [6] So *we are* always confident, knowing that while we are at home in the body we are absent from the Lord. [7] For we walk by faith, not by sight. [8] We are confident, yes, well pleased rather to be absent from the body and to be present with the Lord.

Is Governed by Senses

There are five senses that the human body is governed by, hearing, seeing, smelling, tasting, and feelings. These abilities of mankind allow them to gain knowledge of the physical world, communicate with each other, and to meet mental and physical needs. God will redeem the body of the believer from corruption and mortality giving them a glorious new body in the likeness of Christ.

(1 Corinthians 15:51-58 NKJV) [51] Behold, I tell you a mystery: We shall not all sleep, but we shall all be changed-- [52] in a moment, in the twinkling of an eye, at the last trumpet. For the trumpet will sound, and the dead will be raised incorruptible, and we shall be changed. [53] For this corruptible must put on incorruption, and this mortal *must* put on immortality. [54] So when this corruptible has put on incorruption, and this mortal has put on immortality, then shall be brought to pass the saying that is written: *"Death is swallowed up in victory." [55] "O Death, where is your sting? O Hades, where is your victory?" [56]* The sting of death *is* sin, and the strength of sin *is* the law. [57] But thanks *be* to God, who gives us the victory through our Lord

Jesus Christ. [58] Therefore, my beloved brethren, be steadfast, immovable, always abounding in the work of the Lord, knowing that your labor is not in vain in the Lord.

God's Purpose for Mankind

God's purpose for man is consistent with His person and who He is. God being love will be directed by this love which will in effect equate to a purpose of love concerning mankind. Of all the descriptions of God in the Bible, perhaps the most all inclusive one is the title "Father". God's Father-heart compels Him to have a family that He can be a Father to. His purposes are easily illustrated centering on this theme.

(Ephesians 3:9-11 NKJV) [9] and to make all see what *is* the fellowship of the mystery, which from the beginning of the ages has been hidden in God who created all things through Jesus Christ; [10] to the intent that now the manifold wisdom of God might be made known by the church to the principalities and powers in the heavenly *places,* [11] according to the eternal purpose which He accomplished in Christ Jesus our Lord,

(2 Timothy 1:9 NKJV) [9] who has saved us and called *us* with a holy calling, not according to our works, but according to His own purpose and grace which was given to us in Christ Jesus before time began,

(Romans 8:28 NKJV) [28] And we know that all things work together for good to those who love God, to those who are the called according to *His* purpose.

The Bible reveals God's purpose for mankind which is summarized as being four-fold; relationship, character, function and reproduction.

Relationship

Throughout Scripture God's desire for fellowship and communion with mankind is revealed. Since the fall of Adam which hindered mankind's relationship with God, it is now through the New Covenant that God's purpose of relationship with mankind is fully accomplished. Now God indwells each believer making fellowship constantly available.

(John 14:16-21 KJV) [16] And I will pray the Father, and he shall give you another Comforter, that he may abide with you for ever; [17] *Even* the Spirit of truth; whom the world cannot receive, because it seeth him not, neither knoweth him: but ye know him; for he dwelleth with you, and shall be in you. [18] I will not leave you comfortless: I will come to you. [19] Yet a little while, and the world seeth me no more; but ye see me: because I live, ye shall live also. [20] At that day ye shall know that I *am* in my Father, and ye in me, and I in you. [21] He that hath my commandments, and keepeth them, he it is that loveth me: and he that loveth me shall be loved of my Father, and I will love him, and will manifest myself to him

Character

The word character means distinguishing features and attributes that one possesses. God wanted His creation of mankind to have the image and likeness of Himself. Being holy and righteous, abiding in truth, and encompassed in love God desired that same for mankind. Character is one of the main thoughts in the word "image". Hebrews 1:3 states that Jesus is described as being "the express image" of His father's person. In this verse the Greek word translated image is pronounced *character* and it is the word from which our English word character is obtained. Disobedience corrupted the character of mankind and severed the relationship with God. The need now for mankind is to repent and change their character, restoring it and restoring their relationship with God. This can only be done through the repenting of one's life and the belief in Jesus Christ, allowing the Holy Spirit to indwell ones very spirit. This will replace mankind's nature to the righteous, holy, loving and self-giving nature of God, what God intended for mankind.

(Hebrew 1:3 KJV) 3 Who being the brightness of *his* glory, and the express image of his person, and upholding all things by the word of his power, when he had by himself purged our sins, sat down on the right hand of the Majesty on high;

(2 Peter 1:4-7 NKJV) 4 by which have been given to us exceedingly great and precious promises, that through these you may be partakers of the divine nature, having escaped the corruption *that is* in the world through lust. 5 But also for this very reason, giving all diligence, add to your faith virtue, to virtue knowledge, 6 to knowledge self-control, to self-control perseverance, to perseverance godliness, 7 to godliness brotherly kindness, and to brotherly kindness love.

Function/Purpose

One purpose for the creation of mankind is the function of ruling the universe headed by God and shared responsibilities assigned to redeemed mankind. God the Father, wants His Children the redeemed saints, to be involved in His working of creation. Only through Jesus Christ, who has conquered all, can mankind's dominion be restored.

(Genesis 1:26-28 KJV) 26 And God said, Let us make man in our image, after our likeness: and let them have dominion over the fish of the sea, and over the fowl of the air, and over the cattle, and over all the earth, and over every creeping thing that creepeth upon the earth. 27 So God created man in his *own* image, in the image of God created he him; male and female created he them. 28 And God blessed them, and God said unto them, Be fruitful, and multiply, and replenish the earth, and subdue it: and have dominion over the fish of the sea, and over the fowl of the air, and over every living thing that moveth upon the earth male and female.

Reproduction Physically and Spiritually

God also created mankind to share some of His creative powers. He wanted mankind to reproduce bearing children and growing the family of God. He told Adam and Eve to "be fruitful, and multiply, and replenish the earth". In the New Testament we are told to "be fruitful" and that the disciples of Jesus "multiply" both a reproduction from a physical and also a spiritual perspective. As believers in Jesus Christ we should raise our families according to God's will and Word, as friends and neighbors we should reach out within our communities to bring a new birth, Born again spirit, to all those outside the family of God. The purposes of God are progressive and interdependent. Character development can only occur with a true relationship with God. The purpose for mankind has never changed and will yet be fulfilled through the Church exemplifying God truths and teachings.

(Genesis 1:28 KJV) 28 And God blessed them, and God said unto them, Be fruitful, and multiply, and replenish the earth, and subdue it: and have dominion over the fish of the sea, and over the fowl of the air, and over every living thing that moveth upon the earth

(Acts 6:1 NKJV) 1 Now in those days, when *the number of* the disciples was multiplying, there arose a complaint against the Hebrews by the Hellenists, because their widows were neglected in the daily distribution.

(Acts 6:7 NKJV) Then the word of God spread, and the number of the disciples multiplied greatly in Jerusalem, and a great many of the priests were obedient to the faith.

Begin With Prayer

Biblical Teaching/Doctrine of Sin

Biblical Building Block # 10

(1 Peter 4:7-8 HCSB)
7 Now the end of all things is near; therefore, be serious and disciplined for prayer. **8** Above all, maintain an intense love for each other, since love covers a multitude of sins.

God is a holy and righteous God. His nature is love and when He created mankind He created them in His image to be holy and righteous, with a love nature. But then sin, a rebellious nature, entered into mankind and disrupted the relationship between God and mankind. Pride and self-will along with greed and lust became mankind's focus and God was only something that they invented with their own hands and imaginations. But God, because of His love for mankind gave His Word to be read, studied, taught and obeyed. Then He gave His only begotten Son Jesus Christ the Living Word to cover all of the sins of mankind through the shedding of His blood, one last sacrifice. Today we have a victorious God Who has given mankind a way back to a sinless nature and that is by believing and accepting that Jesus Christ is your Savior and Lord. There is no other way. Only through Jesus Christ can your sins be forgiven.

1. Define sin.

2. What is the origin of sin?

3. How did sin come upon mankind?

4. Describe the nature of sin?

5. How is pride related to sin?

6. How are covetousness and sin related?

7. What is the penalty for sin?

8. What must mankind do about their sin?

Introduction Doctrine of Sin

The word Hamartiology, the doctrine of Sin, comes from the Greek words, *hamartia* meaning sin and *logos* meaning word or discourse. So, Hamartiology is the Biblical teaching concerning sin, its origin, definition, expression and final end.

The Bible defines sin as being a violation of God's standard for human behavior. The Greek word *hamartia* means "miss the mark, fail in duty". Another frequent Greek term *parabasis* describes sin as "transgression", meaning over stepping set limits. Another similar Greek term *paratoma* is a "false step, a trespass on forbidden ground". The New Testament also has two other Greek terms *anomia*, meaning "lawlessness" and *paranomia*, meaning "lawbreaking".

(Romans 3:23 KJV) 23 For all have sinned, and come short of the glory of God;

There are certain questions concerning sin's origin that man struggles to answer. The Word of God to Israel (Deuteronomy 29:29 KJV) 29 The secret *things belong* unto the LORD our God: but those *things which are* revealed *belong* unto us and to our children for ever, that *we* may do all the words of this law.

The doctrine of sin must be studied through the information that is available in the Scriptures. Mankind must be careful to not seek or go beyond what is revealed to us. We must realize that God will provide answers to all of our questions in His own time.

Facts of Sin

The earth and its occupants can honestly say that there is something wrong, causing disorder and confusion. The existence of sin is the reason for all of the chaotic conditions, disharmony and strife we see in the world today, including sickness and death.

Creation Reveals Sin

Nature in itself makes a declaration that there is something wrong. The differences between life and death, harmony and discord, beauty and ugliness, light and darkness, right and wrong, obedience and disobedience, proclaim the fact of the existence of sin. The earth and the forces of nature seem to be turned against mankind being unpredictable, sometimes good, sometimes disastrous. The original intent of the earth and nature was to be a blessing for mankind, but with the introduction of sin a curse fell upon all of nature and mankind.

(Genesis 3:17 KJV) 17 And unto Adam he said, Because thou hast hearkened unto the voice of thy wife, and hast eaten of the tree, of which I commanded thee, saying, Thou shalt not eat of it: cursed *is* the ground for thy sake; in sorrow shalt thou eat *of* it all the days of thy life;

Human History Reveals Sin

The history of humanity delivers a picture of chaos, confusion, wars, bloodshed, a spirit of hate and murder, moral corruption, covetousness, and tyranny indicating that there is something wrong about all of this. Where does all of this injustice come from and why does it continue? The answer is found in the existence of sin.

(James 4:1-4 NKJV) [1] Where do wars and fights *come* from among you? Do *they* not *come* from your *desires for* pleasure that war in your members? [2] You lust and do not have. You murder and covet and cannot obtain. You fight and war. Yet you do not have because you do not ask. [3] You ask and do not receive, because you ask amiss, that you may spend *it* on your pleasures. [4] Adulterers and adulteresses! Do you not know that friendship with the world is enmity with God? Whoever therefore wants to be a friend of the world makes himself an enemy of God.

Human Logic Reveals Sin

From deep inside, mankind knows that something is wrong, but logic alone does not seem to properly identify, the what and why. Within their own being they can sense the confusion, the disharmony and discord that are so apparent within their being and around the globe. Logic would seek to deny the fact of sin but logic in itself cannot make it go away or make anything different. Sin must be dealt with from its origin, which was disobedience to God, and each person must repent and make a change in their life starting with the acceptance of the one and only Savior, Jesus Christ. Within every person resides the knowledge that ultimately there is something more than logic can identify, that something and someone created all of this. Where they decide to put their trust in what to believe will be critical for finding the answer to what is wrong. For mankind knows that when they do good, evil is present with them, so we must face the fact that sin does exist and must be dealt with.

(Romans 7:14-21 KJV) [14] For we know that the law is spiritual: but I am carnal, sold under sin. [15] For that which I do I allow not: for what I would, that do I not; but what I hate, that do I. [16] If then I do that which I would not, I consent unto the law that *it is* good. [17] Now then it is no more I that do it, but sin that dwelleth in me. [18] For I know that in me (that is, in my flesh,) dwelleth no good thing: for to will is present with me; but *how* to perform that which is good I find not. [19] For the good that I would I do not: but the evil which I would not, that I do. [20] Now if I do that I would not, it is no more I that do it, but sin that dwelleth in me. [21] I find then a law, that, when I would do good, evil is present with me.

Human Conscience Reveals Sin

Conscience which is closely linked to human logic is a further witness to the fact of sin. This conscience reacts immediately once a person does something wrong. It alerts them and their thoughts begin to accuse or excuse ones actions. Sin's reality is revealed under the law of conscience.

(Romans 2:14-15 NKJV) ¹⁴ for when Gentiles, who do not have the law, by nature do the things in the law, these, although not having the law, are a law to themselves, ¹⁵ who show the work of the law written in their hearts, their conscience also bearing witness, and between themselves *their* thoughts accusing or else excusing *them*)

Human Experience Reveals Sin

There is an abundance of evidence in every day human experiences concerning the reality of sin. All one has to do is read Scriptures to gain a list of sins that mankind is capable of committing. Just by watching and reading today's news will also provide an additional evidence of sin. All types of sin are currently at work. Immorality, crime, violence, perversion and all forms of lawlessness abound. In modern civilization sin's desire to express itself is seen in the corruption of society providing more evidence of the fact of sin. Scripture indicates that this will increase in the last days. Sin also is becoming more and more transparent within the global societies. Because there are less absolutes accepted as to what is right and wrong, sinfulness is being whitewashed over. In reality it is still there like a cancerous growth, not being seen but destroying and eventually bringing on death.

(Matthew 24:12 NKJV) ¹² And because lawlessness will abound, the love of many will grow cold.

(2 Timothy 3:1-5 KJV) ¹ This know also, that in the last days perilous times shall come. ² For men shall be lovers of their own selves, covetous, boasters, proud, blasphemers, disobedient to parents, unthankful, unholy, ³ Without natural affection, trucebreakers, false accusers, incontinent, fierce, despisers of those that are good, ⁴ Traitors, heady, highminded, lovers of pleasures more than lovers of God; ⁵ Having a form of godliness, but denying the power thereof: from such turn away.

Human Religions Reveals Sin

The belief in God or gods is in every nation of the world. They all have developed some form of religion involving priesthood and sacrifices of appeasement, to satisfy something or someone. Due to the sin nature of mankind, their desire or attempt to appease God or gods comes from the inner sense of some kind of guilt and a realization of their need of redemption. So another witness of the reality of sin is religion itself. However, it is only the true believers in Jesus Christ who have God's answer to the sin problem, as dealt with in the person of Christ. All other attempts of religion outside of the belief in Jesus Christ and His Word are futile.

Believers Reveal Sin

By being a believer in Jesus Christ one will become quite aware of the fact of sin. They will become more conscious of sin because of their salvation and the two laws of conflict within them; the law of death and the law of the Spirit of life. Paul's words in Roman 7 testify to this fact. No believer is perfect and without sin, yet is vitally aware that sin is a reality and must be dealt with by cleansing and overcoming it by the True Word of the Living God, guided by His Spirit.

(Romans 3:20 KJV *7:14-25 KJV) **20** Therefore by the deeds of the law there shall no flesh be justified in his sight: for by the law *is* the knowledge of sin

*NOTE →these verses are back in Human Logic Reveals Sin

Scriptures Reveal Sin

The Word of God is the highest court of appeal in all of creation. It declares that all of mankind are sinners and need salvation, and that salvation is through Jesus Christ and there is no other way, no alternate plan. It can not be done by doing only good works, but obedience to God's Word acting upon His salvation plan.

(Romans 3:23 KJV) **23** For all have sinned, and come short of the glory of God;

There are two mysteries at work in the universe that the Scriptures reveal and are stated as "The Mystery of Godliness" and "The Mystery of Iniquity". In the Word of God all other mysteries that are referred to are within these two. At work in the universe are light and darkness, good and evil, life and death, and godliness and iniquity. The creations of God, being mankind and angelic, will need to make their choice of either godliness or iniquity under one mystery or the other and the choice they make will settle their eternal destiny.

(Psalms 14:1-3 KJV) **1** The fool hath said in his heart, *There is* no God. They are corrupt, they have done abominable works, *there is* none that doeth good. **2** The LORD looked down from heaven upon the children of men, to see if there were any that did understand, *and* seek God. **3** They are all gone aside, they are *all* together become filthy: *there is* none that doeth good, no, not one.

(Romans 5:12 NKJV) **12** Therefore, just as through one man sin entered the world, and death through sin, and thus death spread to all men, because all sinned--

Biblical Definitions of Sin

The Thought of Foolishness

Sin is the thought of foolishness and the place where sin is planted. Acting on this thought will bring about sin in one's life. When Satan, and Adam and Eve entertained the thought of being "as God", it was indeed foolishness and once acted on, this covetous thought itself became sin and lead to rebellion. A foolish scheme is sin.

(Proverbs 24:9 KJV) **9** The thought of foolishness *is* sin: and the scorner *is* an abomination to men.

Transgression of Law

Transgress means, to go across a forbidden boundary line breaking the law. Adam and Eve transgressed God's law in the Garden of Eden. Laws are made to keep order, and for protection.

God's laws are exactly that, to keep order in the universe and to protect that which He has created. It is foolishness when one breaks mankind's laws but even more foolish to break Gods.

(1 John 3:4 KJV) 4 Whosoever committeth sin transgresseth also the law: for sin is the transgression of the law.

Unrighteousness is Sin

All unrighteousness (wickedness) which separates mankind from God is sin. Adam and Eve committed an injustice to God and mankind by selling himself out to Satan's lie.

(1 John 5:17 KJV) 17 All unrighteousness is sin: and there is a sin not unto death.

Not Doing Good is Sin

Knowing that doing something is a good thing but avoiding doing it can be considered sin. An example would be knowing that you got an extra dollar of change, and not giving it back.

(James 4:17 NKJV) 17 Therefore, to him who knows to do good and does not do *it,* to him it is sin

Unbelief is Sin

Although knowing the will of God, both Adam and Eve sinned. They fell because they believed in the lie of words spoken by Satan instead of believing what God had told them. Their unbelief and disobedience caused them to fall away from faith in God and in His Word. Just knowing God's Word is not enough we must trust it and put our entire faith in it. We cannot be lukewarm in our beliefs.

(Romans 14:23 NKJV) 23 But he who doubts is condemned if he eats, because *he does* not *eat* from faith; for whatever *is* not from faith is sin.

Hebrew Words for Sin

Hebrew word for sin "chattath" - *chattath* – means an offense, sometimes habitual sinfulness, and its penalty, occasion sacrifice, or expiation, also meaning "to miss, to sin, by inference to forfeit, to lack".

(Leviticus 4:2-2 NKJV) ² "Speak to the children of Israel, saying: 'If a person sins unintentionally against any of the commandments of the LORD *in anything* which ought not to be done, and does any of them, ³ if the anointed priest sins, bringing guilt on the people, then let him offer to the LORD for his sin which he has sinned a young bull without blemish as a sin offering.

(Isaiah 53:10 KJV) **10** Yet it pleased the LORD to bruise him; he hath put *him* to grief: when thou shalt make his soul an offering for sin, he shall see *his* seed, he shall prolong *his* days, and the pleasure of the LORD shall prosper in his hand.

Transgression (Hebrew "pawsah" or "pehshah") - This word means "to break away from just authority; trespass, apostatize, quarrel, a revolt (national, moral or religious)". It is translated by the words "offend, rebel, revolt, transgression" .

(Exodus 34:7 KJV) **7** Keeping mercy for thousands, forgiving iniquity and transgression and sin, and that will by no means clear *the guilty*; visiting the iniquity of the fathers upon the children, and upon the children's children, unto the third and to the fourth *generation*.

Iniquity (Hebrew "avon, or avown") means "perversity, evil" translated "to amiss, bow down, make crooked, commit iniquity, pervert, fault".

(Psalms 52:3 NKJV) ³ You love evil more than good, lying rather than speaking righteousness.

(Daniel 9:24 KJV) **24** Seventy weeks are determined upon thy people and upon thy holy city, to finish the transgression, and to make an end of sins, and to make reconciliation for iniquity, and to bring in everlasting righteousness, and to seal up the vision and prophecy, and to anoint the most Holy.

Trespass (Hebrew "asham") - Meaning "to be guilty" or "a fault".

(Leviticus 6:2 KJV) ² If a soul sin, and commit a trespass against the LORD, and lie unto his neighbour in that which was delivered him to keep, or in fellowship, or in a thing taken away by violence, or hath deceived his neighbour;

Greek Words for Sin

Harmartia - This word is used in the New Testament and is always translated "sin" or "sins" (except in 2 Corinthians 11:7 –"offense"). This means "to miss the mark, or to seek to attain results which lie beyond the limits of one's capabilities". In the New Testament it became the general term for sin, referring to both the inner principle of sin and its outward expression; to both the power of sin and its fruit (Matthew 1:21; 26:28; Luke 11:4; 24:47; John 1:29; 8:34, Acts 2:38; Romans 3:20; 5:12; 6:10-23; 8:2; 14:23; 2 Corinthians 5:21; James 1:15; 5:17; 1 John 1:9; 5:17).

Hamartema - Used in the New Testament and is always translated "sin or sins". It only differs in meaning from the word (*Harmartia*) in that its meaning is limited to the outward expression of sin. It denotes an actual act of disobedience against the divine law (Romans 5:19; 2 Corinthians 10:6; Hebrews 2:2).

Parakoe – Is used in the New Testament. The noun form is translated "disobedience" and the verb form of it is translated "neglect to hear". It means "to hear amiss" and it refers most likely to a refusal to listen to God speaking or possibly an imperfect hearing of His Word/voice. Both of these display a carelessness in attitude toward the Word of God. (Matthew 18:17; Romans 5:19; 2 Corinthians 10:6; Hebrews 2:2)

Anomia - Used in the New Testament and is always translated "iniquity" (except in 2 Corinthians 6:14 → "unrighteousness" and in 1 John 3:4 → "transgressions of the law"). It means lawlessness both to the inward opposition of the heart and to the outward acts of violating that law. (Matthew 7:23; 23:28; 24:12; Romans 4:7; 6:19; 2 Thessalonians 2:7; Titus 2:14; Hebrews 1:9; 8:12; 10:17)

Paranomia - This word is used only once in the New Testament and is translated "iniquity". Refers to a breaking of a law. (2 Peter 2:16)

Parabasis - This word is used in the New Testament. The noun forms are translated "transgressor and transgression" (except in Romans 2:23 "breaking" and Romans 2:25 "breaker"). The verb form is translated "transgress". Means to step beyond as when crossing a line or boundary. In the New Testament it refers to a direct action of violation of God's Law/s. This insists that a law be in existence in that unless there is a boundary line drawn, there can be no stepping across it. (Matthew 15:2-3; Romans 4:15; 5:14; Galatians 2:18; 1 Timothy 2:14; Hebrews 2:2; James 2:9,11; 2 John 9)

Paraptoma - This word is used in the New Testament. It's translations are "trespasses, offences, offence, fall, fault, faults". It means to fall aside, to fall away, and to blunder. In the New Testament it refers to a deviation or falling away from uprightness and truth. (Matthew 6:14-15; Romans 4:24;515-20; 11:11,12; 2 Corinthians 5:19; Galatians 6:1; Ephesians 1:7; 2:1; Colossians 2:13; James 5:16)

Agnoema - This word is used only once in the New Testament. Translated "errors". Means an act of ignorance and refers to a sin of ignorance. It regards sin in the mildest light possible without making excuses for it. Not an open act of rebellion. (Hebrews 9:7)

Hettema - This word is used 2 times in the New Testament. It is translated "diminishing" in Romans 11:12 and "fault" in 1 Corinthians 6:7. Means a lessening or a loss and it refers in 1 Corinthians to a defect, a flaw (the lost of their unity).

Law of God in Relation to Sin

Within the Scriptures we see that the doctrine of sin and the subject of law are linked together. In the Epistle to the Romans this link between law and sin is what Paul is dealing with as he answers the objections raised by the Jews of his time.

(Romans 3:20 NKJV) [20] Therefore by the deeds of the law no flesh will be justified in His sight, for by the law *is* the knowledge of sin.

(Romans 7:7 NKJV) What shall we say then? *Is* the law sin? Certainly not! On the contrary, I would not have known sin except through the law. For I would not have known covetousness unless the law had said, *"You shall not covet."*

(Romans 4:15 NKJV) [15] because the law brings about wrath; for where there is no law *there is* no transgression.

Necessity of the Law

In Romans 7:11 the Apostle Paul told the Jews who knew the law and who expected a reaction, that it was the law that gave him the knowledge of sin. He also stated that without the law sin was dead and that when the commandment of the law of God was given it caused sin to come alive.

If there was no law to violate, then sin would not have taken place, for "sin is not imputed when there is no law" (Romans 5:13). Paul anticipated the reaction that the law of God must be the real problem. "What shall we say then? Is the Law sin? God forbid" (Romans 7:7). He further adds that the law is holy, just, good and spiritual (Romans 7:12,4).

> Text Message → The first law for mankind was given to Adam and Eve – not to eat of the Tree of Knowledge. They broke it, crossed the line, caused a fault, an offense, blundered, trespassed, and rebelled - against God. Sin then was upon mankind.

The law of God then is not the problem but those who violate it. God did not author sin nor does He need it to exist to glorify Himself. This is what brings us to the absolute necessity of law in the universe as well as human or angelic beings. Sin is violation of the law for both mankind and angels. Transgression is the breaking, disobeying, and violation of the law of God leading to sin.

(1 John 3:4 KJV) [4] Whosoever committeth sin transgresseth also the law: for sin is the transgression of the law.

Origin of Sin

In dealing with the beginning of sin and the origin of evil, the Apostle James gives us insight in James 1:13. It aides in the answers to such questions as "who tempted Lucifer?" and "did

Lucifer's temptation come from within or without?" And this principle that he states applies to both mankind and angels.

(James 1:13 KJV)– "Let no man (and we can rightly say 'let no angel') say when he is tempted, I am tempted of God, God CANNOT be tempted with evil, neither tempted He any man (or angel)." So God did not and could not tempt angels or mankind to sin. This would violate His moral attributes. God did not create or decree sin. He does not approve of it nor incite His creatures to sin. To charge God with such is an attack on His holiness and moral attributes.

The angelic hosts who were the first moral beings created were the first and original sinners, led by Lucifer and his followers (angels). The angelic order is where sin began, rebellion and disobedience against God. Then Lucifer/Satan deceived mankind who then entered into sin.

Lucifer the original sinner - Under the figurative statements of the King of Tyre and the King of Babylon, we have a description of Lucifer, who, as most expositors believe, became the devil.

(Isaiah 14:12-14 KJV) 12 How art thou fallen from heaven, O Lucifer, son of the morning! *how* art thou cut down to the ground, which didst weaken the nations! 13 For thou hast said in thine heart, I will ascend into heaven, I will exalt my throne above the stars of God: I will sit also upon the mount of the congregation, in the sides of the north: 14I will ascend above the heights of the clouds; I will be like the most High.

(Ezekiel 28:11-19 KJV) 11 Moreover the word of the LORD came unto me, saying, 12 Son of man, take up a lamentation upon the king of Tyrus, and say unto him, Thus saith the Lord GOD; Thou sealest up the sum, full of wisdom, and perfect in beauty. 13 Thou hast been in Eden the garden of God; every precious stone *was* thy covering, the sardius, topaz, and the diamond, the beryl, the onyx, and the jasper, the sapphire, the emerald, and the carbuncle, and gold: the workmanship of thy tabrets and of thy pipes was prepared in thee in the day that thou wast created. 14 Thou *art* the anointed cherub that covereth; and I have set thee *so*: thou wast upon the holy mountain of God; thou hast walked up and down in the midst of the stones of fire. 15 Thou *wast* perfect in thy ways from the day that thou wast created, till iniquity was found in thee. 16 By the multitude of thy merchandise they have filled the midst of thee with violence, and thou hast sinned: therefore I will cast thee as profane out of the mountain of God: and I will destroy thee, O covering cherub, from the midst of the stones of fire. 17 Thine heart was lifted up because of thy beauty, thou hast corrupted thy wisdom by reason of thy brightness: I will cast thee to the ground, I will lay thee before kings, that they may behold thee. 18 Thou hast defiled thy sanctuaries by the multitude of thine iniquities, by the iniquity of thy traffick; therefore will I bring forth a fire from the midst of thee, it shall devour thee, and I will bring thee to ashes upon the earth in the sight of all them that behold thee. 19 All they that know thee among the people shall be astonished at thee: thou shalt be a terror, and never *shalt* thou *be* any more."

and it consumed you. I reduced you to ashes on the ground in the sight of everyone watching you. 19 All those who know you among the nations are appalled at you. You have become an object of horror and will never exist again."

There is a double application in the prophecy stated. The expression used could not apply to a king of humanity, such as the prince of Tyre or of Babyon. Throughout Scripture this interpretation principle is used. For example in Genesis 3:14-15 where God is speaking to the serpent, He is also speaking to Satan/the devil behind the serpent. The serpent in the Garden of Eden was the mouthpiece and instrument of the evil one. Matthew 16:16-23 illustrates this also. When Jesus spoke to Peter, he was speaking to Satan behind Peter's utterance. So in Isaiah and Ezekiel, when God is speaking of the Princes of Tyre and Babylon, He is referring also to the instigator behind these earthly princes, Satan.

Lucifer/Satan was created with wisdom, light and beauty. He was skilled in music being the leader of the angelic ministry of worship. He was also the anointed Cherub guarding the throne of God. He was created as a free-will moral agent, a dependent being and created for God's glory and pleasure.

We have a description in the following statements of Lucifer before his fall.

He is called Lucifer, the Day Star, the Shining One, the Light-bearer.
He was full of beauty and wisdom. Nothing could be hidden from him.
Every precious stone was his covering, as the colors of the rainbow for beauty.
He was in the Holy Mountain of God and given a high position in heaven as a created being.
He walked up and down in the midst of the stones of fire, the fire of God's holiness.
He was perfect in all his ways from the day that he was created.
He was in Eden, the Garden of God.
He was the anointed Cherub and guardian of the throne of God.
He is called Son of the Morning because of his brightness.

In 2 Thessalonians 2:7, it is stated that – the mystery of the lawlessness is already at work – the beginning of the "mystery of iniquity" began with Lucifer, the created archangel. Questions such as how did this happen, what was the sin of Lucifer, what caused or tempted him, and did God create him to be the devil often arise? When one seeks the answers to these questions it becomes obvious that God has kept back certain answers for Himself (Deuteronomy 29:29). There is enough information given in Scriptures to give us a degree of understanding. Ezekiel 28:15 tells us that the Prince of Tyre was perfect in all ways from the day he was created, until iniquity was found in him; this could not refer to any created man because only Adam was created perfect/without sin, before Jesus Christ. Other Scriptures speak also of the devil as a sinner (1 John 3:8; Ezekiel 28:16; John 8:44).

Iniquity, evil and disobedience began in the heart of Lucifer. He became the author, the originator of all sin. Sin overtook him and he is now the personification of sin. The mystery of iniquity began its work in the universe, in this fallen Archangel. Lucifer became corrupted in his entire nature and being and became the devil.

He is a fallen spirit being who has sinned in the light of God's holiness, becoming unredeemable and will be judged as so. At this time God has not taken away Satan's wisdom, and beauty but it is now corrupted and perverted. This wisdom that he had became earthly, sensual and devilish.

(James 3:15 HCSB) Such wisdom does not come down from above, but is earthly, sensual, demonic.

God did not create this Archangel to be the devil.

God did not create a wicked creature, but He created a free-will being who had the power of choice and became evil by choice.

Nature of Lucifer's Sin

Self-centeredness is a major theme of the nature of sin. It contains three aspects which are of pride, covetousness or lust, and self-will exercised against God's will.

Pride

The word pride means "inordinate self-esteem, conceit, vanity, self-exaltation" and an unwarranted excessively high opinion of oneself. (Obadiah 1:3 NKJV) *The pride of your heart has deceived you...* Pride is a deceiver and this is exactly what Lucifer became, the king of deception. The Prophet Ezekiel speaks of this pride and self-assertion in Ezekiel 28:1-19. In verses 2, 4, 5, and 17 he speaks of Lucifer's heart being "lifted up" because of riches and beauty. In verses 2, 6, and 9 he "lifted himself" up to be a god, to sit in the throne of God, and set his heart as the heart of God. Pride turned this Archangel into a devil. Lucifer's God-given beauty, wisdom and anointing became a temptation to lust after that worship which only belonged to God.

(Proverbs 16:18 HCSB) **18** Pride comes before destruction, and an arrogant spirit before a fall

(Proverbs 18:12 KJV) 12 Before destruction the heart of man is haughty, and before honour *is* humility.

(Isaiah 14:12-14 KJV) 12 How art thou fallen from heaven, O Lucifer, son of the morning! *how* art thou cut down to the ground, which didst weaken the nations! 13 For thou hast said in thine heart, I will ascend into heaven, I will exalt my throne above the stars of God: I will sit also upon the mount of the congregation, in the sides of the north: 14 I will ascend above the heights of the clouds; I will be like the most High.

(Luke 10:18 KJV) 18 And he said unto them, I beheld Satan as lightning fall from heaven.

Covetousness & Lust

Lust is overwhelming desire or craving. It is very much the same as covetousness, which takes it to the next step: excessive desire of possession of that which is being lusted over. It becomes sin when it overtakes one's action and the law of God is broken allowing the lust to grow into covetousness and over take their being. This is something that is spawned from within. So Lucifer's pride led to lust and lust led to covetousness and all of this led to an unlawful desire for something that was forbidden. Paul tied lust to covetousness in Romans 7:7 KJV… for I had not known lust, except the law had said "Thou shalt not covet", by referring to the tenth commandment (Exodus 20:17).

(James 1:14-15 KJV) But every man is tempted, when he is drawn away of his own lust, and enticed. Then when lust hath conceived, it bringeth for sin: and sin, when it is finished, bringeth forth death.

Satan, the devil covets being worshiped as a god. He stated this lustful desire when he said "I will be like the Most High" (Isaiah 14:14). He coveted the position of God and desired the worship that only belongs to God.

It has been implied that Lucifer went against the Word, the eternal Son, when the Father said in Hebrews 1:6 "…And let all the angels of God worship Him". Lucifer coveted the position and the worship given to the, Word/Jesus. It was this reason that, The Word, humbled Himself and took upon Himself flesh, in order to deal with the original sinner and all of sin.

(John 1:13-18 KJV) 13 Which were born, not of blood, nor of the will of the flesh, nor of the will of man, but of God. 14 And the Word was made flesh, and dwelt among us, (and we beheld his glory, the glory as of the only begotten of the Father,) full of grace and truth. 15 John bare witness of him, and cried, saying, This was he of whom I spake, He that cometh after me is preferred before me: for he was before me. 16 And of his fulness have all we received, and grace for grace. 17 For the law was given by Moses, *but* grace and truth came by Jesus Christ. 18 No man hath seen God at any time; the only begotten Son, which is in the bosom of the Father, he hath declared *him*.

(Hebrews 2:14-16 HCSB) 14 Now since the children have flesh and blood in common, Jesus also shared in these, so that through His death He might destroy the one holding the power of death—that is, the Devil — 15 and free those who were held in slavery all their lives by the fear of death. 16 For it is clear that He does not reach out to help angels, but to help Abraham's offspring.

Self-will

Self-will is something that comes about from pride and covetousness. Pride, lust, and covetousness created in Lucifer self-will to go against God's will. He exercised the free will that God had created in him in a disobedient manner, corrupting his being and corrupting others. This action was a deliberate action (choice) of the will, as all sin is.

In the following Scripture there are five illustrations of self-will concerning Lucifer's fall.

(Isaiah 14:12-14 KJV) **12** How art thou fallen from heaven, O Lucifer, son of the morning! *how* art thou cut down to the ground, which didst weaken the nations! **13** For thou hast said in thine heart, I will ascend into heaven, I will exalt my throne above the stars of God: I will sit also upon the mount of the congregation, in the sides of the north: **14** I will ascend above the heights of the clouds; I will be like the most High.

1. I will ascend into heaven *(self ascension)*.
2. I will exalt my throne above the stars of God (*self exaltation*).
3. I will sit also upon the mount of the congregation in the sides of the north (*self enthronement*).
4. I will ascend above the heights of the clouds (*self-dependence*).
5. I will be like the Most High (*self deification*).

Self-centeredness is ego-centric. It is ego-theistic, when self is lifted up as God. From being God-centered, Lucifer became self-centered, self-directing, self-reliant, and self-supporting. He became selfishness personified. He turned "in" upon himself. Beholding his own beauty, wisdom, anointing and ministry, he was lifted up in pride, forgetting that all he had was God-given. He then coveted a higher position, even God's.

The Sinning Angels

Scriptures indicate that other angels sinned with Lucifer. They transgressed a given law and, like Lucifer, became totally apostate and unredeemable.

(2 Peter 2:4 KJV) **4** For if God spared not the angels that sinned, but cast *them* down to hell, and delivered *them* into chains of darkness, to be reserved unto judgment;

(Jude 1:6 KJV) **6** And the angels which kept not their first estate, but left their own habitation, he hath reserved in everlasting chains under darkness unto the judgment of the great day

NOTE → Many expositors believe that the devil drew a third part of the angelic hosts with him in his original sin and fall from this verse.

(Revelation 12:3-4 NKJV) **3** And another sign appeared in heaven: behold, a great, fiery red dragon having seven heads and ten horns, and seven diadems on his heads. **4** His tail drew a third of the stars of heaven and threw them to the earth. And the dragon stood before the woman who was ready to give birth, to devour her Child as soon as it was born.

The Entrance of Sin into Humanity

The same basic principles are at play when we discuss the entrance of sin upon mankind. These actions that took place among the angelic order will aid in the understanding of this happening to the human race.

Creation of Man

The Book of Genesis gives the account of the creation of mankind as a free-will, morally responsible and intelligent creature in the image and likeness of God.

(Genesis 1:26-28 KJV) 26 And God said, Let us make man in our image, after our likeness: and let them have dominion over the fish of the sea, and over the fowl of the air, and over the cattle, and over all the earth, and over every creeping thing that creepeth upon the earth. 27 So God created man in his *own* image, in the image of God created he him; male and female created he them. 28 And God blessed them, and God said unto them, Be fruitful, and multiply, and replenish the earth, and subdue it: and have dominion over the fish of the sea, and over the fowl of the air, and over every living thing that moveth upon the earth.

Probation of Man

Mankind was placed under a period of probation just as the angelic creations had been. Because mankind was created with freewill they had to be placed under the law of God. Adam and Eve made their choice between God's will and their own, choosing to covet the fruit (the law that was given them).

(Genesis 3:1-7 KJV) 1 Now the serpent was more subtil than any beast of the field which the LORD God had made. And he said unto the woman, Yea, hath God said, Ye shall not eat of every tree of the garden? 2 And the woman said unto the serpent, We may eat of the fruit of the trees of the garden: 3 But of the fruit of the tree which *is* in the midst of the garden, God hath said, Ye shall not eat of it, neither shall ye touch it, lest ye die. 4 And the serpent said unto the woman, Ye shall not surely die: 5 For God doth know that in the day ye eat thereof, then your eyes shall be opened, and ye shall be as gods, knowing good and evil. 6 And when the woman saw that the tree *was* good for food, and that it *was* pleasant to the eyes, and a tree to be desired to make *one* wise, she took of the fruit thereof, and did eat, and gave also unto her husband with her; and he did eat. 7 And the eyes of them both were opened, and they knew that they *were* naked; and they sewed fig leaves together, and made themselves aprons.

Temptation of Man

The Scriptures give an account of the temptation of mankind and the entrance of sin upon them in Genesis 3:1-6. The word "temptation" means to entice, to be inviting or attractive. There was a certain tree in the Garden of Eden, The Tree of Knowledge of good and evil that was a test for Adam and Eve. It was the only tree they were not allowed to eat from, a direct commandment/order from God (Genesis 2:17). This test of the one commandment involved total obedience. Just as the desire of Lucifer to choose against God came from within so did the desire to disobey and fall victim to lust of the heart from within, befall Adam and Eve. So it was the yielding to temptation, going against God's will, that sin was made.

Tempted in Body, Soul and Spirit

The temptation of Satan/Lucifer was to all parts of mankind's being, spirit, soul and body. His approach was from without to within (body → soul → spirit).

(1 Thessalonians 5:23 HCSB) **23** Now may the God of peace Himself sanctify you completely. And may your spirit, soul, and body be kept sound and blameless for the coming of our Lord Jesus Christ.

Body →	Lust of the flesh →	The tree was good to eat
Soul →	Lust of the eyes →	The tree was pleasant to the eyes.
Spirit →	Pride of life →	The tree was desired to make one wise, making them as gods, knowing good and evil.

There are five basic instincts that God created in mankind. Satan seeks to exploit, pervert and use them for his evil purpose against God. His temptation through the serpent to Adam and Eve were aimed at these basic instincts. This was an appeal to the flesh enacting pride and self-will, corrupting and perverting the basic instincts within mankind.

1. Self Preservation → enabling man to take care of himself.
2. Self Acquisition → which enables man to acquire the necessities of life for self-support.
3. Self sustenance → the food seeking instinct.
4. Self propagation → the sex instinct to multiply on the earth.
5. Self assertion → whereby man can subdue and have dominion over the earth.

Pride

The temptation also involved pride, which arises out of inordinate desire. Satan's statement, "You will be like God, knowing good and evil." was an appeal to the ego. It was an appeal of pride, exploiting the law of self-assertion. The temptation appealed to mankind to gain wisdom and knowledge which they did not have and which was forbidden by the law of God.

Self-will

Satan's purpose of temptation was to appeal to and impact the free will of mankind, causing it to act in a manner that would put self first, instead of God. The will of mankind and the action it takes will affect all of mankind, their spirit, soul and body. Satan's aim was to get to the will of mankind and to have them exercise self-will against God's will, causing disobedience and corrupting the whole being. Satan fell due to his self-will and Adam and Eve also fell victim to their self-will.

Because of mankind exercising their self-will making the choice to be disobedient to God's law, will, and Word, sin was upon them. Sin did not originate with Adam and Eve. They fell victim to it by a deliberate choice. This choice brought along with it death in which the entire unborn human race must bear.

(Romans 5:12 HCSB) **12** Therefore, just as sin entered the world through one man, and death through sin, in this way death spread to all men, because all sinned

Tempted in Relation to the Law

The law of God is another area that should be observed concerning the temptation in Eden and also temptation taking place to date. The one decree given by God to mankind in Genesis 2:17 were God's Law, Commandment, Word and Will. The devil, "lawless one", made a direct attack by using the temptation against God's law that mankind was to adhere to. Breaking the one law given them was like breaking all the laws, as stated in (James 2:10 NKJV) *¹⁰ For whoever shall keep the whole law, and yet stumble in one* point, *he is guilty of all.*

The plan of Satan in his temptation was to create doubt. His lies were an attack against God's real intention by slandering and distorting the Word of God.

Text Message → these are used today in all cults and false beliefs of God even some claiming Christianity.

Fall of Man and its Effects

Sin brought on by the actions of Adam and Eve was a result of a deliberate choice and act of the will against a given law of God. This was total disobedience. Rebellion and selfishness are high treason against God. The affects did not only impact Adam and Eve but the human race on a whole and all of their unborn descendants.

Immediate Effects

Forfeited Purity	Knowing they were naked, this was a sense of shame that came	Genesis 3:7 with 2:25

	upon Adam and Eve after their act of disobedience.	
Knowledge of Good and Evil	They became aware of the knowledge of good and evil.	Romans 7:18-24
Law of Conscience at Work	Guilt came upon them the moment they sinned and the law of conscience began to work.	Romans 2:14-15
Law of Works	Making themselves coverings with fig was a result of the guilty conscience at work.	Genesis 3:7
Blame of Others	No one took the blame – Adam blamed Eve, Eve blamed the Serpent for their sin.	Genesis 3:13-19
Mans Nature Corrupted	Sin took over and corrupted the whole being of mankind, their spirit, soul and body.	

Long Range Effects of the Fall

The effects of the fall of Adam and Eve were not immediately realized. These effects are now impacting all of the human race and earth itself.

Sin Passed to All Mankind

Because of Adam and Eve's sin, sin has entered the entire world and all of mankind. Being the first parents of mankind and having a sin nature, they passed it on to all their offspring. Therefore, having this sin nature of Adam and Eve, mankind is also subject to lusts being stirred up from without, causing them to rise up in pride and set their will against God's.

Lucifer's sin began within: pride which led to lust and enacted by self-will. Adam and Eve's sin began from outside: lust leading to pride and enacting by self-will. Mankind now is subjected to sin coming from within and outside influences. The self-centeredness and pride that now resides in mankind's nature causes them to have lusts that arise within and to lead them to exalt their will against God's.

Sin inherited from Adam is called original sin. Actual sin is what mankind commits. Both are present in mankind. The sinful nature within mankind causes them to act sinful. They are not a sinner because they sin, but sin because they are a sinner, being accountable to God.

Sin can be considered both hereditary and universal in regards to mankind. All are born with the sinful and depraved natures that sin carries, because we all trace back to Adam and Eve. All need to be born again in the spirit in which Jesus Christ has provided by His life/death/victory upon the earth establishing mankind's relationship back to God their creator.

(Romans 5:19 NKJV) ¹⁹ For as by one man's disobedience many were made sinners, so also by one Man's obedience many will be made righteous.

(Romans 3:23 KJV) ²³ For all have sinned, and come short of the glory of God;

(1 Kings 8:46 KJV) ⁴⁶ If they sin against thee, (for *there is* no man that sinneth not,) and thou be angry with them, and deliver them to the enemy, so that they carry them away captives unto the land of the enemy, far or near;

Death Passed Upon All Mankind

The penalty of sin is death, and was brought upon mankind by one man and one woman. All sinned and all died "in Adam", the father and representative of the human race (1 Corinthians 15:21-23; 45-50). God created mankind to be immortal and not to die, death was foreign to them, but because of the sin committed in the Garden of Eden death came upon them.

(Genesis 2:17 KJV) ¹⁷ But of the tree of the knowledge of good and evil, thou shalt not eat of it: for in the day that thou eatest thereof thou shalt surely die.

Law of Sin

The word 'Law' in relation to sin is used here to refer to a principle of action, or how a thing works (as with the 'law of gravity'). The best Scriptural synopsis of the law of sin is to be found in (James 1:15 HCSB) **15** *Then after desire has conceived, it gives birth to sin, and when sin is fully grown, it gives birth to death.*

Once a person reacts to temptation, beginning within, the conception of sin has been seeded within their heart. If this conception is not dealt with immediately it will begin to grow and blossom into sin, becoming a willful act contrary to God's will. The mind leads to the heart and must always be guarded against things that would lead us away from God. There is a spiritual battle raging war against your mind lead by Satan and his evil spirits and demons. The only sure weapon mankind has available to them is the Word of God, and acting within His will. God will provide the rest if we truly trust, walk, pray, study, praise and worship the one and only true God, believing that our salvation can only be possible through Jesus Christ.

Text Message → Garbage in, garbage out so be careful and on guard of what you let into yourself

---

Begin With Prayer

Biblical Teaching/Doctrine of Eternal States

Biblical Building Block # 11

(Jude 1:20-21 NKJV)
²⁰ But you, beloved, building yourselves up on your most holy faith, praying in the Holy Spirit, ²¹ keep yourselves in the love of God, looking for the mercy of our Lord Jesus Christ unto eternal life.

Eternity is something that most people have a hard time understanding. God created mankind to live an eternal life with no death. God's love is an eternal love forever and ever. Though it was God's intent for mankind never to experience death, sin entered through disobedience - making the decision to go against God's command, and brought with it death to the human race. God has provided a way, to experience death once and then live with Him in eternity, to those who believe in Jesus Christ as their Savior and accept Him in their heart. Those who choose not to accept God's provision will experience a second death, eternity which means a forever separation from God and all that is good. Eternity has no end so the decision one makes about Jesus Christ is the most important decision one will ever make in this life time and forever. Jesus Christ offers an eternal life to those who believe and put their faith in Him. Remember God is Love and He wants nothing more than to share that Love with you.

1. Define time and eternity.

2. Do you know what a covenant is pertaining to the Bible?

3. Do you know the different covenants stated in the Bible and what they were?

4. What are the two types of resurrections concerning mankind that are identified in Scripture?

5. Describe the nature of the redeemed resurrected body.

6. Do you know what the different judgments are? Explain them.

7. What is heaven?

8. What is hell?

Time and Eternity

Scripture identifies God as being eternal and not limited to time. God speaks of Himself as the "I AM THAT I AM", that is, the eternal (Exodus 3:14-15 KJV). He is the first and the last, the beginning and the ending, the Alpha and the Omega. Mankind, however, is subject to time. They are finite and limited by time and space. Though mankind is a creature of time, they were made for eternity. They have a beginning but exist eternally. Mankind will be rewarded by God according to mankind's actions of their life on earth towards God.

(Revelation 1:8 KJV) 8 I am Alpha and Omega, the beginning and the ending, saith the Lord, which is, and which was, and which is to come, the Almighty.

(Isaiah 41:4 NKJV) 4 Who has performed and done *it,* Calling the generations from the beginning? ' I, the LORD, am the first; And with the last I *am* He.' "

Time (Probation of Mankind)

During the time Adam and Eve spent in the Garden of Eden (earthly paradise) they were to obey God's given commandment to not eat of the tree of Good and Evil.

(Genesis 2:16-17 KJV) 16 And the LORD God commanded the man, saying, Of every tree of the garden thou mayest freely eat: 17 But of the tree of the knowledge of good and evil, thou shalt not eat of it: for in the day that thou eatest thereof thou shalt surely die.

This would be like a test of mankind's obedience to God, a probation test of mankind's free will. They failed in this probationary period. God extended grace to them and gave them space to repent and be restored to His fellowship by the atoning sacrifice. God pronounced the death penalty on mankind's sin of disobedience. However, there was a period of probation given to Adam and Eve as well as the entire human race. To mankind this period is called time.

Each person born has been given a period of time that we can call their life-span. This life-span
is the probation period of each person and only God knows the length of it. It is this period of time that mankind must use to repent of sin and establish their relationship and peace with God. This period of time is mankind's only opportunity to repent and accept God's salvation and once it is passed it to will be passed forever. One's eternal state and destiny are settled, unchanged and unchangeable. So in this period of probation called time a person must settle their account with God and their eternal destiny. God has made a plan of salvation for all of mankind to turn from their sin, by accepting Jesus Christ as their Savior and coming under His redeeming grace.

(Revelation 2:21 NKJV) 21 And I gave her time to repent of her sexual immorality, and she did not repent.

(2 Peter 3:8-9 NKJV) [8] But, beloved, do not forget this one thing, that with the Lord one day *is* as a thousand years, and a thousand years as one day. [9] The Lord is not slack concerning *His* promise, as some count slackness, but is longsuffering toward us, not willing that any should perish but that all should come to repentance.

Eternity (Rewarding of Mankind)

When mankind experiences death of this life and enters the event of eternity it will lead into the rewarding of the redeemed. According to their works, all of mankind will be rewarded whether good or worthless, concerning God. Everyone will be judged according to the deeds done in the body. A person's character, life style, and life choices determine their eternal state and destiny. What a person has done, their works, will be the determining factor of their eternal rewards. One cannot separate character and works. The character of a person will dictate their works and so what a person is, determines what a person does and both settle their eternal state.

(2 Corinthians 5:10 NKJV) [10] For we must all appear before the judgment seat of Christ, that each one may receive the things *done* in the body, according to what he has done, whether good or bad.

(Romans 14:10 NKJV) [10] But why do you judge your brother? Or why do you show contempt for your brother? For we shall all stand before the judgment seat of Christ.

Dispensations/Arrangement of Time

What God is going to do in eternity He has illustrated in time. He determines certain judgments and rewards to both the righteous and unrighteous during their time on earth. In eternity He follows the same principle. Each of God's dispensations/arrangements/covenants closed with judgment on the wicked and rewards or promises of reward to the righteous. So as it is in time, it will be in eternity. *It should be noted that the word "dispensation" as used here and in Scripture (KJV)* has **no direct allusion to the ages of time** but rather a **specific arrangement /system by which something is dispensed** (HCSB)** a dealing of God relative to mankind. The word "dispensation" as used by Paul in his writings distinctly mean "specific arrangement/system by which something is dispensed or administered" such as the different covenants.*

(Ecclesiastes 11:9 KJV) [9] Rejoice, O young man, in thy youth; and let thy heart cheer thee in the days of thy youth, and walk in the ways of thine heart, and in the sight of thine eyes: but know thou, that for all these *things* God will bring thee into judgment.

(Matthew 12:36 NKJV) [36] But I say to you that for every idle word men may speak, they will give account of it in the day of judgment.
*(1 Corinthians 9:17 KJV) [17] For if I do this thing willingly, I have a reward: but if against my will, a dispensation *of the gospel* is committed unto me.

(Ephesians 1:10 HCSB) 10 for the administration of the days of fulfillment —to bring everything together in the Messiah, both things in heaven and things on earth in Him.

There is one plan of salvation that God has revealed to mankind. In His dealing with them throughout time He has unfolded it in a progressive manner using different methods but to one ultimate purpose. He also used various ways of dealing with mankind in relation to this plan.

All of the different dispensations/arrangements should not be separated from the divine covenant. They were a particular arrangement between God and mankind, during a particular period of time, having their own distinctive emphasis as God desired to unfold it. Therefore the word "dispensations" as used here refers to the dealings of God with mankind under their respective covenant. As each covenant closed, judgment was made on the wicked and reward given to the righteous, each will find their fulfillment in the final judgments and rewards of eternity.

Eden Covenant (Dispensation of Innocence)

This dispensation was characterized by innocence. Adam and Eve (mankind) was subjected to a simple test of obedience under a period of probation. They were forbidden to partake of the tree of the knowledge of good and evil. Mankind exercised their free-will and chose to partake of the forbidden tree. They brought themselves and all of future mankind under the power of sin, Satan, and death.

(Genesis 1:26-30 KJV) **26** And God said, Let us make man in our image, after our likeness: and let them have dominion over the fish of the sea, and over the fowl of the air, and over the cattle, and over all the earth, and over every creeping thing that creepeth upon the earth. **27** So God created man in his *own* image, in the image of God created he him; male and female created he them. **28** And God blessed them, and God said unto them, Be fruitful, and multiply, and replenish the earth, and subdue it: and have dominion over the fish of the sea, and over the fowl of the air, and over every living thing that moveth upon the earth. **29** And God said, Behold, I have given you every herb bearing seed, which *is* upon the face of all the earth, and every tree, in the which *is* the fruit of a tree yielding seed; to you it shall be for meat. **30** And to every beast of the earth, and to every fowl of the air, and to every thing that creepeth upon the earth, wherein *there is* life, *I have given* every green herb for meat: and it was so.

(Genesis 2:15-17 KJV) **15** And the LORD God took the man, and put him into the garden of Eden to dress it and to keep it. **16** And the LORD God commanded the man, saying, Of every tree of the garden thou mayest freely eat: **17** But of the tree of the knowledge of good and evil, thou shalt not eat of it: for in the day that thou eatest thereof thou shalt surely die.

(Genesis 3:17-19 KJV) **17** And unto Adam he said, Because thou hast hearkened unto the voice of thy wife, and hast eaten of the tree, of which I commanded thee, saying, Thou shalt not eat of it: cursed *is* the ground for thy sake; in sorrow shalt thou eat *of* it all the days of thy life; **18** Thorns also and thistles shall it bring forth to thee; and thou shalt eat the herb of the field; **19** In the sweat of thy face shalt thou eat bread, till thou return unto the ground; for out of it wast thou taken: for dust thou *art*, and unto dust shalt thou return.

Adam Covenant (Dispensation of Conscience)

Conscience came into operation the instant mankind sinned. Through this conscience mankind would be able to know and distinguish between good and evil. So, mankind came under conscience behavior and God's dealings with them were according to their conscience. Conscience allows mankind to define good and evil but it leaves them powerless to overcome this evil and do the good. This arrangement brought in judgment on the ungodly world by the flood and the reward of the righteous remnant who knew the preservation in the Ark of Noah.

(Genesis 6:7-8 KJV) **7** And the LORD said, I will destroy man whom I have created from the face of the earth; both man, and beast, and the creeping thing, and the fowls of the air; for it repenteth me that I have made them. **8** But Noah found grace in the eyes of the LORD.

Noah Covenant (Dispensation of Human Government)

During this time God entrusted mankind with governmental authority. The details of this are stated within Genesis 8-9. This is when God identified forms of punishment for violation of human rights. The handling of this government mankind proved to be inadequate and God brought in judgment upon them at the tower of Babel. The sons of Noah were divided and scattered to their respective inheritances. God promised a reward of a city to Abraham that He-Himself would build. Abraham responded and came out of Babel, Ur or the Chaldees.

(Hebrews 11:10-16 NKJV) **10** for he waited for the city which has foundations, whose builder and maker *is* God. **11** By faith Sarah herself also received strength to conceive seed, and she bore a child when she was past the age, because she judged Him faithful who had promised. **12** Therefore from one man, and him as good as dead, were born *as many* as the stars of the sky in multitude--innumerable as the sand which is by the seashore. **13** These all died in faith, not having received the promises, but having seen them afar off were assured of them, embraced *them* and confessed that they were strangers and pilgrims on the earth. **14** For those who say such things declare plainly that they seek a homeland. **15** And truly if they had called to mind that *country* from which they had come out, they would have had opportunity to return. **16** But now they desire a better, that is, a heavenly *country*. Therefore God is not ashamed to be called their God, for He has prepared a city for them.

Abraham Covenant (Dispensation of Patriarchal)

God chose Abraham after the tower of Babel, then Isaac, followed by Jacob to be the fathers of a new nation. The promises given involve the great Abraham Covenant. Seed, land, and blessings, both national or natural and spiritual were promised. In Genesis 12-50, are stated the details of these promises. In Egypt Israel became a nation and an enslaved people. This period was closed by the divine judgments on Egypt and the deliverance of God's chosen people from slavery, in fulfillment of the promises made to the fathers.

(Exodus 3:12 NKJV) [12] So He said, "I will certainly be with you. And this *shall be* a sign to you that I have sent you: When you have brought the people out of Egypt, you shall serve God on this mountain."

Mosaic Covenant (Dispensation of Law)

With the chosen nation of Israel at Mt. Sinai after their exodus from Egypt the Mosaic Covenant was made. This Covenant involved the Tabernacle, Priesthood, Sacrifices, Feasts and the Law. It continued from the period of Moses to the first coming of Christ and the ministry of the early Church (receiving the Holy Spirit). The reward for the believers at this period of time was escape from the terrible judgments and destruction which came upon the Jewish people as a nation.

(Matthew 24:1-2 NKJV) [1] Then Jesus went out and departed from the temple, and His disciples came up to show Him the buildings of the temple. [2] And Jesus said to them, "Do you not see all these things? Assuredly, I say to you, not *one* stone shall be left here upon another, that shall not be thrown down."

(Luke 19:41-44 NKJV) [41] Now as He drew near, He saw the city and wept over it, [42] saying, "If you had known, even you, especially in this your day, the things *that make* for your peace! But now they are hidden from your eyes. [43] For days will come upon you when your enemies will build an embankment around you, surround you and close you in on every side, [44] and level you, and your children within you, to the ground; and they will not leave in you one stone upon another, because you did not know the time of your visitation."

New Covenant (Dispensation of Grace)

Jesus introduced this "the New Testament" or literally "the new arrangement". It fulfilled/cancelled out the Mosaic Covenant and brought in the dispensation/period of grace, God's dealing with mankind in this present time. "The Law was given by Moses from God, but grace and truth came by Jesus Christ (God directly)". It is the grace of God which accomplishes the eternal purposes of God in relation to mankind for all who receive and believe. However, all of mankind will not receive the free grace of God and this dispensation will consummate with the judgments of God upon the ungodly. When grace is rejected, there is no alternative but to judge mankind. The second coming of Christ will usher in both judgments on the wicked and rewards for the righteous.

(Matthew 26:26-28 KJV) **26** And as they were eating, Jesus took bread, and blessed *it*, and break *it*, and gave *it* to the disciples, and said, Take, eat; this is my body. **27** And he took the cup, and gave thanks, and gave *it* to them, saying, Drink ye all of it; **28** For this is my blood of the new testament, which is shed for many for the remission of sins.

(John 1:17 HCSB) **17** for the law was given through Moses, grace and truth came through Jesus Christ.

(2 Thessalonians 1:7-10 NKJV) and to *give* you who are troubled rest with us when the Lord Jesus is revealed from heaven with His mighty angels, **8** in flaming fire taking vengeance on those who do not know God, and on those who do not obey the gospel of our Lord Jesus Christ. **9** These shall be punished with everlasting destruction from the presence of the Lord and from the glory of His power,

Everlasting Covenant (Dispensation of the Kingdom)

During the second coming of Jesus Christ, the arrangement/covenant between God and mankind will be distinguished by mankind's place of dominion in the kingdom of God. According to the Word of God, the Kingdom of God has always been in existence, note what the Psalmist says; "*Thy kingdom is an everlasting Kingdom*" (Psalm 145:13 KJV). So the Kingdom of God and relating it to earth has been articulated in different forms, each a part of the progressive representation of the eternal Kingdom. It is this aspect of the Kingdom which fulfills all other arrangements/covenants. ***It brings mankind back to the original purpose of God through the redemption in Christ. It also ushers in the eternal order.***

During this period of time the final judgments and rewards will be appraised and given. This will comprise of both eternal Judgment and rewards being distributed to both angelic and human beings. Everything will be dealt with at the Judgment Seat of Christ, the Great White Throne of God.

(Hebrews 6:1-2 NKJV) **1** Therefore, leaving the discussion of the elementary *principles* of Christ, let us go on to perfection, not laying again the foundation of repentance from dead works and of faith toward God, **2** of the doctrine of baptisms, of laying on of hands, of resurrection of the dead, and of eternal judgment.

(Revelation 20:11-15 KJV) **11** And I saw a great white throne, and him that sat on it, from whose face the earth and the heaven fled away; and there was found no place for them. **12** And I saw the dead, small and great, stand before God; and the books were opened: and another book was opened, which is *the book* of life: and the dead were judged out of those things which were written in the books, according to their works. **13** And the sea gave up the dead which were in it; and death and hell delivered up the dead which were in them: and they were judged every man according to their works. **14** And death and hell were cast into the lake of fire. This is the second death. **15** And whosoever was not found written in the book of life was cast into the lake of fire.

Resurrections and Judgments

The final judgments of God and the resurrections are very much associated and need to be reviewed as such. Resurrection precedes judgment and judgment necessitates resurrection. The principles of the Doctrine of Christ involve "the resurrection of the dead/asleep and eternal judgment". Revelation 20:1-15 deals with the Doctrine of Resurrection and then the Great White Throne judgment. So resurrection and judgment are tightly linked together.

(Acts 17:30-31 KJV) **30** And the times of this ignorance God winked at; but now commandeth all men every where to repent: **31** Because he hath appointed a day, in the which he will judge the world in righteousness by *that* man whom he hath ordained; *whereof* he hath given assurance unto all *men*, in that he hath raised him from the dead.

Resurrection

Two types of resurrections are identified in Scripture related to mankind, for the righteous and for the unrighteous. The righteous will awake to everlasting life called a better resurrection. The unrighteous will awake to shame and to an everlasting damnation and contempt.

In the Book of Revelation chapter 20 John describes that there are 1000 years between the two resurrections stating that the second resurrection points to the second death.

(Revelation 20:13-15 NKJV) **13** The sea gave up the dead who were in it, and Death and Hades delivered up the dead who were in them. And they were judged, each one according to his works. **14** Then Death and Hades were cast into the lake of fire. This is the second death. **15** And anyone not found written in the Book of Life was cast into the lake of fire.

(Acts 24:15 KJV) **15** And have hope toward God, which they themselves also allow, that there shall be a resurrection of the dead, both of the just and unjust.

(John 5:29 KJV) **29** And shall come forth; they that have done good, unto the resurrection of life; and they that have done evil, unto the resurrection of damnation.

(Revelation 20:4-6 KJV) **4** And I saw thrones, and they sat upon them, and judgment was given unto them: and *I saw* the souls of them that were beheaded for the witness of Jesus, and for the word of God, and which had not worshipped the beast, neither his image, neither had received *his* mark upon their foreheads, or in their hands; and they lived and reigned with Christ a thousand years. **5** But the rest of the dead lived not again until the thousand years were finished. This *is* the first resurrection. **6** Blessed and holy *is* he that hath part in the first resurrection: on such the second death hath no power, but they shall be priests of God and of Christ, and shall reign with him a thousand years.

The resurrection is taught and illustrated in both Old and New Testaments. The resurrection of Jesus Christ is the sure proof of the resurrection of all mankind (Acts 17:30-31). Actual physical resurrections in the New Testament are identified during the ministries of Jesus, Paul and Peter. (Matthew 9:18-26; 27:50-53; Luke 7:11-23; John 2:43-44; Acts 9:36-42; 20:7-12)

In The New Testament Jesus taught the resurrection of the physical body as well as a spiritual resurrection (John 5:28-29; 6:39-54; Luke 16:19-31; 20:35-36). Also, Paul wrote about the bodily resurrection (Acts 24:15; 1 Corinthians 15:3-5; 1 Thessalonians 4:14-18; Philippians 3:11,21). And John spoke of the resurrections (Revelation 20:4-6).

In the Old Testament the testimony of Job and the prophet David speak of the resurrection. (Job 19:25-27; Psalm 16:9; 17:15). The Prophets spoke of the resurrection of the body also (Isaiah 26:19; Daniel 12:1-3; Hosea 13:14). In actuality, Elijah and Elisha knew the power of resurrection in the persons they raised from the dead (1 Kings 17:17-24; 2 Kings 4:18-37; 8:5; 13:20-21; Jude 9).

Nature of the Resurrection Body

The resurrected body of the redeemed is to *be like* Christ's glorious body – Body of bones and flesh	(Luke 24:39 KJV) 39 Behold my hands and my feet, that it is I myself: handle me, and see; for a spirit hath not flesh and bones, as ye see me have. (John 5:28-29 KJV) 28 Marvel not at this: for the hour is coming, in the which all that are in the graves shall hear his voice, 29 And shall come forth; they that have done good, unto the resurrection of life; and they that have done evil, unto the resurrection of damnation.
Redeemed Body	(Romans 8:11 KJV) 11 But if the Spirit of him that raised up Jesus from the dead dwell in you, he that raised up Christ from the dead shall also quicken your mortal bodies by his Spirit that dwelleth in you.
Glorious body	(Philippians 3:21 NKJV) 21 who will transform our lowly body that it may be conformed to His glorious body, according to the working by which He is able even to subdue all things to Himself.
Incorruptible body and Spiritual body	(1 Corinthians 15:42 KJV) 42 So also *is* the resurrection of the dead. It is sown in corruption; it is raised in incorruption:
Heavenly Body	(1 Corinthians 15:47-49 KJV) 47 The first man *is* of the earth, earthy: the second man *is* the Lord from heaven. 48 As *is* the earthy, such *are* they also that are earthy: and as *is* the heavenly, such *are* they also that are heavenly. 49 And as we have borne the image of the earthy, we shall also bear the image of the heavenly.

> **The unredeemed** → There is no description given of the resurrected body of the unredeemed, but, it suggests that one is temporarily given (<u>Matthew 10:28 with Daniel 7:11 HCSB</u>) *"Don't fear those who kill the body but are able to kill the soul; rather, fear Him who is able to destroy both soul and body in hell." – "I watched, then because of the sound of the arrogant words the horn was speaking. As I continued watching, the beast was killed and its body destroyed and given over to the burning fire."* → It is this that will constitute the second death.
>
> (<u>Revelation 2:11 KJV</u>) **11** He that hath an ear, let him hear what the Spirit saith unto the churches; He that overcometh shall not be hurt of the second death.
>
> (<u>Revelation 21:8 KJV</u>) **8** But the fearful, and unbelieving, and the abominable, and murderers, and whoremongers, and sorcerers, and idolaters, and all liars, shall have their part in the lake which burneth with fire and brimstone: which is the second death.

Judgments

The resurrection precedes judgment and judgment necessitates resurrection. Judgment is necessary because the conscience of mankind, history, and justice all demand it. The law of conscience, when violated, may be silent, but it comes alive and active in the judgment before God's throne, and will accuse the guilty. Through history the injustices of mankind and the perversion of God's righteous laws demand that they be judged before the one Holy and Righteous God. God will need to judge all sin for the sake of justice which stems from His law that is Holy and Righteous.

(<u>Romans 2:14-15 KJV</u>) **14** For when the Gentiles, which have not the law, do by nature the things contained in the law, these, having not the law, are a law unto themselves: **15** Which shew the work of the law written in their hearts, their conscience also bearing witness, and *their* thoughts the mean while accusing or else excusing one another;

Day of Judgment

This is the day that God will bring all mankind before His throne to give an account of their lives. This day will be for believers and unbelievers. The judge will be Jesus Christ. And the Purpose of this judgment will be to reveal the true character of each person to determine the value of the works. Christ will render public reward or punishment to exonerate the righteousness of God in His dealings with mankind. His justice will be acknowledged.

(<u>Acts 17:31 KJV</u>) **31** Because he hath appointed a day, in the which he will judge the world in righteousness by *that* man whom he hath ordained; *whereof* he hath given assurance unto all *men*, in that he hath raised him from the dead.

(2 Corinthians 5:10 KJV) 10 For we must all appear before the judgment seat of Christ; that every one may receive the things *done* in *his* body, according to that he hath done, whether *it be* good or bad.

(John 5:22-27 KJV) 22 For the Father judgeth no man, but hath committed all judgment unto the Son: 23 That all *men* should honour the Son, even as they honour the Father. He that honoureth not the Son honoureth not the Father which hath sent him. 24 Verily, verily, I say unto you, He that heareth my word, and believeth on him that sent me, hath everlasting life, and shall not come into condemnation; but is passed from death unto life. 25 Verily, verily, I say unto you, The hour is coming, and now is, when the dead shall hear the voice of the Son of God: and they that hear shall live. 26 For as the Father hath life in himself; so hath he given to the Son to have life in himself; 27 And hath given him authority to execute judgment also, because he is the Son of man.
(Revelation 19:1-2 KJV) 1 And after these things I heard a great voice of much people in heaven, saying, Alleluia; Salvation, and glory, and honour, and power, unto the Lord our God: 2 For true and righteous *are* his judgments: for he hath judged the great whore, which did corrupt the earth with her fornication, and hath avenged the blood of his servants at her hand.

Principles and Standards Will Apply

Mankind will be judged with righteous judgment according to God's holy standards and according to their attitudes; to Christ, to the measure of light and opportunity given them with Jesus Christ as the judge. There will be no chance of mistaken judgment for He has all things (all hidden facts), deeds, motives and thoughts of mankind before Him. He will use different degrees of rewards or punishment as He sees fits.

(Luke 12:47-48 KJV) 47 And that servant, which knew his lord's will, and prepared not *himself*, neither did according to his will, shall be beaten with many *stripes*. 48 But he that knew not, and did commit things worthy of stripes, shall be beaten with few *stripes*. For unto whomsoever much is given, of him shall be much required: and to whom men have committed much, of him they will ask the more.

(John 12:48 NKJV) 48 He who rejects Me, and does not receive My words, has that which judges him--the word that I have spoken will judge him in the last day.

(Ecclesiastes 12:14 KJV) 14 For God shall bring every work into judgment, with every secret thing, whether *it be* good, or whether *it be* evil.

Judgment and Rewards of Eternity

Believers –Judgment & Rewards

Believers will be judged by Jesus Christ for their works giving an account of themselves. Responsibility will have a need of accountability. This judgment takes place at the second coming of Christ. It is not a judgment concerning the believer's salvation that was settled at Calvary (the believer's acceptance of Jesus Christ as they lived on earth), it is a judgment of his works and service for the lord.

(1 Corinthians 3:11-15 NKJV) ¹¹ For no other foundation can anyone lay than that which is laid, which is Jesus Christ. ¹² Now if anyone builds on this foundation *with* gold, silver, precious stones, wood, hay, straw, ¹³ each one's work will become clear; for the Day will declare it, because it will be revealed by fire; and the fire will test each one's work, of what sort it is. ¹⁴ If anyone's work which he has built on *it* endures, he will receive a reward. ¹⁵ If anyone's work is burned, he will suffer loss; but he himself will be saved, yet so as through fire.

The statement of rewards is used over 100 times in the NT. It is spoken of for both the righteous and the wicked. They are not to be considered as bribes but as incentives to God's redeemed to live a life that will bring glory to God. Some rewards mentioned in the Bible are: rewards of faithfulness, crown of life, of glory, of rejoicing, of righteousness, of the incorruptible crown, of the prophet and the righteous man's crown of gold.

(James 1:12 KJV) 12 Blessed *is* the man that endureth temptation: for when he is tried, he shall receive the crown of life, which the Lord hath promised to them that love him.

(Revelation 2:10 KJV) 10 Fear none of those things which thou shalt suffer: behold, the devil shall cast *some* of you into prison, that ye may be tried; and ye shall have tribulation ten days: be thou faithful unto death, and I will give thee a crown of life.

Unbelievers – Judgment

The final judgment and eternal judgment of the ungodly will take place at the Great White Throne during the close of the 1,000 years of the kingdom period mentioned in the book of Revelation. All are judged out of the books according to their works. The unbelievers and ungodly will be rewarded by their works "the reward of iniquity".

(Revelation 20:11-15 KJV) 11 And I saw a great white throne, and him that sat on it, from whose face the earth and the heaven fled away; and there was found no place for them. 12 And I saw the dead, small and great, stand before God; and the books were opened: and another book was opened, which is *the book* of life: and the dead were judged out of those things which were written in the books, according to their works. 13 And the sea gave up the dead which were in it; and death and hell delivered up the dead which were in them: and they were judged every man according to their works. 14 And death and hell were cast into the lake of fire. This is the second death. 15 And whosoever was not found written in the book of life was cast into the lake of fire.

(Daniel 7:10 KJV) 10 A fiery stream issued and came forth from before him: thousand thousands ministered unto him, and ten thousand times ten thousand stood before him: the judgment was set, and the books were opened.

(Romans 2:5-13 KJV) **5** But after thy hardness and impenitent heart treasurest up unto thyself wrath against the day of wrath and revelation of the righteous judgment of God; **6** Who will render to every man according to his deeds: **7** To them who by patient continuance in well doing seek for glory and honour and immortality, eternal life: **8** But unto them that are contentious, and do not obey the truth, but obey unrighteousness, indignation and wrath, **9** Tribulation and anguish, upon every soul of man that doeth evil, of the Jew first, and also of the Gentile; **10** But glory, honour, and peace, to every man that worketh good, to the Jew first, and also to the Gentile: **11** For there is no respect of persons with God. **12** For as many as have sinned without law shall also perish without law: and as many as have sinned in the law shall be judged by the law; **13** (For not the hearers of the law *are* just before God, but the doers of the law shall be justified.

Eternal States

The eternal and ultimate state of the wicked will be the punishment of hell, the dwelling place for the unredeemed. The eternal and ultimate state of the righteous is stated in Scripture as called heaven. Whatever other rewards the believer or unbeliever receives the eternal reward of heaven or hell will be the ultimate reward.

NOTE → Many people want to believe in a heaven without a hell, but it is inconsistent to have one without the other – Scripture will show this.

Heaven (Dwelling Place of the Redeemed)

Heaven is the dwelling place of God and the elected angels. It is the everlasting home of the redeemed of all mankind. Scriptures identify three heavens and that these heavens are the reality of the shadow cast on earth in the three places in the Tabernacle of Moses and the Temple of Solomon. The earthly sanctuary was the shadow of the heavenly sanctuary, as the books of Hebrews and Revelation state.

(Genesis 2:1 KJV) **1** Thus the heavens and the earth were finished, and all the host of them.

(Hebrews 8:1-7 KJV) **1** Now of the things which we have spoken *this is* the sum: We have such an high priest, who is set on the right hand of the throne of the Majesty in the heavens; **2** A minister of the sanctuary, and of the true tabernacle, which the Lord pitched, and not man. **3** For every high priest is ordained to offer gifts and sacrifices: wherefore *it is* of necessity that this man have somewhat also to offer. **4** For if he were on earth, he should not be a priest, seeing that there are priests that offer gifts according to the law: **5** Who serve unto the example and shadow of heavenly things, as Moses was admonished of God when he was about to make the tabernacle: for, See, saith he, *that* thou make all things according to the pattern shewed to thee in the mount.
6 But now hath he obtained a more excellent ministry, by how much also he is the mediator of a better covenant, which was established upon better promises. **7** For if that first *covenant* had been faultless, then should no place have been sought for the second.

First Heaven

This is the atmospheric heaven above the surrounding earth. This is the heaven that mankind depends on for breath, sustenance and earth productions, which include sun, wind, and rain. It corresponds to the Outer Court of the Tabernacle of Moses. This heaven is to be followed by a new heaven and new earth in due time. It is to be rolled up as a scroll and melted with fervent heat. It is this heaven that is "shut up" and withholds the rain from mankind when they sin against God.

(Genesis 1:8 KJV) **8** And God called the firmament Heaven. And the evening and the morning were the second day.

(2 Chronicles 6:26 KJV) **26** When the heaven is shut up, and there is no rain, because they have sinned against thee; *yet* if they pray toward this place, and confess thy name, and turn from their sin, when thou dost afflict them;

(Revelation 6:13 KJV) **13** And the stars of heaven fell unto the earth, even as a fig tree casteth her untimely figs, when she is shaken of a mighty wind.

Other Scriptures to Review
2 Peter 3:5-16; Revelation 21:1-2: 1 Kings 17:1; Deuteronomy 28:23; Leviticus 26:19; Job 1:16; Revelation 20:11; 21:1; 12:7-12

Second Heaven

This is the central - planetary heaven. It corresponds with the Holy Place of the earthly sanctuary of Moses. This heaven has the untold billions of planets, and galaxies. When the prophets speak of being darkened in the *Last Days* in judgment prior to and at the coming of the Lord Jesus Christ it is this second heaven. This heaven is to be shaken.

(Joel 2:10 KJV) **10** The earth shall quake before them; the heavens shall tremble: the sun and the moon shall be dark, and the stars shall withdraw their shining:

(Joel 2:30-32 KJV) **30** And I will shew wonders in the heavens and in the earth, blood, and fire, and pillars of smoke. **31** The sun shall be turned into darkness, and the moon into blood, before the great and the terrible day of the LORD come. **32** And it shall come to pass, *that* whosoever shall call on the name of the LORD shall be delivered: for in mount Zion and in Jerusalem shall be deliverance, as the LORD hath said, and in the remnant whom the LORD shall call.

(Isaiah 50:3 KJV) **3** I clothe the heavens with blackness, and I make sackcloth their covering.

Third Heaven

The third Heaven is the place of the immediate presence of God and called Paradise. This is the Most Holy Place of all. It is this heaven which is the center of the universe subjected to God's will. Scripture states it is the third heaven, Paradise, heaven itself, the presence of God, God's dwelling place, the Throne of God.

(Revelation 2:7 KJV) 7 He that hath an ear, let him hear what the Spirit saith unto the churches; To him that overcometh will I give to eat of the tree of life, which is in the midst of the paradise of God.

(Hebrews 9:24 KJV) 24 For Christ is not entered into the holy places made with hands, *which are* the figures of the true; but into heaven itself, now to appear in the presence of God for us:

(2 Corinthians 12;1-4 NKJV) It is doubtless not profitable for me to boast. I will come to visions and revelations of the Lord: 2 I know a man in Christ who fourteen years ago-- whether in the body I do not know, or whether out of the body I do not know, God knows-- such a one was caught up to the third heaven. 3 And I know such a man--whether in the body or out of the body I do not know, God knows-- 4 how he was caught up into Paradise and heard inexpressible words, which it is not lawful for a man to utter.

(Luke 23:43 KJV) 43 And Jesus said unto him, Verily I say unto thee, To day shalt thou be with me in paradise.

New Heaven, Earth, and Jerusalem

Scriptures state in time there will be a new heaven, earth and Jerusalem. This will be the eternal dwelling place of the redeemed and where all eternal activity is worked. The New Jerusalem will be the new capitol of the universe and the place where the redeemed gather for worship and service.

Some characteristics of the new heaven, earth, and Jerusalem that have been stated in the Scriptures are; it will be new, no seas to separate the land, a holy city, a dwelling place of the redeemed with God, no pain, no tears, no sorrow, no death, filled with God's presence and glory, and it will be a center of worship of God.

(Genesis 1:1 KJV) 1 In the beginning God created the heaven and the earth
And
(Revelation 21:1 KJV) 1 And I saw a new heaven and a new earth: for the first heaven and the first earth were passed away; and there was no more sea.

(Hebrews 11:10-16 KJV) 10 For he looked for a city which hath foundations, whose builder and maker *is* God. 11 Through faith also Sara herself received strength to conceive seed, and was delivered of a child when she was past age, because she judged him faithful who had promised. 12 Therefore sprang there even of one, and him as good as dead, *so many* as the stars of the sky in multitude, and as the sand which is by the sea shore innumerable. 13 These all died in faith, not having received the promises, but having seen them afar off, and were persuaded of *them*, and embraced *them*, and confessed that they were strangers and pilgrims on the earth. 14 For they that say such things declare plainly that they seek a country. 15 And truly, if they had been mindful of that *country* from whence they came out, they might have had opportunity to have returned. 16 But now they desire a better *country*, that is, an heavenly: wherefore God is not ashamed to be called their God: for he hath prepared for them a city.

Other Scriptures that describe Heaven
Psalm 73:24; 16:11; John 14:2; 14:2-3; Jude 24; Philippians 1:23; Matthew 6:19-20; 1 John 5:11-12; 2 Corinthians 12:2-4; Hebrews 11:10-16; 13:14; Revelation 21:1-2; Hebrews 11:10-16; 2; Isaiah 65:17; Hebrews 13:14; Galatians 4:26; Revelation 3:12; 21:2; Exodus 19:4-6; Jeremiah 31:31-34; Revelation 21:3; Revelation 21:4; Revelation 21:4; Isaiah 65:17; 66:22

Hell (Dwelling Place of the Unredeemed)

This is the place of punishment for the wicked/unrighteous that die in their sins without repentance or being saved by the grace of God. It is an actual place. Hell was not made for mankind but prepared for the devil and his rebellious angels. Then sin entered upon mankind and now they can either repent and accept God and his salvation or follow after the devil and be rebellious to the creator of all, God.

(Matthew 5:22 NKJV) 22 But I say to you that whoever is angry with his brother without a cause shall be in danger of the judgment. And whoever says to his brother, 'Raca!' shall be in danger of the council. But whoever says, 'You fool!' shall be in danger of hell fire.

(Matthew 25:42 NKJV) 41 Then He will also say to those on the left hand, 'Depart from Me, you cursed, into the everlasting fire prepared for the devil and his angels:

Scripture speaks of three divisions and a final hell Gehenna - **Sheol or Hades** as being "the place of departed spirits or "the unseen state" and also referred to as the grave. Both OT and NT confirm this information – Hebrew word Sheol is translated as hell, grave, and pit – Consideration of these references show that Sheol is "down", "in the depths", "beneath" and it is a place of pain and sorrows.

(Deuteronomy 32:22 KJV) 22 For a fire is kindled in mine anger, and shall burn unto the lowest hell, and shall consume the earth with her increase, and set on fire the foundations of the mountains.

(2 Samuel 22:6 NKJV) 6 The sorrows of Sheol surrounded me; The snares of death confronted me.

(Proverbs 23:14 NKJV) ¹⁴ You shall beat him with a rod, And deliver his soul from hell.

Greek word "Hades" is translated "hell" 10 times and "grave" one time. It seems to be "down", having gates, and is a place for the spirits of the departed dead and is to lose its victory over the righteous, and then is eventually to be cast into the Lake of Fire, final Hell.

(Matthew 11:23 NKJV) ²³ And you, Capernaum, who are exalted to heaven, will be brought down to Hades; for if the mighty works which were done in you had been done in Sodom, it would have remained until this day.

(Acts 2:27 NKJV) ²⁷ *For You will not leave my soul in Hades, Nor will You allow Your Holy One to see corruption.*

(Luke 10:15 NKJV) ¹⁵ And you, Capernaum, who are exalted to heaven, will be brought down to Hades

Tartarus - This Greek word is used once in the New Testament and is translated "Hell". Tartarus is shown to be a prison or a jail specifically for sinning angelic spirit beings, when one reviews
2 Peter 2:4 with Jude 1:6. These fallen angels are held in this place of darkness it being "down" and reserved to be judged at the Great White Throne.

(2 Peter 2:4 HCSB) **4** For if God didn't spare the angels who sinned but threw them down into Tartarus. (NOTE the word Tartarus is translated 'hell' in the KJV and NKJV)

(Jude 1:6 HCSB) **6** and He has kept, with eternal chains in darkness for the judgment of the great day, the angels who did not keep their own position but deserted their proper dwelling.

(1 Corinthians 6:3 KJV) **3** Know ye not that we shall judge angels? how much more things that pertain to this life?

Abyss - This third division is in the deep or the bottomless pit. Various translations describe it – *Hebrew "abaddon"* translated "destruction". *Greek "apollyon"* is the word translated "destruction". *The Deep* is also the Abyss in Revelation and the Bottomless Pit is also considered this.

(Revelation 9:1 HCSB) The fifth angel blew his trumpet, and I saw a star that had fallen from heaven to earth. The key to the shaft of the abyss was given to him
NKJV & KJV translates the word 'abyss' to bottomless pit note below

(Revelation 9:1 NKJV) ¹ Then the fifth angel sounded: And I saw a star fallen from heaven to the earth. To him was given the key to the bottomless pit.

(Job 26:5-6 HCSB) **5** The departed spirits tremble beneath the waters and ⌊all⌋ that inhabit them. **6** Sheol is naked before God, and Abaddon has no covering.

NKJV & KJV translates the word "abaddon" to destruction

(Job 26:5-6 NKJV) 5 "The dead tremble, Those under the waters and those inhabiting them. 6 Sheol *is* naked before Him, And Destruction has no covering.

Additional Scriptures to review
Job 26:6; 28:22; 31:12; Psalm 88:11; Proverbs 27:20; 15:11; Matthew 7:13; Romans 9:22; Philippians 3:19; 2 Peter 2:1; 3:16; Revelation 9:11; Romans 10:7; Luke 8:31; Revelation 9:1-3; 20:1-3,7

Gehenna (Greek word- Geenna) - Means the valley of hinnom south of Jerusalem. It is translated as hell and also several times called "the lake of fire". This Greek word is used in a number of New Testament texts to designate the fiery place for punishment of sinners and is often translated "hell" or "the fires of hell". Gehenna is also usually used in connection with the final judgment and its use suggests that the punishment spoken of is eternal, final hell.

(Revelation 19:20 KJV) 20 And the beast was taken, and with him the false prophet that wrought miracles before him, with which he deceived them that had received the mark of the beast, and them that worshipped his image. These both were cast alive into a lake of fire burning with brimstone.

(Matthew 5:22 KJV) 22 But I say unto you, That whosoever is angry with his brother without a cause shall be in danger of the judgment: and whosoever shall say to his brother, Raca, shall be in danger of the council: but whosoever shall say, Thou fool, shall be in danger of hell fire.

(Revelation 20:10 KJV) 10 And the devil that deceived them was cast into the lake of fire and brimstone, where the beast and the false prophet *are*, and shall be tormented day and night for ever and ever.

The Old Testament equivalent is found in the Hebrew word "Tophet" or "Topheth" which means "alter." When Israel fell into idolatry and began to worship Baal, they used a certain part of the valley on the east side of Jerusalem to burn their children alive and to burn the refuse of the city with fire and brimstone. This part of the valley was called "Tophet" or "Valley of the Dead Bodies". Here wicked kings made their children pass through the fire unto the gods of Baal and Molech, the "sun" and "fire" gods. These thousands of children were placed upon the red hot metal hands of the great idol, and as they were being roasted alive, their agonizing screams were drowned by cymbals and the shouts of frenzied worshippers. They also beat drums to drown out the cries of the children. So it was called the Valley of Hinnom, Valley of the Children of Hinnom, Valley of the Son of Hinnon, Valley of Dead Bodies, and Valley of the groans of the Children– Also this place was the place of all the refuse of the city of Jerusalem. So, Gehenna of the New Testament is equivalent to the Tophet of the Old Testament. ***This is a horrible place and the final hell.***

(Deuteronomy 18:10 NKJV) [10] There shall not be found among you *anyone* who makes his son or his daughter pass through the fire, *or one* who practices witchcraft, *or* a soothsayer, or one who interprets omens, or a sorcerer,

(Jeremiah 7:31 KJV) [31] And they have built the high places of Tophet, which *is* in the valley of the son of Hinnom, to burn their sons and their daughters in the fire; which I commanded *them* not, neither came it into my heart.

Location of Hell

The location of hell is somewhat uncertain. Two major views are held on this. One view holds that it is some special place somewhere in the universe where God will confine the damned criminals of heaven and earth. The other view is that this present earth will become the final hell at the close of the Kingdom period and God's plan, relative to earth. This seems to be the consistent view, as a consideration of 2 Peter 3:3-9 with Revelation 20:11-15; 21:1 seems to indicate.

(2 Peter 3:3-8 KJV) [3] Knowing this first, that there shall come in the last days scoffers, walking after their own lusts, [4] And saying, Where is the promise of his coming? for since the fathers fell asleep, all things continue as *they were* from the beginning of the creation. [5] For this they willingly are ignorant of, that by the word of God the heavens were of old, and the earth standing out of the water and in the water: [6] Whereby the world that then was, being overflowed with water, perished: [7] But the heavens and the earth, which are now, by the same word are kept in store, reserved unto fire against the day of judgment and perdition of ungodly men. [8] But, beloved, be not ignorant of this one thing, that one day *is* with the Lord as a thousand years, and a thousand years as one day.

(Revelation 20:11-15 KJV) [11] And I saw a great white throne, and him that sat on it, from whose face the earth and the heaven fled away; and there was found no place for them. [12] And I saw the dead, small and great, stand before God; and the books were opened: and another book was opened, which is *the book* of life: and the dead were judged out of those things which were written in the books, according to their works. [13] And the sea gave up the dead which were in it; and death and hell delivered up the dead which were in them: and they were judged every man according to their works. [14] And death and hell were cast into the lake of fire. This is the second death. [15] And whosoever was not found written in the book of life was cast into the lake of fire.

Begin With Prayer

Biblical Teaching/Doctrine of Angels

Biblical Building Block # 12

(1 John 4:19 NCSB)

19 We love because He first loved us.

God the creator of all things created them with the nature of Love. The angels of God who were created before mankind were made to worship God and obey His laws of the universe. Sadly a group rebelled and led by one who was known as Lucifer. He was created with beauty and was given much responsibility in the heavens. This same fallen angel now leads a spiritual battle against all that is righteous, holy and of God. So, mankind must be aware of this environment that truly exists and does influence mankind in both good and bad events. Mankind must never praise or worship angels lifting them above or equal to God. Angels have a place such as mankind has a place in the creation of Gods heavens and both have a future of eternity either with God or judged to be outside of the paradise of heaven that Our Lord offers to all those who are obedient to the Godhead.

1. Do you know what the term angel means?

2. Describe the different types of angels.

3. What is the nature of angels?

4. Can you identify some of the characteristics of angels?

5. What are some other titles given to angels?

6. Define the ministry of angels.

7. Do you know what the term Seraphim means?

8. Do you know what the term Cherubim means?

9. Can you explain what the 'Angel of the Lord' is, pertaining to Scripture?

10. Should mankind praise, worship or pray to angels?

Angels

Scripture clearly teaches the existence of angels as mighty created spirit beings, whose chief duties are to worship and serve God. They are not a race, reproducing themselves, but a company created to minister to the heirs of salvation. There are two classes of angels, elect and fallen, and ***MAN IS FORBIDDEN TO WORSHIP EITHER***.

Existence of Angels

Scripture reveals that God has an everlasting kingdom, and in the kingdom there are created spirit beings called angels. These can be identified in two classes; good and evil. The good angels (or elect angels) are concerned with our welfare, the evil (or fallen) angels are out to cause harm to the human race. There are about 300 references to angels in the Bible which substantiates their existence.

The Hebrew word for angel is "*malak*" and means "an agent, a messenger". It is generally translated "angel" or "messenger". The Greek word for angel is "*angelos*" which also means "messenger". These words are used of God, of men, and of the angelic beings. Only the surrounding context will clarify which is being referred to, but in most instances it is the angelic beings.

In both the Old Testament and New Testament there are accounts of angels ministering to the people of God. Nearly all of the great men of the Bible exhibited a belief in the existence of angels. The Lord Jesus Christ Himself spoke often of the angels, and was also ministered to by them. In fact, the Bible reports that at times people unwittingly entertained angels.

(Mark 8:38 KJV) 38 Whosoever therefore shall be ashamed of me and of my words in this adulterous and sinful generation; of him also shall the Son of man be ashamed, when he cometh in the glory of his Father with the holy angels.

(Hebrews 12:22 KJV) 22 But ye are come unto mount Sion, and unto the city of the living God, the heavenly Jerusalem, and to an innumerable company of angels,

(2 Thessalonians 1:7 KJV) 7 And to you who are troubled rest with us, when the Lord Jesus shall be revealed from heaven with his mighty angels,

Order of Angels

The universe is a kingdom that belongs to God, the King. There is a divine order within this kingdom. This divine order involves the Eternal Godhead as the Father, Son and Holy Spirit and various orders of created angelic beings. Scripture speaks about archangels, principalities, powers, seraphim, cherubim, the Angel of the Lord and then also an indefinite number of angels.

The Godhead

Angels are created beings which are to worship and serve their creator. Their creator is the Eternal Godhead being the Father, Son and Holy Spirit.

(Matthew 28:19-20 KJV) **19** Go ye therefore, and teach all nations, baptizing them in the name of the Father, and of the Son, and of the Holy Ghost: **20** Teaching them to observe all things whatsoever I have commanded you: and, lo, I am with you alway, *even* unto the end of the world. Amen.

(1 Peter 3:22 KJV) **22** Who is gone into heaven, and is on the right hand of God; angels and authorities and powers being made subject unto him.

(Colossians 1:16 NKJV) **16** For by Him all things were created that are in heaven and that are on earth, visible and invisible, whether thrones or dominions or principalities or powers. All things were created through Him and for Him.

The Archangels

There are 12 archangels which is the number of divine government in the Hebrew tradition. Scripture in the whole context would confirm this tradition of the number 12. Jesus said that He could have prayed to His Father and immediately be given twelve legions of angels to deliver Him from the multitude. Three archangels are specifically mentioned in the Bible.

Lucifer

The name Lucifer has a meaning of "Day Star", or "Son of the Morning". He is shown as the archangel who was associated with the throne of God, as the leader of the worship of God among the angelic hosts. Because of his pride, rebellion and disobedience he fell from this holy place.

(Isaiah 14:12-15 HCSB) **12** Shining morning star, how you have fallen from the heavens! You destroyer of nations, you have been cut down to the ground. **13** You said to yourself: "I will ascend to the heavens; I will set up my throne above the stars of God. I will sit on the mount of the ⌊gods'⌋ assembly, in the remotest parts of the North. **14** I will ascend above the highest clouds; I will make myself like the Most High." **15** But you will be brought down to Sheol into the deepest regions of the Pit.

Michael

Michael is specifically called an archangel. Michael's name has a meaning of "Who is like God" or "God-Like". His activities are mentioned in four specific accounts. He is stated as being the chief prince of the nation of Israel in the Old Testament. His activities are always seen in connection with warfare with Satan and with the resurrection of the body.

(Daniel 10:21 KJV) **21** But I will shew thee that which is noted in the scripture of truth: and *there is* none that holdeth with me in these things, but Michael your prince.

(Jude 1:9 NKJV) **9** Yet Michael the archangel, in contending with the devil, when he disputed about the body of Moses, dared not bring against him a reviling accusation, but said, "The Lord rebuke you!"

(Revelation 12:7-9 KJV) **7** And there was war in heaven: Michael and his angels fought against the dragon; and the dragon fought and his angels, **8** And prevailed not; neither was their place found any more in heaven. **9** And the great dragon was cast out, that old serpent, called the Devil, and Satan, which deceiveth the whole world: he was cast out into the earth, and his angels were cast out with him.

Gabriel

The angel Gabriel is generally accepted as an archangel. Gabriel's name means "Strength of God". He is mentioned as a prophetic angel, the messenger and interpreter of the prophetic Word concerning the Christ of God. He also appeared to Daniel twice and then to Zacharias, John the Baptist's father, and then to Mary the virgin mother of Jesus. Each of these visitations involved Messianic revelation.

(Daniel 8:16-17 KJV) **16** And I heard a man's voice between *the banks of* Ulai, which called, and said, Gabriel, make this *man* to understand the vision. **17** So he came near where I stood: and when he came, I was afraid, and fell upon my face: but he said unto me, Understand, O son of man: for at the time of the end *shall be* the vision.

(Luke 1:19 HCSB) **19** The angel answered him, "I am Gabriel, who stands in the presence of God, and I was sent to speak to you and tell you this good news.

The Multitude of the Angelic Hosts

Scripture clearly show that there are innumerable legions of angelic beings. They speak of thousands or multitudes of spirit beings that worship and serve God. Two groups are mentioned in Scripture, Elect angels who are the angels who DID NOT join or follow Lucifer's rebellion against God and the Fallen angels who fell to sin by joining Lucifer in his rebellion against God.

(Daniel 7:9-10 KJV) **9** I beheld till the thrones were cast down, and the Ancient of days did sit, whose garment *was* white as snow, and the hair of his head like the pure wool: his throne *was like* the fiery flame, *and* his wheels *as* burning fire. **10** A fiery stream issued and came forth from before him: thousand thousands ministered unto him, and ten thousand times ten thousand stood before him: the judgment was set, and the books were opened.

(Revelation 5:11 KJV) **11** And I beheld, and I heard the voice of many angels round about the throne and the beasts and the elders: and the number of them was ten thousand times ten thousand, and thousands of thousands;

(1 Timothy 5:21 NKJV) [21] I charge *you* before God and the Lord Jesus Christ and the elect angels that you observe these things without prejudice, doing nothing with partiality.

(2 Peter 2:4 NKJV) [4] For if God did not spare the angels who sinned, but cast *them* down to hell and delivered *them* into chains of darkness, to be reserved for judgment;

(Jude 1:6-9 KJV) [6] And the angels which kept not their first estate, but left their own habitation, he hath reserved in everlasting chains under darkness unto the judgment of the great day. [7] Even as Sodom and Gomorrha, and the cities about them in like manner, giving themselves over to fornication, and going after strange flesh, are set forth for an example, suffering the vengeance of eternal fire. [8] Likewise also these *filthy* dreamers defile the flesh, despise dominion, and speak evil of dignities. [9] Yet Michael the archangel, when contending with the devil he disputed about the body of Moses, durst not bring against him a railing accusation, but said, The Lord rebuke thee.

The Heavenly Sanhedrin (theory) → *(the point is, there is an Order)*

The heavenly order and pattern in the Kingdom of God may be understood by the earthly shadow and manifestation in the Kingdom of God on earth. The Scriptures speak of principalities, powers, rulers and wicked spirits in the Kingdom of Satan, which is simply a counterfeit of God's Kingdom. We have some clues as to what the divine order seems to be.

Within the Jewish Sanhedrin, there consisted of 70 elders of Israel with the High Priest who was the President. Jewish tradition states that there are 70 angels as princes over the 70 nations of which the human family was divided at the Tower of Babel. These 70 angels constituted the heavenly Sanhedrin. Shadows of this seem to be seen on earth in the order of the seventies in Israel's history, and in the New Testament. Angels or princes of the nations are spoken of.

Moses set 12 pillars up at Mt. Sinai and had 70 elders with him from the camp of Israel. There were 12 wells of water and 70 palm trees at Elim which blessed the nation of Israel. The Jewish nation had 70 elders which comprised their council. The Lord Jesus chose 12 apostles and then 70 others for the ministry of healing and preaching the Gospel of the Kingdom. If this order was but the earthly shadow and manifestation of the heavenly pattern, then it indeed points to the 12 archangels and the 70 angels of the heavenly council of Sanhedrin.

Heavenly order	Israel's Order	New Testament Order
Father, Son, and Spirit	Abraham, Isaac, Jacob	Father, Son, and Spirit
12 Archangels	12 Sons of Israel	12 Apostles
70 Angels	70 Souls	70 Others
Multitude of Angelic hosts	Multitude of Israel's hosts	Multitude of Believers, the Church

(Ephesians 6:12 NKJV) ¹² For we do not wrestle against flesh and blood, but against principalities, against powers, against the rulers of the darkness of this age, against spiritual *hosts* of wickedness in the heavenly *places.*

(Exodus 15:27 NKJV) ²⁷ Then they came to Elim, where there *were* twelve wells of water and seventy palm trees; so they camped there by the waters.

(Luke 9:1-2 NKJV) ¹ Then He called His twelve disciples together and gave them power and authority over all demons, and to cure diseases. ² He sent them to preach the kingdom of God and to heal the sick.

(Luke 10:1-2 NKJV) ¹ After these things the Lord appointed seventy others also, and sent them two by two before His face into every city and place where He Himself was about to go. ² Then He said to them, "The harvest truly *is* great, but the laborers *are* few; therefore pray the Lord of the harvest to send out laborers into His harvest.

(Exodus 24:1-11 KJV) ¹ And he said unto Moses, Come up unto the LORD, thou, and Aaron, Nadab, and Abihu, and seventy of the elders of Israel; and worship ye afar off. ² And Moses alone shall come near the LORD: but they shall not come nigh; neither shall the people go up with him. ³ And Moses came and told the people all the words of the LORD, and all the judgments: and all the people answered with one voice, and said, All the words which the LORD hath said will we do. ⁴ And Moses wrote all the words of the LORD, and rose up early in the morning, and builded an altar under the hill, and twelve pillars, according to the twelve tribes of Israel. ⁵ And he sent young men of the children of Israel, which offered burnt offerings, and sacrificed peace offerings of oxen unto the LORD. ⁶ And Moses took half of the blood, and put *it* in basons; and half of the blood he sprinkled on the altar. ⁷ And he took the book of the covenant, and read in the audience of the people: and they said, All that the LORD hath said will we do, and be obedient. ⁸ And Moses took the blood, and sprinkled *it* on the people, and said, Behold the blood of the covenant, which the LORD hath made with you concerning all these words. ⁹ Then went up Moses, and Aaron, Nadab, and Abihu, and seventy of the elders of Israel: ¹⁰ And they saw the God of Israel: and *there was* under his feet as it were a paved work of a sapphire stone, and as it were the body of heaven in *his* clearness. ¹¹ And upon the nobles of the children of Israel he laid not his hand: also they saw God, and did eat and drink.

Nature of Angels

They are created beings under the authority of God their creator, both the elect and fallen angels.	(Revelation 4:11 KJV) ¹¹ "You are worthy, O Lord, To receive glory and honor and power; For You created all things, And by Your will they exist and were created."
They are Spirit Beings active in the heavens.	(Hebrews 1:13-14 KJV) ¹³ But to which of the angels said he at any time, Sit on my right hand, until I make thine enemies thy footstool? ¹⁴ Are they not all ministering spirits, sent forth to minister for them who

	shall be heirs of salvation?
They are a company of beings, not a race. Not involved in marriage and do not reproduce their kind. They were created as individual spirit beings. The angels which sinned each sinned as individuals, therefore sin is not transmitted as it is in the human race from Adam to his unborn offspring.	(Luke 20:34-36 NKJV) ³⁴ And Jesus answered and said to them, "The sons of this age marry and are given in marriage. ³⁵ But those who are counted worthy to attain that age, and the resurrection from the dead, neither marry nor are given in marriage; ³⁶ nor can they die anymore, for they are equal to the angels and are sons of God, being sons of the resurrection.
Are innumerable, angels are great in number.	(Hebrews 12:22 NKJV) ²² But you have come to Mount Zion and to the city of the living God, the heavenly Jerusalem, to an innumerable company of angels, (Revelation 5:11 NKJV) ¹¹ Then I looked, and I heard the voice of many angels around the throne, the living creatures, and the elders; and the number of them was ten thousand times ten thousand, and thousands of thousands,
They are higher than mankind, in the order of created beings, angels are the first before mankind. The Scriptures show that mankind was made a little lower than the angels. Mankind is a triune being consisting of spirit, soul and body, angels are spirit beings, a higher order. Angels are inferior to their creator, God.	(Hebrews 2:7 NKJV) ⁶ But one testified in a certain place, saying: *"What is man that You are mindful of him, Or the son of man that You take care of him? ⁷ You have made him a little lower than the angels; You have crowned him with glory and honor, And set him over the works of Your hands.* (Psalm 8:4-5 NKJV) ⁴ What is man that You are mindful of him, And the son of man that You visit him? ⁵ For You have made him a little lower than the angels, And You have crowned him with glory and honor.
They have the power of choice, a free will.	(Jude 1:6 NKJV) ⁶ And the angels who did not keep their proper domain, but left their own abode, He has reserved in everlasting chains under darkness for the judgment of the great day;
Have personalities and are not mere good or evil influences, having intelligence and assignments.	(Matthew 18:10 NKJV) ¹⁰ "Take heed that you do not despise one of these little ones, for I say to you that in heaven their angels always see the face of My Father who is in heaven.

Character of Angels

Worship → Elect angels direct all worship to God and are symbolic of the "church in heaven".	(Luke 2:13 NKJV) ¹³ And suddenly there was with the angel a multitude of the heavenly host praising God and saying:
Obedience →Is immediate and with out question.	(Matthew 26:53 NKJV) ⁵³ Or do you think that I cannot now pray to My Father, and He will provide

	Me with more than twelve legions of angels?
Can have Knowledge → They are intelligent beings.	(Mark 13:32 NKJV) ³² "But of that day and hour no one knows, not even the angels in heaven, nor the Son, but only the Father.
They are Powerful → They are mighty as God has given them might but are humble in character.	(2 Peter 2:11 NKJV) ¹¹ whereas angels, who are greater in power and might, do not bring a reviling accusation against them before the Lord.
Holiness → Their character is of holiness towards God.	(Mark 8:38 NKJV) ³⁸ For whoever is ashamed of Me and My words in this adulterous and sinful generation, of him the Son of Man also will be ashamed when He comes in the glory of His Father with the holy angels."
Joy → Angels rejoiced in heaven over anyone who is redeemed.	(Luke 15:10 NKJV) ¹⁰ Likewise, I say to you, there is joy in the presence of the angels of God over one sinner who repents."

Titles of Angels

Watchers	(Daniel 4:13 NKJV) ¹³ "I saw in the visions of my head *while* on my bed, and there was a watcher, a holy one, coming down from heaven.
Heavenly Host	(Luke 2:13 NKJV) ¹³ And suddenly there was with the angel a multitude of the heavenly host praising God and saying:
Holy angels	(Matthew 25:31 NKJV) ³¹ When the Son of man shall come in his glory, and all the holy angels with him, then shall he sit upon the throne of his glory:
Ministering Spirits → servants of God.	(Hebrews 1:13-14 KJV) ¹³ But to which of the angels said he at any time, Sit on my right hand, until I make thine enemies thy footstool? ¹⁴ Are they not all ministering spirits, sent forth to minister for them who shall be heirs of salvation?
The Elect → angels who refused to follow Satan against God.	(1 Timothy 5:21 NKJV) ²¹ I charge *you* before God and the Lord Jesus Christ and the elect angels that you observe these things without prejudice, doing nothing with partiality.
Sons of God → created sons of God not begotten sons of God, as are human born again believers.	(Luke 20:34-36 NKJV) ³⁴ And Jesus answered and said to them, "The sons of this age marry and are given in marriage. ³⁵ But those who are counted worthy to attain that age, and the resurrection from the dead, neither marry nor are given in marriage; ³⁶ nor can they die anymore, for they are equal to the angels and are sons of God, being sons of the resurrection.

Ministry of Angels

The ministry and function of angels is primarily worship and service to doing Gods will. The elect angels are also ministering spirits to heirs of salvation. Angels have been given a charge over the saints to keep them in all their ways. Eternity alone will reveal the ministry that angels have rendered to the believers, the heirs of salvation. The angels will have kept their charge over us. The believer may thank God for the unseen ministry of these ministering spirits.

(Hebrews 1:14 KJV) **14** Are they not all ministering spirits, sent forth to minister for them who shall be heirs of salvation?

(Psalms 103:20-21 KJV) **20** Bless the LORD, ye his angels, that excel in strength, that do his commandments, hearkening unto the voice of his word. **21** Bless ye the LORD, all *ye* his hosts; *ye* ministers of his, that do his pleasure.

(Psalms 91:11-12 KJV) **11** For he shall give his angels charge over thee, to keep thee in all thy ways. **12** They shall bear thee up in *their* hands, lest thou dash thy foot against a stone.

Angels and the Gospel

The Gospel is never to be preached by the angels to sinners because they can never experience being redeemed from sin, as mankind can. Peter tells us that the angels desire to look into the mystery of our great salvation as foretold by the Old Testament prophets. However, God did use the angels to make special announcements relative to the Gospel.

(1 Peter 1:9-12 NKJV) **9** receiving the end of your faith--the salvation of *your* souls. **10** Of this salvation the prophets have inquired and searched carefully, who prophesied of the grace *that would come* to you, **11** searching what, or what manner of time, the Spirit of Christ who was in them was indicating when He testified beforehand the sufferings of Christ and the glories that would follow. **12** To them it was revealed that, not to themselves, but to us they were ministering the things which now have been reported to you through those who have preached the gospel to you by the Holy Spirit sent from heaven--things which angels desire to look into.

(Luke 2:10-11 NKJV) **10** Then the angel said to them, "Do not be afraid, for behold, I bring you good tidings of great joy which will be to all people. **11** For there is born to you this day in the city of David a Savior, who is Christ the Lord.

(Acts 8:26 NKJV) **26** Now an angel of the Lord spoke to Philip, saying, "Arise and go toward the south along the road which goes down from Jerusalem to Gaza." This is desert.

Angels in Old Testament, New Testament and in the Book of Revelation

Angels in Old Testament	
Ministered to Hagar and Ishmael.	(Genesis 16:10-11 KJV) **10** And the angel of the LORD said unto her, I will multiply thy seed exceedingly, that

	it shall not be numbered for multitude. ¹¹ And the angel of the LORD said unto her, Behold, thou *art* with child, and shalt bear a son, and shalt call his name Ishmael; because the LORD hath heard thy affliction.
3 angels visited Abraham and Sarah.	(Genesis 18:2 KJV) ² And he lift up his eyes and looked, and, lo, three men stood by him: and when he saw *them*, he ran to meet them from the tent door, and bowed himself toward the ground,
2 angels rescued Lot out of Sodom.	(Genesis 19:1 KJV) ¹ And there came two angels to Sodom at even; and Lot sat in the gate of Sodom: and Lot seeing *them* rose up to meet them; and he bowed himself with his face toward the ground;
Moses received the revelation of the Name of God from the Angel of the Lord in the burning bush.	(Exodus 3:2 NKJV) ² And the angel of the LORD appeared unto him in a flame of fire out of the midst of a bush: and he looked, and, behold, the bush burned with fire, and the bush *was* not consumed.
Angels were involved in the giving of the Law to Moses at Sinai.	(Galatians 3;19 NKJV) ¹⁹ What purpose then *does* the law *serve?* It was added because of transgressions, till the Seed should come to whom the promise was made; *and it was* appointed through angels by the hand of a mediator.
An Angel destroyed 70,000 Israelites when David sinned in numbering the people without the atonement money.	(2 Samuel 24:16-17 KJV) ¹⁶ And when the angel stretched out his hand upon Jerusalem to destroy it, the LORD repented him of the evil, and said to the angel that destroyed the people, It is enough: stay now thine hand. And the angel of the LORD was by the threshingplace of Araunah the Jebusite. ¹⁷ And David spake unto the LORD when he saw the angel that smote the people, and said, Lo, I have sinned, and I have done wickedly: but these sheep, what have they done? let thine hand, I pray thee, be against me, and against my father's house
Daniel was preserved by an angel in the lion's den.	(Daniel 6:22 KJV) ²² My God hath sent his angel, and hath shut the lions' mouths, that they have not hurt me: forasmuch as before him innocency was found in me; and also before thee, O king, have I done no hurt.
Angels in the New Testament	
Ministry of the Lord Jesus.	(1 Timothy 3:16 NKJV) ¹⁶ And without controversy great is the mystery of godliness: God was manifested in the flesh, Justified in the Spirit, Seen by angels,

	Preached among the Gentiles, Believed on in the world, Received up in glory.
During the birth of Jesus, spoke to Mary.	(Luke 1:26-28 NKJV) 26 Now in the sixth month the angel Gabriel was sent by God to a city of Galilee named Nazareth, 27 to a virgin betrothed to a man whose name was Joseph, of the house of David. The virgin's name *was* Mary. 28 And having come in, the angel said to her, "Rejoice, highly favored *one,* the Lord *is* with you; blessed *are* you among women!"
During the birth of Jesus, spoke to Joseph.	(Matthew 1:20 NKJV) 20 But while he thought about these things, behold, an angel of the Lord appeared to him in a dream, saying, "Joseph, son of David, do not be afraid to take to you Mary your wife, for that which is conceived in her is of the Holy Spirit.
Spoke to the shepherds.	(Luke 2:9-10 NKJV) 9 And behold, an angel of the Lord stood before them, and the glory of the Lord shone around them, and they were greatly afraid. 10 Then the angel said to them, "Do not be afraid, for behold, I bring you good tidings of great joy which will be to all people
In His temptation angels ministered to Jesus afterwards.	(Matthew 4:11 NKJV) 11 Then the devil left Him, and behold, angels came and ministered to Him.
During Jesus Ministry they ascended and descended upon the Son of Man.	(John 1:51 NKJV) 51 And He said to him, "Most assuredly, I say to you, hereafter you shall see heaven open, and the angels of God ascending and descending upon the Son of Man."
At the Resurrection, angels were seen in the empty tomb after the resurrection.	(Luke 24:23 NKJV) 23 When they did not find His body, they came saying that they had also seen a vision of angels who said He was alive
Angels opened the prison doors to release the apostles to witness.	(Acts 5:19 NKJV) 19 But at night an angel of the Lord opened the prison doors and brought them out, and said, ,
Phillip was sent by an angel to the desert to witness to the Ethiopian.	(Acts 8:26 NKJV) 26 Now an angel of the Lord spoke to Philip, saying, "Arise and go toward the south along the road which goes down from Jerusalem to Gaza." This is desert
An angel instructed Cornelius to send for Peter to hear the words of the Gospel.	(Acts 10:3 NKJV) 3 About the ninth hour of the day he saw clearly in a vision an angel of God coming in and saying to him, "Cornelius!"
The saints are forbidden to worship angels.	(Revelation 22:8-9 KJV) 8 And I John saw these things, and heard *them.* And when I had heard and seen, I fell down to worship before the feet of the angel which shewed me these things. 9 Then saith he unto me, See *thou do it* not: for I am thy fellowservant, and of thy brethren the prophets, and of them which keep the

	sayings of this book: worship God.
Saints are to judge the angels in due time.	(1 Corinthians 6:3 NKJV) ³ Do you not know that we shall judge angels? How much more, things that pertain to this life?

Angels in the Book of Revelation

Innumerable angels worship God and the Lamb.	(Revelation 5:11 KJV) ¹¹ And I beheld, and I heard the voice of many angels round about the throne and the beasts and the elders: and the number of them was ten thousand times ten thousand, and thousands of thousands;
Four angels restrain the winds of judgment.	(Revelation 7:1 KJV) ¹ And after these things I saw four angels standing on the four corners of the earth, holding the four winds of the earth, that the wind should not blow on the earth, nor on the sea, nor on any tree.
Seven angels sounded the 7 trumpets of judgment.	(Revelation 8:2 KJV) ² And I saw the seven angels which stood before God; and to them were given seven trumpets.
Michael and his angels engage in war with Satan and his angels and cast them out.	(Revelation 12:7 KJV) ⁷ And there was war in heaven: Michael and his angels fought against the dragon; and the dragon fought and his angels,
Angelic ministry is evident in the judgments of the earth.	(Revelation 14:6 KJV) ⁶ And I saw another angel fly in the midst of heaven, having the everlasting gospel to preach unto them that dwell on the earth, and to every nation, and kindred, and tongue, and people,
John saw an angel standing in the sun calling for the birds and beasts to the supper of the wicked.	(Revelation 19:17 KJV) ¹⁷ And I saw an angel standing in the sun; and he cried with a loud voice, saying to all the fowls that fly in the midst of heaven, Come and gather yourselves together unto the supper of the great God;

Usage of the word Angel

The word "angel" is used in Scripture of various groupings of persons, and only the immediate context will determine who the "angel-messenger" referred to may be. Ministers of the churches or God's prophets are also spoken of as being "angels". Israel was God's messenger. Haggai the prophet was God's messenger, John the Baptist was spoken of as the "messenger of the Lord" and Jesus Christ Himself is spoken of as "The Messenger of the Covenant".

(Malachi 2:7 KJV) ⁷ For the priest's lips should keep knowledge, and they should seek the law at his mouth: for he *is* the messenger of the LORD of hosts.

(Haggai 1:13 KJV) **13** Then spake Haggai the LORD'S messenger in the LORD'S message unto the people, saying, I *am* with you, saith the LORD.

(Revelation 22:16 KJV) **16** I Jesus have sent mine angel to testify unto you these things in the churches. I am the root and the offspring of David, *and* the bright and morning star.

The Seraphim

In Scripture there are only two references to the angelic being call Seraphims. The title means "The Burning Ones". They are especially seen in relation to the throne and holiness of God.

Seraphim's have six wings; two to cover their feet (significant of holy service); two to cover their face (significant of their awe and reverence) and two to fly with (significant of their obedience to God's Will). Their constant cry "Holy, Holy, Holy is the Lord of Hosts, the whole earth is full of His glory" magnifies the holiness of God. Also, the Seraphims is seen ministering the coal of cleansing from the alter to the lips of the prophet Isaiah. In this vision of Isaiah Jesus said it was of the messiah Himself.

(Isaiah 6:2-4 KJV) **2** Above it stood the seraphims: each one had six wings; with twain he covered his face, and with twain he covered his feet, and with twain he did fly. **3** And one cried unto another, and said, Holy, holy, holy, *is* the LORD of hosts: the whole earth *is* full of his glory. **4** And the posts of the door moved at the voice of him that cried, and the house was filled with smoke.

(Isaiah 6:6 KJV) **6** Then flew one of the seraphims unto me, having a live coal in his hand, *which* he had taken with the tongs from off the altar:

The Cherubim

Many expositors hold that the Cherubim are a distinct order of angelic beings. A second opinion is that the Cherubim are representatives or symbolic of the blessed Godhead and a third opinion held by some expositors is that the Cherubim, especially those seen in visions by Ezekiel and John, are symbolic of the redeemed saints.

(Ezekiel 10:15-19 KJV) **15** And the cherubims were lifted up. This *is* the living creature that I saw by the river of Chebar. **16** And when the cherubims went, the wheels went by them: and when the cherubims lifted up their wings to mount up from the earth, the same wheels also turned not from beside them. **17** When they stood, *these* stood; and when they were lifted up, *these* lifted up themselves *also*: for the spirit of the living creature *was* in them. **18** Then the glory of the LORD departed from off the threshold of the house, and stood over the cherubims. **19** And the cherubims lifted up their wings, and mounted up from the earth in my sight: when they went out, the wheels also *were* beside them, and *every one* stood at the door of the east gate of the LORD'S house; and the glory of the God of Israel *was* over them above.

(Hebrews 9:5 KJV) **5** And over it the cherubims of glory shadowing the mercyseat; of which we cannot now speak particularly.

The Angel of the Lord

The most prominent angelic manifestation of the Godhead is that of the "Angel of the Lord", the pre-incarnate Christ of God. The Lord Jesus is revealed as the Angel of the Lord

(Exodus 3:2-4 KJV) **2** And the angel of the LORD appeared unto him in a flame of fire out of the midst of a bush: and he looked, and, behold, the bush burned with fire, and the bush *was* not consumed. **3** And Moses said, I will now turn aside, and see this great sight, why the bush is not burnt. **4** And when the LORD saw that he turned aside to see, God called unto him out of the midst of the bush, and said, Moses, Moses. And he said, Here *am* I.

The Angel of the Lord is the final area pertaining to Angelology which has some mystery around it. In the Old Testament this mystery of the Angel of the Lord or more correctly stated, "The Jehovah Angel" appears. Some expositors understand these appearances often to be a theophany or an appearance of the Lord Jesus Christ before His incarnation.

The word theophany comes from two Greek words: "theos" meaning "God" and "phaneroo", meaning "appearance". A theophany is simply an appearance of God and more particularly in the OT was an appearance of the Son of God before His incarnation. A theophany was a temporary manifestation in human form.

Incarnation is the embodiment of God in the human form of Jesus. This is God manifested in the flesh (1 Timothy 3:16). When the eternal Son of God was born of the Virgin Mary, it was not a mere temporary appearance (theophany), it was an incarnation. Jesus now has an eternal body.
Before the cross, God the Son would appear temporarily. The incarnation is the eternal manifestation of God the Son. The incarnation was begotten and born in human form, and then, after the resurrection, eternally glorified. Glorified humanity is upon the Christ of God, the eternal Son.

Jesus Christ the Lord is NOT an angel or a created being, but God. The theophanies were only temporary manifestations of Him appearing as an angel, or as a man, this happened all before His incarnation. During the Old Testament times Jesus Christ was seen as the Jehovah-Angel, temporary manifestations. Now in the New Testament times, He is the Jehovah-Man in the incarnation. Following are some verses describing the Angel of the Lord.

The Angel of the Lord slew 185,000 Assyrians in one night, thus saving Judah.	(2 Kings 19:35 KJV) **35** And it came to pass that night, that the angel of the LORD went out, and smote in the camp of the Assyrians an hundred fourscore and five thousand: and when they arose early in the morning,

	behold, they *were* all dead corpses.
Balaam saw the Angel of the Lord with the drawn sword.	(Numbers 22:22-23 KJV) **22** And God's anger was kindled because he went: and the angel of the LORD stood in the way for an adversary against him. Now he was riding upon his ass, and his two servants *were* with him. **23** And the ass saw the angel of the LORD standing in the way, and his sword drawn in his hand: and the ass turned aside out of the way, and went into the field: and Balaam smote the ass, to turn her into the way
Appeared to Moses in a flame of fire within a bush.	(Exodus 3:2 KJV) **2** And the angel of the LORD appeared unto him in a flame of fire out of the midst of a bush: and he looked, and, behold, the bush burned with fire, and the bush *was* not consumed.
Appeared to Gideon supporting him as a warrior.	(Judges 6:11-12 KJV) **11** And there came an angel of the LORD, and sat under an oak which *was* in Ophrah, that *pertained* unto Joash the Abiezrite: and his son Gideon threshed wheat by the winepress, to hide *it* from the Midianites. **12** And the angel of the LORD appeared unto him, and said unto him, The LORD *is* with thee, thou mighty man of valour.

The Book of Revelation contains accounts of the risen, glorified Son of God who is seen by John as the Jehovah Angel.	
The Angel-Sealer who comes with the seal of the living God points to the Lord Jesus Christ. No ordinary angel can perform such a sealing of the Spirit and name of God.	(Revelation 7:2 KJV) **2** And I saw another angel ascending from the east, having the seal of the living God: and he cried with a loud voice to the four angels, to whom it was given to hurt the earth and the sea,
The Angel-Priest with the golden censer, who offers the prayers of the saints on the golden alter before God points to the Lord Jesus Christ. No angel can take the prayers of the saints and offer them to God. There is only one Mediator between God and man, the man Christ Jesus.	(Revelation 8:1-3 KJV) **1** And when he had opened the seventh seal, there was silence in heaven about the space of half an hour. **2** And I saw the seven angels which stood before God; and to them were given seven trumpets. **3** And another angel came and stood at the altar, having a golden censer; and there was given unto him much incense, that he should offer *it* with the prayers of all saints upon the golden altar which was before the throne.

Prayer and worship to angels is forbidden.	
The Angel-Redeemer, clothed with a cloud, His face as the sun, having the little open book in His hand, whose voice is as the voice of a lion, and who speaks of "My two witnesses" points to the Lord Jesus Christ not to any servant angelic being.	(Revelation 10:1-5 KJV) And I saw another mighty angel come down from heaven, clothed with a cloud: and a rainbow *was* upon his head, and his face *was* as it were the sun, and his feet as pillars of fire: **2** And he had in his hand a little book open: and he set his right foot upon the sea, and *his* left *foot* on the earth, **3** And cried with a loud voice, as *when* a lion roareth: and when he had cried, seven thunders uttered their voices. **4** And when the seven thunders had uttered their voices, I was about to write: and I heard a voice from heaven saying unto me, Seal up those things which the seven thunders uttered, and write them not. **5** And the angel which I saw stand upon the sea and upon the earth lifted up his hand to heaven,
The "Angel-Avenger" who lightens the earth with His glory points to Christ also.	(Revelation 18:1 KJV) **1** And after these things I saw another angel come down from heaven, having great power; and the earth was lightened with his glory.
The "Angel-Binder", who binds Satan and casts him into the bottomless pit for one thousand years also points to Jesus Christ. He is the stronger man who binds the strong man, and then spoils his house. This was judicially accomplished at Calvary.	(Revelation 20:1-3 KJV) **1** And I saw an angel come down from heaven, having the key of the bottomless pit and a great chain in his hand. **2** And he laid hold on the dragon, that old serpent, which is the Devil, and Satan, and bound him a thousand years, **3** And cast him into the bottomless pit, and shut him up, and set a seal upon him, that he should deceive the nations no more, till the thousand years should be fulfilled: and after that he must be loosed a little season. (with Matthew 12:28-29 HCSB)**28** If I drive out demons by the Spirit of God, then the kingdom of God has come to you. **29** How can someone enter a strong man's house and steal his possessions unless he first ties up the strong man? Then he can rob his house.

HOWEVER ☐ **it should be constantly remembered that mankind is forbidden to worship angels, or to go beyond that which is revealed in the Word of God. All worship must go the Eternal Godhead, the Father, Son and Holy Spirit. Also, saints are not to be worshiped or prayed to, this includes Mary who gave birth to Jesus; only God should be prayed to.**

(Colossians 2:18 NKJV) 18 Let no one cheat you of your reward, taking delight in false humility and worship of angels, intruding into those things which he has not seen, vainly puffed up by his fleshly mind,

(1 Peter 3:22 NKJV) 22 who has gone into heaven and is at the right hand of God, angels and authorities and powers having been made subject to Him.

(Revelation 22:8-9 NKJV) Now I, John, saw and heard these things. And when I heard and saw, I fell down to worship before the feet of the angel who showed me these things. 9 Then he said to me, "See that you do not do that. For I am your fellow servant, and of your brethren the prophets, and of those who keep the words of this book. Worship God."

Begin With Prayer

Biblical Teaching/Doctrine of Demonology and Satan

Biblical Building Block # 13

(Colossians 1:13-14 HCSB)

13 He has rescued us from the domain of darkness and transferred us into the kingdom of the Son He loves. **14** We have redemption, the forgiveness of sins, in Him.

As we venture into this doctrine we must put into perspective the fact that God loves mankind so much that He has given us a pathway from the darkness of the kingdom of lies and deception. Through Jesus Christ we have victory over all evil of this world and any in the heavens. We must never believe that the evil one/s has power over God or His children, but that through Jesus Christ and walking in the Holy Spirit we are empowered to conquer anything in Christ. At the same time we must also realize that we fight a spiritual battle and must be well aware of what we should be doing to avoid being tripped up. We must put on the armor of God. Not worldly armor of man's philosophies or his wisdom but using the Word of the Living God, Jesus.

1. Can you explain the origin of Satan?

2. Describe the difference between Lucifer and Satan.

3. What is the nature of Satan?

4. Describe the activities of Satan.

5. What are evil spirits?

6. What are demons?

7. What activities do evil spirits and demons do?

8. What does occult mean to you?

9. As a believer in Jesus Christ what must one do to protect themselves from the attacks of Satan and his followers?

10. What is the major battle ground in the spiritual warfare against Satan's evil kingdom?

Kingdom of Darkness

The Reality

There is a kingdom of darkness in the universe and encompassing the planet earth as the Scriptures indicate. It is antithesis (direct contrast – exact opposite) of the kingdom of God. This kingdom is under the control of Satan and also under his authority are numerous fallen angels and demon spirits.

There is a tremendous increase of activity in the satanic realm within all nations of the world (Hollywood leading the charge in promoting curiosity). In 1Timothy 4:1-3 Paul warned us that in the last day's people would depart from the faith and give heed to seducing spirits and to doctrines of devils. There are many teachings today that are not of God being accepted by mankind and causing a drifting from the faith.

(1 Timothy 4:1-3 HCSB) **1** Now the Spirit explicitly says that in later times some will depart from the faith, paying attention to deceitful spirits and the teachings of demons, **2** through the hypocrisy of liars whose consciences are seared. **3** They forbid marriage and demand abstinence from foods that God created to be received with gratitude by those who believe and know the truth.

Satan's existence, power, and influence is either ignored or over-emphasized by believers and non-believers disregard his presence completely. A position Satan enjoys. Only through the Scriptures can one gain a proper understanding of this subject as well as helping others to.

God Kingdom	Satan's Kingdom
Of Light	Of Darkness
Of Holiness and Righteousness	Of Sin and Unrighteousness
Of Healing and Health (referring to spirit, mind and body)	Of Sickness and Disease
Of Truth	Of Deception and Lies
Of Joy and Life (eternal)	Of Sorrow and Death (eternal separation form God and all that is good)

Domain

The word "domain" refers to "the rule, reign and territory over which a king rules". The domain of the kingdom of darkness is wherever Satan exercises his dominion. Satan's domain and kingdom is completely opposite and contrary to the Kingdom of God in all aspects, nature, character and purpose. **It is essential to understand that the extent of Satan's domain is limited by God. He cannot exercise authority where God does not allow.**

Following References Describe this Kingdom

It is called Satan's kingdom.	(Matthew 12:25-26 NKJV) [25] But Jesus knew their thoughts, and said to them: "Every kingdom divided against itself is brought to desolation, and every city or house divided against itself will not stand. [26] If Satan casts out Satan, he is divided against himself. How then will his kingdom stand?
It is a kingdom of darkness.	(Colossians 1:13 NKJV) [13] He has delivered us from the power of darkness and conveyed *us* into the kingdom of the Son of His love,
It influences the kingdoms of this world's system.	(Luke 4:5-6 NKJV) [5] Then the devil, taking Him up on a high mountain, showed Him all the kingdoms of the world in a moment of time. [6] And the devil said to Him, "All this authority I will give You, and their glory; for *this* has been delivered to me, and I give it to whomever I wish.
It influences the world kingdoms from the atmospheric heavens or "the heavenly places".	(Ephesians 2:1-3 NKJV) [1] And you *He made alive,* who were dead in trespasses and sins, [2] in which you once walked according to the course of this world, according to the prince of the power of the air, the spirit who now works in the sons of disobedience, [3] among whom also we all once conducted ourselves in the lusts of our flesh, fulfilling the desires of the flesh and of the mind, and were by nature children of wrath, just as the others. (Ephesians 6:12 NKJV) [12] For we do not wrestle against flesh and blood, but against principalities, against powers, against the rulers of the darkness of this age, against spiritual *hosts* of wickedness in the heavenly *places.*

His Origin

God's kingdom, the kingdom of light, is modeled after its king, God. So in direct contrast, Satan's kingdom, the kingdom of darkness, is modeled after its king, Satan. The nature and the character of each kingdom is an example of its leader. The king represents the kingdom and the kingdom represents the king.

The Scriptures give limited direct information concerning the origin and fall of Satan and his hosts, which took place ages past before the creation of mankind.

Based on the law of double reference (speaking of or to one person there is reference to another person beyond or behind them) we see this used in the following pertaining to Satan:

(Genesis 3:14-15 NKJV) ¹⁴ So the LORD God said to the serpent: "Because you have done this, You *are* cursed more than all cattle, And more than every beast of the field; On your belly you shall go, And you shall eat dust All the days of your life. ¹⁵ And I will put enmity Between you and the woman, And between your seed and her Seed; He shall bruise your head, And you shall bruise His heel."

(Matthew 16:23 NKJV) ²³ But He turned and said to Peter, "Get behind Me, Satan! You are an offense to Me, for you are not mindful of the things of God, but the things of men."

Within Scriptures there are two main passages describing Satan's origin and fall Ezekiel 28:1-19 and Isaiah 14:4-23. The terms used in these descriptions of the King of Tyre and the King of Babylon certainly goes beyond what could be applied to any earthly rulers, and is indicating the king behind the kings of this world order, Satan.

(Ezekiel 28:1-19 KJV) ¹ The word of the LORD came again unto me, saying, ² Son of man, say unto the prince of Tyrus, Thus saith the Lord GOD; Because thine heart *is* lifted up, and thou hast said, I *am* a God, I sit *in* the seat of God, in the midst of the seas; yet thou *art* a man, and not God, though thou set thine heart as the heart of God: ³ Behold, thou *art* wiser than Daniel; there is no secret that they can hide from thee: ⁴ With thy wisdom and with thine understanding thou hast gotten thee riches, and hast gotten gold and silver into thy treasures: ⁵ By thy great wisdom *and* by thy traffick hast thou increased thy riches, and thine heart is lifted up because of thy riches: ⁶ Therefore thus saith the Lord GOD; Because thou hast set thine heart as the heart of God; ⁷ Behold, therefore I will bring strangers upon thee, the terrible of the nations: and they shall draw their swords against the beauty of thy wisdom, and they shall defile thy brightness. ⁸ They shall bring thee down to the pit, and thou shalt die the deaths of *them that are* slain in the midst of the seas. ⁹ Wilt thou yet say before him that slayeth thee, I *am* God? but thou *shalt be* a man, and no God, in the hand of him that slayeth thee. ¹⁰ Thou shalt die the deaths of the uncircumcised by the hand of strangers: for I have spoken *it*, saith the Lord GOD. ¹¹ Moreover the word of the LORD came unto me, saying, ¹² Son of man, take up a lamentation upon the king of Tyrus, and say unto him, Thus saith the Lord GOD; Thou sealest up the sum, full of wisdom, and perfect in beauty. [13] Thou hast been in Eden the garden of God; every precious stone *was* thy covering, the sardius, topaz, and the diamond, the beryl, the onyx, and the jasper, the sapphire, the emerald, and the carbuncle, and gold: the workmanship of thy tabrets and of thy pipes was prepared in thee in the day that thou wast created. [14] Thou *art* the anointed cherub that covereth; and I have set thee *so*: thou wast upon the holy mountain of God; thou hast walked up and down in the midst of the stones of fire. [15] Thou *wast* perfect in thy ways from the day that thou wast created, till iniquity was found in thee. [16] By the multitude of thy merchandise they have filled the midst of thee with violence, and thou hast sinned: therefore I will cast thee as profane out of the mountain of God: and I will destroy thee, O covering cherub, from the midst of the stones of fire. [17] Thine heart was lifted up because of thy beauty, thou hast corrupted thy wisdom by reason of thy brightness: I will cast thee to the ground, I will lay thee before kings, that they may behold thee. [18] Thou hast defiled thy sanctuaries by the multitude of thine iniquities, by the iniquity of thy traffick; therefore will I bring forth a fire from the midst of thee, it shall devour thee, and I will bring thee to ashes upon the earth in the sight of all them that behold thee. [19] All they that know thee among the people shall be astonished at thee: thou shalt be a terror, and never *shalt* thou *be* any more.

Daniel's prophecy confirms the fact that there are princes of Satan's kingdom behind the princes of the world kingdoms.

(Daniel 10:10-13 NKJV) [10] Suddenly, a hand touched me, which made me tremble on my knees and *on* the palms of my hands. [11] And he said to me, "O Daniel, man greatly beloved, understand the words that I speak to you, and stand upright, for I have now been sent to you." While he was speaking this word to me, I stood trembling. [12] Then he said to me, "Do not fear, Daniel, for from the first day that you set your heart to understand, and to humble yourself before your God, your words were heard; and I have come because of your words. [13] But the prince of the kingdom of Persia withstood me twenty-one days; and behold, Michael, one of the chief princes, came to help me, for I had been left alone there with the kings of Persia.

The expressions used in this writing cannot fully be relevant to earthly kings, but insinuates to a king behind them of another kingdom outside of this world. This description indicated that Lucifer was a mighty being, and had been given a high position near the throne of God; an anointed ministry to lead heaven's angelic worship of the triune God.

About Satan	Scripture
Real personality and a spirit being – He is evil personified and characteristics are ascribed to him. He is not an impersonal influence or power. Personal Pronouns, intelligence, knowledge, will	(2 Timothy 2:26 NKJV) [26] and *that* they may come to their senses *and escape* the snare of the devil, having been taken captive by him to *do* his will. (2 Corinthians 2:11 NKJV) [11] lest Satan should take advantage of us; for we are not ignorant of his devices.

and action are attributed to him.	
Created being - Was in Eden – was blameless - Therefore dependent on God for his very existence.	(Ezekiel 28:13 NKJV) [13] You were in Eden, the garden of God; Every precious stone *was* your covering: The sardius, topaz, and diamond, Beryl, onyx, and jasper, Sapphire, turquoise, and emerald with gold. (Ezekiel 28:15 NKJV) [15] You *were* perfect in your ways from the day you were created, Till iniquity was found in you.
Was called Lucifer - Which means 'day star, son of the morning, or light bearer'.	(Isaiah 14:12 with 2 Corinthians 11:14 NKJV) [12] "How you are fallen from heaven, O Lucifer, son of the morning! *How* you are cut down to the ground, You who weakened the nations! --- [4] And no wonder! For Satan disguises himself as an angel of light.
Was an anointed cherub in the heavenly sanctuary - Just as OT prophets, priests and kings were anointed for office.	(Ezekiel 28:14 KJV) [14] Thou *art* the anointed cherub that covereth; and I have set thee *so*: thou wast upon the holy mountain of God; thou hast walked up and down in the midst of the stones of fire.
Was full of wisdom and beauty.	(Ezekiel 28:12 NKJV) [12] "Son of man, take up a lamentation for the king of Tyre, and say to him, 'Thus says the Lord GOD: "You *were* the seal of perfection, Full of wisdom and perfect in beauty.
He is a murderer and the Father of lies.	(John 8:44 NKJV) [44] You are of *your* father the devil, and the desires of your father you want to do. He was a murderer from the beginning, and *does not* stand in the truth, because there is no truth in him. When he speaks a lie, he speaks from his own *resources,* for he is a liar and the father of it.

His Fall

He was lifted up in Pride over his God-given wisdom, anointing and beauty.		(Ezekiel 28:17 NKJV) [17] "Your heart was lifted up because of your beauty; You corrupted your wisdom for the sake of your splendor; I cast you to the ground, I laid you before kings, That they might gaze at you.
He exalted himself, and came under condemnation		(Isaiah 14:13-14 NKJV) [13] For you have said in your heart: 'I will ascend into heaven, I will exalt my throne above the stars of God; I will also sit on the mount of the congregation On the farthest sides of the north; [14] I will ascend above the heights of the clouds, I will be
Self-exaltation	*I will exalt my throne above the stars of God.*	
Self- enthronement	*I will sit also upon the mount of the congregation in the sides of the north.*	
Self-ascension	*I will ascend above the heights of the clouds.*	

Self-will	I will ascend into heaven.	like the Most High.'
Self-deification	I will be like the Most High.	

He fell through pride and self-will, the very essence of sin. He wanted to be independent of God.	(Isaiah 14:12 NKJV) 12 "How you are fallen from heaven, O Lucifer, son of the morning! *How* you are cut down to the ground, You who weakened the nations!
He fell as lightning.	(Luke 10:18 NKJV) 18 And He said to them, "I saw Satan fall like lightning from heaven.
He was also cast down by God in this self-deification - He was permitted to retain his God-given wisdom which became corrupted, and by which he deceives mankind today.	(Ezekiel 28:16-17 NKJV) 16 "By the abundance of your trading You became filled with violence within, And you sinned; Therefore I cast you as a profane thing Out of the mountain of God; And I destroyed you, O covering cherub, From the midst of the fiery stones. 17 "Your heart was lifted up because of your beauty; You corrupted your wisdom for the sake of your splendor; I cast you to the ground, I laid you before kings, That they might gaze at you.
He was the original sinner, and iniquity (lawlessness) was found in him.	(Ezekiel 28:15 NKJV) 15 You *were* perfect in your ways from the day you were created, Till iniquity was found in you. (1 John 3:7-8 NKJV) 8 He who sins is of the devil, for the devil has sinned from the beginning. For this purpose the Son of God was manifested, that He might destroy the works of the devil.
He did not abide in the truth and He became a liar and murderer.	(John 8:44 NKJV) 44 You are of *your* father the devil, and the desires of your father you want to do. He was a murderer from the beginning, and *does not* stand in the truth, because there is no truth in him. When he speaks a lie, he speaks from his own *resources,* for he is a liar and the father of it.
He is the source of all sin and in him "The Mystery of Iniquity" is personified. He is the original Antichrist. He was the first apostate and caused other angels to sin in heaven.	(2 Thessalonians 2:7-9 NKJV) 7 For the mystery of lawlessness is already at work; only He who now restrains *will do so* until He is taken out of the way. 8 And then the lawless one will be revealed, whom the Lord will consume with the breath of His mouth and destroy with the brightness of His coming. 9 The coming of the *lawless one* is according to the working of Satan, with all power, signs, and lying wonders, working, with all kinds of false miracles, signs, and wonders
He will eventually be destroyed by fire. Many expositor believe that his fall took place before the creation of mankind, that he was cast out of the immediate presence of God, and that he fell to the earth bringing about the chaotic	(Matthew 25:41 NKJV) 41 Then He will also say to those on the left hand, 'Depart from Me, you cursed, into the everlasting fire prepared for the devil and his angels:,

condition seen in Genesis 1:1-2.	

His Nature

A person's name in Scripture generally meant to signify the nature, experience or function of that person. This is true of the many names of God, of the names of persons, and also of the many names of Satan. The following table indentifies Scriptural names and titles of Satan revealing the nature, character and work of this fallen archangel. The name with its interpretation is given along with suitable Scriptural references:

Names	Scriptures of reference
Satan - Adversary, Hater, Opponent, Enemy	1 Chronicles 21:1; Job 1:6-12; 2:1-7; Zechariah 3:1-7; 1 Kings 11:1, 23-25; 2 Corinthians 2:11
Devil - Slanders God to man and man to God. Accuser, Slanderer, Whisperer	Matthew 4:1; 13:39; 25:41; John 8:44; Ephesians 4:27; 6:11; Hebrews 2:14; James 4:7; Revelation 12:10
Serpent - Wisdom perverted to evil ends – Enchanter, beguiler, speaker of subtlety	Matthew 10:16; 2 Corinthians 11:3; James 3:15; Genesis 3:1-14; Revelation 12:9, 14-15; 20:2; Isaiah 27:1
Dragon - Speaks of the vicious beastly nature and rage of Satan – Great Enchanting Serpent	Isaiah 51:9; Ezekiel 29:3; 32:2; Revelation 12:3-17; 13:2,4,11; 16:13; 20:2
Beelzebub - This was a heathen god believed to be ruler of all evil spirits – Prince of Devils; Derived from Beelzebub or Lord of the Flies	2 King 1:2; Matthew 10:25; 12:24,27; Mark 3:22; Luke 11:15-19
Lucifer - Daystar, Morning Star, Light-bearer, Shining One	Isaiah 14:12
Belial - Worthless, Perverse, Lawless	1 Samuel 30:22: 10:27; 2 Corinthians 6:15;2 Samuel 23:6
Prince of this World - Prince of this world system	John 12:31; 14:30; 16:11
The Enemy - Hater, hostility	Matthew 13:39
The Tempter - Enticer	Matthew 4:3; 1 Thessalonians 3:5; 1 Chronicles 21:1; 7:5
The Wicked One	Matthew 13:19, 38-39; 1 John 5:18-19; 3:12

Names Interpretation	Scripture
Angel of Light	Luke 10:18; 2 Corinthians 11:13-15
Accuser of the Brethren - One against, one charging with an offence	Revelation 12:10; with Job 1:6-7; 2:1-2; Zechariah 3:1
Antichrist - One over against Christ. Spirit of Antichrist	1 John 2:18-22; 4:1-4; 2 John 7
Adversary - The enemy, the opposer	1 Peter 5:8
Murderer - Killer, destroyer of life	John 8:44
Liar	John 8:44
Sinner	1 John 3:8
Abaddon or Apollyon - Destroyer	Revelation 9:11
Roaring Lion	1 Peter 5:8
Wolf	John 10:12
Wicked One - Hurtful, evil one	Matthew 13:19
Fowler - One out to entrap and ensnare	Psalms 91:3
King of a Kingdom	Matthew 12:26-29; Acts 26:18; Colossians 1:13
Angel of the Bottomless Pit	Revelation 9:11
Leviathan - Great Water Animal	Isaiah 27:1
Son of Perdition - Lost soul, eternal damnation	2 Thessalonians 2:1-12

His Activity

Though Satan is mighty, he is not all-mighty; though he is wise and knowing, he is not omniscient; though he is powerful, he is not all-powerful. Nor is he omnipresent; he is on God's chain and can only go as far as God permits in affecting mankind. This is seen clearly in the experience of Job and Satan's attacks against his person, household and possessions (Job 1-2 with Luke 22:31).

His activities can be stated in seven main areas, but his main activity is to deceive.

Temptation	(Mark 1:13 NKJV) [13] And He was there in the wilderness forty days, tempted by Satan, and was with the wild beasts; and the angels ministered to Him. (Luke 4:13 NKJV) [13] Now when the devil had ended every temptation, he departed from Him until an opportune time.
Sin -He is the originator of rebellion against divine authority.	(1 John 3:8 NKV) [8] He who sins is of the devil, for the devil has sinned from the beginning. For this purpose the Son of God was manifested, that He might destroy the works of the devil.

Deception - This is the greatest power of Satan. Using trickery, misleading, dishonest, lying, misrepresenting the truth, Ensnare, falseness, to cause a person to believe in something that is not true, Lead into error.	(Genesis 3:1-5 NKJV) ¹ Now the serpent was more cunning than any beast of the field which the LORD God had made. And he said to the woman, "Has God indeed said, 'You shall not eat of every tree of the garden'?" ² And the woman said to the serpent, "We may eat the fruit of the trees of the garden; ³ but of the fruit of the tree which *is* in the midst of the garden, God has said, 'You shall not eat it, nor shall you touch it, lest you die.' " ⁴ Then the serpent said to the woman, "You will not surely die. ⁵ For God knows that in the day you eat of it your eyes will be opened, and you will be like God, knowing good and evil." (1 John 4:6 HCSB) **6** We are from God. Anyone who knows God listens to us; anyone who is not from God does not listen to us. From this we know the Spirit of truth and the spirit of deception.
Accusation - Satan hurls his accusations against the saints continually but the believer as an Advocate, Jesus Christ, interceding on his behalf.	(Revelation 12:10 NKJV) ¹⁰ Then I heard a loud voice saying in heaven, "Now salvation, and strength, and the kingdom of our God, and the power of His Christ have come, for the accuser of our brethren, who accused them before our God day and night, has been cast down.
Affliction - He seeks to afflict both physically and mentally.	(1 Corinthians 5:5 NKJV) ⁵ deliver such a one to Satan for the destruction of the flesh, that his spirit may be saved in the day of the Lord Jesus.
Opposition - Satan and his hosts are involved in a great spiritual war against God and Gods Kingdom.	(Acts 10:38 NKJV) ³⁸ how God anointed Jesus of Nazareth with the Holy Spirit and with power, who went about doing good and healing all who were oppressed by the devil, for God was with Him. (2 Timothy 2:25-26 NKJV) ²⁵ in humility correcting those who are in opposition, if God perhaps will grant them repentance, so that they may know the truth, ²⁶ and *that* they may come to their senses *and escape* the snare of the devil, having been taken captive by him to *do* his will.
Death - Has been brought on by Satan but Jesus has conquered death by His resurrection.	(Hebrews 2:14 NKJV) ¹⁴ Inasmuch then as the children have partaken of flesh and blood, He Himself likewise shared in the same, that through death He might destroy him who had the power of death, that is, the devil,

His Counterfeit

Religion is something that comes naturally for mankind because they were made to worship. They were made to worship the one and only God their creator by the power of the Holy Spirit. But if they do not accept and worship the one and only true God they will resort to counterfeit forms of belief systems, religion, worshipping all that is not of God. Which Satan will use and create with the help of his evil spirits to kill, steal and destroy all those that fall victim to his lies. This is the reason that Satan has set up many counterfeit religions. When Satan said "I will be like God (Isaiah 14:12-14), he did not mean that he would be like God in character in holiness, but he wanted to be like God in the sense of independence and running his own show.

He wanted to be God and to be worshipped as God. So he set up rival false religions and philosophies which are a complete imitation of all that God is and does.

Satan's imitation of God is seen in the following list of counterfeits.	
Has a throne.	(Revelation 2:13 NKJV) [13] I know your works, and where you dwell, where Satan's throne *is.* And you hold fast to My name, and did not deny My faith even in the days in which Antipas *was* My faithful martyr, who was killed among you, where Satan dwells.
Has great depth of teachings/doctrines.	(Revelation 2:24 NKJV) [24] Now to you I say, and to the rest in Thyatira, as many as do not have this doctrine, who have not known the depths of Satan, as they say, I will
Has a synagogue.	(Revelation 2:9 NKJV) [9] I know your works, tribulation, and poverty (but you are rich); and *I know* the blasphemy of those who say they are Jews and are not, but *are* a synagogue of Satan.
Has a counterfeit cup; has a communion table.	(1 Corinthians 10:20-21 NKJV) [20] Rather, that the things which the Gentiles sacrifice they sacrifice to demons and not to God, and I do not want you to have fellowship with demons. [21] You cannot drink the cup of the Lord and the cup of demons; you cannot partake of the Lord's table and of the table of demons.
Gives his doctrines to men to teach.	(1 Timothy 4:1 NJKV) [1] Now the Spirit speaketh expressly, that in the latter times some shall depart from the faith, giving heed to seducing spirits, and doctrines of devils;
Imitates the revelation of him. Godhead in his Satanic three in Revelation 13: the Beast (anti-Father); the Antichrist (Anti-Son); and the False	(Revelation 16:13-14 NKJV) [13] And I saw three unclean spirits like frogs *come* out of the mouth of the dragon, and out of the mouth of the beast, and out of the mouth of the false prophet. [14] For they are the spirits of devils, working miracles, *which* go forth unto the kings of the

| Prophet (Anti-Spirit). 14 - Does counterfeit miracles, signs and wonders. | earth and of the whole world, to gather them to the battle of that great day of God Almighty. |

His Judgment

In God's overall plan, it is evident that He is dealing with Satan in a progressive manner. There are seven steps in the judgment of Satan.	
The moment he sinned he was cast out of Paradise, the third heaven, which is the immediate presence of God.	(Ezekiel 28:16 KJV) [16] By the multitude of thy merchandise they have filled the midst of thee with violence, and thou hast sinned: therefore I will cast thee as profane out of the mountain of God: and I will destroy thee, O covering cherub, from the midst of the stones of fire.
He was judged in Eden's earthly Paradise, when Satan caused Adam and Eve to sin.	(Genesis 3:14-15 NKJV) [14] So the LORD God said to the serpent: "Because you have done this, You *are* cursed more than all cattle, And more than every beast of the field; On your belly you shall go, And you shall eat dust All the days of your life. [15] And I will put enmity Between you and the woman, And between your seed and her Seed; He shall bruise your head, And you shall bruise His heel."
He was conquered by Christ at Calvary's cross.	(John 12:31 NKJV) [31] Now is the judgment of this world; now the ruler of this world will be cast out.
He and his hosts are being conquered by the church as they release the captives of the human race who are under his control.	(Romans 16:20 NKJV) [20] And the God of peace will crush Satan under your feet shortly. The grace of our Lord Jesus Christ *be* with you. Amen.
He and his angels are to be cast out of heaven to the earth in the time of tribulation at the close of the age. This casting out is the result of an angelic war in the heavens.	(Revelation 12:7-9 NKJV) [7] And war broke out in heaven: Michael and his angels fought with the dragon; and the dragon and his angels fought, [8] but they did not prevail, nor was a place found for them in heaven any longer. [9] So the great dragon was cast out, that serpent of old, called the Devil and Satan, who deceives the whole world; he was cast to the earth, and his angels were cast out with him.
He will be cast out of the earth into the bottomless pit for a thousand years at the second coming of Christ.	(Revelation 20:2-3 NKJV) [2] He laid hold of the dragon, that serpent of old, who is *the* Devil and Satan, and bound him for a thousand years; [3] and he cast him into the bottomless pit, and shut him up, and set a seal on him, so that he should deceive the nations no more till the thousand years were finished. But after these things he must be released for a little while.
He will be loosed out of the bottomless pit for a season, after which he will be cast into the Lake	(Revelation 20:10 NKJV) [10] The devil, who deceived them, was cast into the lake of fire and brimstone where the beast and the false prophet *are*. And they

of Fire & Brimstone for all eternity. The eternal judgment upon Satan will also be the same for all choose to serve him in this life.	will be tormented day and night forever and ever.

Satan's Servants – Evil Spirits

A vast host of evil spirit beings are available to Satan and they are under his control. In the Bible they are called angels, authorities, principalities and powers, rulers of darkness, wicked spirits, and demons. There are different ranks and levels of authority in Satan's kingdom as suggested by these titles. Though many scholars see all of the titles as referring to the same beings, there does seem to be a distinction in Scripture between fallen angels and demon spirits.

(Romans 8:32 KJV) [38] For I am persuaded, that neither death, nor life, nor angels, nor principalities, nor powers, nor things present, nor things to come, [39] Nor height, nor depth, nor any other creature, shall be able to separate us from the love of God, which is in Christ Jesus our Lord.

(Ephesians 6:12 KJV) [12] For we wrestle not against flesh and blood, but against principalities, against powers, against the rulers of the darkness of this world, against spiritual wickedness in high *places*.

Fallen Angels

In Satan's kingdom of darkness there are angels who function as messengers. The Scriptures speak of a vast company of angels who fell with Satan. The following verse suggests that the possibility of one third of the angels fell.

(Revelation 12:4 NKJV) [4] His tail drew a third of the stars of heaven and threw them to the earth. And the dragon stood before the woman who was ready to give birth, to devour her Child as soon as it was born.

There were certain angels which sinned and were cast down to hell. (2 Peter 2:4 NKJV) *For if God did not spare the angels who sinned, but cast them down to hell and delivered them into chains of darkness, to be reserved for judgment*; Some angels are bound in various places of the earth, and others are loose, able to appear as angels of light. In time Michael and his angels (the angels that did not follow Satan) did cast Satan and his angels out of heaven. The redeemed saints will also judge these fallen angels. Then Satan and the angels who followed him will be cast into the Lake of Fire.

(Revelation 12:7-9 NKJV) [7] And war broke out in heaven: Michael and his angels fought with the dragon; and the dragon and his angels fought, [8] but they did not prevail, nor was a place found for them in heaven any longer. [9] So the great dragon was cast out, that serpent of old, called the Devil and Satan, who deceives the whole world; he was cast to the earth, and his angels were cast out with him.

> Psalm 78:49; Romans 8:38; 2 Peter 2:4; Revelation 9:14-15; 2 Corinthians 11:14-15; 1 Corinthians 6:3; Revelation 12:7-9; Matthew 25:41; Jude 6

Demon Spirits

Demon spirits origin is not specifically stated in the Bible. But it does reveal them having real personalities that are able to think, act, speak and express themselves through mankind and using them as hosts. There seems to be a difference between fallen angels and demons; demons desire and seek out to inhabit a human body as a host but fallen angels do not. The human body is not the only host they seem to seek out or can take residence in, they also can inhabit animal bodies expressing their destructive nature. In the New Testament there are two words most used to refer to demons, "devils" and "spirits". The Greek word "*daimon*" or "*daimonion*" is translated "devil" or "devils". The Greek word "*pneuma*" is translated "spirit" and is used of the Holy Spirit, the human spirit or of evil spirits.

(Matthew 8:28-29 NKJV) [28] When He had come to the other side, to the country of the Gergesenes, there met Him two demon-possessed *men,* coming out of the tombs, exceedingly fierce, so that no one could pass that way. [29] And suddenly they cried out, saying, "What have we to do with You, Jesus, You Son of God? Have You come here to torment us before the time?"

> Mark 5:1-20; John 13:27; Mark 1:34; 16:17; Luke 9:1; 10:17; James 2:19; 1 Corinthians 10:20-21; Matthew 9:33-34

> Text Message → There is one devil, Satan, but many demon spirits who are controlled by Satan and they all are wicked spirits, evil in all aspects, one should never try communicating with them.

They have real personalities possessing both will and intelligence and act according to their evil nature. They are spirit beings invisible, incorporeal, though often manifesting their nature and character through human beings. They are Satan's servants and are slaves to Satan and obligated to do his bidding. They are numerous, on one occasion a demon admitted to Jesus that his name was Legion, for "we are many".

(Matthew 8:31-32 KJV) [31] So the devils besought him, saying, If thou cast us out, suffer us to go away into the herd of swine. [32] And he said unto them, Go. And when they were come out, they went into the herd of swine: and, behold, the whole herd of swine ran violently down a steep place into the sea, and perished in the waters.

> Luke 4:35, 41; James 2:19; Matthew 17:18; 8:16; Luke 10,20; 9:38-42; Matthew 12:22-30; Mark 5:9; Luke 8:30; Matthew 12:26-27

They are symbolized as fowls of the air, unclean birds in a cage, locusts from the bottomless pit, army of horses and horsemen, with lions heads and serpents tails by which they torment, serpents and vipers.

(Revelation 18:1-2 KJV) [1] And after these things I saw another angel come down from heaven, having great power; and the earth was lightened with his glory. [2] And he cried mightily with a strong voice, saying, Babylon the great is fallen, is fallen, and is become the habitation of devils, and the hold of every foul spirit, and a cage of every unclean and hateful bird.

Their Nature

There are many kinds of demon spirits with degrees of wickedness in them.

Devils – evil spirits or servants of the Devil	Leviticus 17; Deuteronomy 32:17; Mark 1:34; 16:17
Evil Spirits	Judges 9:23; I Samuel 16:14,23; Luke 7:21;8:2; Acts 19:12-13
Unclean spirits – used 21 times	Zechariah 13:2; Matthew 10:1; Revelation 16:13
Dumb spirits	Luke 11:14; Mark 9:17
Blind and dumb spirits	Matthew 12:22
Deaf and dumb spirits	Mark 9:25
Foul spirits	Revelation 18:2; Mark 9:25
Lying spirits	1 Kings 22:22-23; 2 Thessalonians 2:9-12
Spirit of infirmity	Luke 13:11
Spirit of divination – fortune telling	Acts 16:16; 8:9
Seducing spirits – bring false doctrine	1 Timothy 4:1
Lunatic spirits - suicidal	Matthew 17:15-18; Mark 9:14-29
Antichrist spirits	1 John 4:3
Spirit of whoredom	Hosea 4:12
Spirit of error	1 John 4:6
Spirit of fear	2 Timothy 1:7
Perverse spirit	Isaiah 19:14
Familiar spirit	1 Samuel 28:7-8

Their Activity

In the Scripture John 10:10 the activity of demon spirits serving Satan is best stated.

"A thief comes only to steal and kill and to destroy"... These spirits attack mankind spiritually, morally, mentally, physically and emotionally.

Oppose Gods Ministers.	Matthew 13:19; 2 Corinthians 4:4
Pervert the Word of God and seek to hinder the Gospel.	1 Thessalonians 2:18
Hold their Captives.	2 Timothy 2:26; 1 Timothy 3:7
Blind the minds of unbelievers.	2 Corinthians 4:4
Sow tares among wheat (the people/church).	Matthew 13:39
Seduce people; The Greek work "Planos", translated "seduce" means that they rove at tramps, and by implication they are imposters and misleaders. They seek to draw aside from the path; to lead astray, allure, tempt, corrupt, defraud and entice **Note → a seducing spirit can cause people to be obsessed with a false idea, or doctrinal imbalance.**	1 Timothy 4:1; Mark 13:22; 1 John 2:26
Trouble people; The Hebrew word for "trouble" means "to make fearful, afraid, to terrify." It speaks of agitation of the mind, being perplexed, uneasy, and molested.	1 Chronicles 10:13-14; 1 Samuel 16:14
Oppress people, meaning to exercise dominion against, oppress, and overburden in body of mind.	Acts 10:38
Vex people; involves a person experiencing sensations or impressions, usually painful, feelings, passions and sufferings. Also, means to mob, to harass, molest or to suffer at the hands of another, to suffer or experience pain.	Matthew 15:22; 17:15; Luke 6:18; Acts 5:16
Deceive people.	Revelation 12:9; Matthew 24:4,5; 11,24
Possess people; Possession denotes both the occupancy and ownership of a person by an evil spirit. It is indwelling control. Possession is to be under the control of a demon that has entered the person and can control their faculties at will. Cases of possession caused lunacy, palsy, dumbness, blindness, and enabled fortune-telling (that we know of from the Bible). NOTE→ no true believer (born-	Matthew 4:24; 8:16,28-34; Mark 5:1-20; Luke 8:26-40; Matthew 9:32,33; 12:22; 15:21-28; Mark 7:24-30; 1:32; 9:14-29; 4:33-35; Acts 8:7; 16:16

again in Christ) can be possessed by demons, because the Holy Spirit dwells within the believer's spirit.	
Torment people.	Revelation 9:1-11; 16:13-14

Their Judgment

The Bible tells us that the judgment of evil spirits will parallel that of Satan. Their judgment just as Satan's judgment is progressive and culminates at the same time. This judgment will involve them being conquered and spoiled, spared not, cast down to hell, made subject to Christ, delivered into chains of darkness, and reserved for final judgment, putting them away for eternity.

(Colossians 2:15 NKJV) ¹⁵ Having disarmed principalities and powers, He made a public spectacle of them, triumphing over them in it.

1 Peter 3:22; 2 Peter 2:4; Jude 6; Revelation 12:9; Matthew 25:41

Occult

Mankind with their curiosity has tried to contact the invisible spirit world through the ages, but not only relating to God but outside of God. The occult and spiritualism has been used by Satan to provide an avenue of contacts to the spirit realm. These occult and spiritualism type practices are only counterfeit forms of communication leading one to an avenue of evil. There will be in the last days, and already has been an increase in this type of activity seeking to communicate with the spirit world outside of God. Satan will continue to increase his use of this among mankind using his army of evil spirits and demons to draw in as many as they can seeking to kill, steal and destroy all who fall victim. Believers in Jesus Christ must be careful not to go outside of the Holy Spirit and the Word of God. Anything else is a lie and counterfeit of Satan. One of the major contributors of creating curiosity is the movie industry, we must be careful of what we and the ones who we are responsible for, watch and listen to.

Occult Activities mentioned in Bible	Modern day designations
Magicians, Wise men, Divination, Observer of Times, Passing (through the fire), Enchanter, Witch, Charmer, Consulter, Wizard, Necromancer (seeker unto the dead for advise and information), Soothsayers, Sorcerers	Ouija Board, Horoscope, Cosmology, Numerology, Yoga, Satanism, Séance, Reincarnation, Talismans, Transference, Rhaddomancy, crystal gazing, ESP, Levitation, Omen, Oracle, Palmistry, Precognition, Black mass, Charming or enchanting, blood pack, automatic writing, fetishes, NOTE → these are only an example of the many designations today --

Warning Against the Occult

The Scriptures are very clear in its warnings and judgments to those who get involved in the world of the occult. Mankind is to be only involved with God through the Holy Spirit and when they do not invite the true God into their life they will seek or respond to evil spirits linking themselves to Satan and his kingdom of evil, lies, counterfeits, and destruction. All such contact is forbidden by the Word of God and comes under divine judgment. Deception, enslavement and separation from God are Satan's objectives for counterfeiting spiritual activities and even using miracles to deceive mankind.

(Leviticus 19:31 NKJV) ³¹ 'Give no regard to mediums and familiar spirits; do not seek after them, to be defiled by them: I *am* the LORD your God.

(Deuteronomy 18:10 KJV) **10** There shall not be found among you *any one* that maketh his son or his daughter to pass through the fire, *or* that useth divination, *or* an observer of times, or an enchanter, or a witch,

Proving Spirits Can be Accomplished by the Following:

Spirits must be tested by the Word of God. *"To the law and to the testimony: if they (the spirits) speak not according to this Word, it is because there is no light in them".* (Isaiah 8:19-20)

Spirit utterances must be proven by fulfillment (Deuteronomy 18:21-22). Spirits must be tested by the truth of Christ's coming in the flesh, both by His incarnation and in the Church, which is His body (1 John 4:2-3).

Spirit's can be tested by the fruit they bring forth (Matthew 7:19-23).

Spirits can be discerned by the gift of the Holy Spirit in the discerning of spirits, which will expose what spirit is at work (1 Corinthians 12:7-10; Acts 16:16-18).

Jesus Christ's Victory

Victory is available for every believer because the Lord Jesus Christ has already conquered Satan and all of his hosts at the Cross of Calvary. Jesus Christ is Lord over all principalities and powers and mankind needs to trust, seek, worship, pray and believe in Him and no other. He is the "Strong Man" who has overcome. Satan has been stripped of his authority and now Christ is dividing His spoil with the Church (Psalm 19:5; Isaiah 53:12).

(Luke 11:20-22 KJV) **22** But when a stronger than he shall come upon him, and overcome him, he taketh from him all his armour wherein he trusted, and divideth his spoils.

The victory of Christ is in three parts: in His Life, Death and Resurrection.

In His Life

One of the greatest Biblical doctrines is the fact that the Lord Jesus Christ overcame and conquered Satan and his evil hosts in two realms. Jesus Christ conquered Satan in a personal way during the three temptations in the wilderness and He acted on mankind's part defeating Satan at Calvary in the fulfillment of His death, burial, resurrection and ascension now being King of Kings and Lord of Lords, all must bow before Him.

Jesus was tempted in the wilderness in the three areas of a mankind's being: spirit, soul, and body; and in the three areas of sin: the lust of the flesh, the lust of the eyes, and the pride of life.
(Matthew 4:1-11: Luke 4:1-13: 1Thessalonians 5:23)

Just as we are tempted and our flesh used against us, so it was for Jesus yet He was without sin. This was a personal victory over Satan and was the first step of gaining victory for all believers. Which Jesus did at the Cross of Calvary, being the representative on behalf of all mankind.

(1 John 2:15-16 KJV) 15 Love not the world, neither the things *that are* in the world. If any man love the world, the love of the Father is not in him. 16 For all that *is* in the world, the lust of the flesh, and the lust of the eyes, and the pride of life, is not of the Father, but is of the world.

(Hebrews 2:18 NKJV) 18 For in that He Himself has suffered, being tempted, He is able to aid those who are tempted.

(Hebrews 4:15 NKJV) 15 For we do not have a High Priest who cannot sympathize with our weaknesses, but was in all *points* tempted as *we are, yet* without sin.

In His substitution death

The temptation that took place in the wilderness against Jesus was a personal victory of Him being in the flesh as mankind is and winning over temptation, being sinless.

The temptation concerning the cross was a victory on behalf of mankind facing humiliation, ridicule, physical beating, and death. He was victorious.

(Colossians 2:14-15 KJV) 14 Blotting out the handwriting of ordinances that was against us, which was contrary to us, and took it out of the way, nailing it to his cross; 15 *And* having spoiled principalities and powers, he made a shew of them openly, triumphing over them in it.

When Jesus died and rose again, he defeated Satan in 5 realms: as the author of sin, of sickness, of death, as the ruler of the kingdoms of this world, and in the realm of the heavens, over principalities and powers in heaven and earth.

> 1 John 3:8; 2 Corinthians 5:19-21; Isaiah 53:4; Matthew 8: 16-17; 1 Corinthians 6:19-20; Acts 10:38; Hebrews 2:13-14; Revelation 1:18; Matthew 4:8-10; Revelation11:15; Ephesians 1:19-23; 4: 8-10; Philippians 2:9-11

In His Resurrection and Ascension

Both on earth and in heaven sin brought disharmony, conflict, and friction. Satan, for now is the accuser against the saints, but because of the finished works of the resurrection, ascension and exaltation of the Lord Jesus to the right hand of the Majesty on High (Hebrews 8:1-2), we have a perfect man, the conqueror of Satan and his demonic hosts, representing us in heaven. The Scriptures proclaim that all principalities, powers and authorities are subject to His control.

Jesus now has all power in both heaven and the earth. Because of Christ's completed victory over Satan's kingdom of darkness, believers can rejoice and be assured of their salvation in Jesus Christ. Giving hope to all mankind. This was and is a complete victory, now all things are subject to Him. Jesus Christ is the head of all things concerning His church and His church worldwide should be under His Living Word the Bible and its revelation and no other.

(1 Peter 3:22 NKJV) [22] who has gone into heaven and is at the right hand of God, angels and authorities and powers having been made subject to Him.

(Ephesians 1:21-23 NKJV) [21] far above all principality and power and might and dominion, and every name that is named, not only in this age but also in that which is to come. [22] And He put all *things* under His feet, and gave Him *to be* head over all *things* to the church, [23] which is His body, the fullness of Him who fills all in all.

(1 Corinthians 15:25-26 NKJV) [25] For He must reign till He has put all enemies under His feet. [26] The last enemy *that* will be destroyed *is* death.

Ministry of the Church

Apostle Paul told the Church at Rome in Romans 16:20 that God would "bruise Satan under your feet shortly". The church of God which is His body of believers in Jesus Christ has been given power to control and combat the influence of Satan upon the earth. Jesus Christ has delegated His authority to the 12 Apostles, then to the 70 Disciples, now to the Church corporately and to the believers individually. The Gospel of Jesus Christ is to be delivered, taught, and practiced in all the nations of the world; this is the working ministry of the church. Too often the church is found doing all but the ministry that it was assigned to do; politics, finding cures for diseases, being caught up in entertaining more than teaching, focusing on how to become wealthy and healthy with worldly programs vs. Biblical teachings, adding confusion by splitting the church into different groups (causing a break in unity), and living like the rest of the world, trying to fit in instead of exemplifying Jesus Christ in their lives, being a peculiar people. And most of all giving love out to the world as Jesus Christ did, praying for our enemies, helping those in need, giving what is most valuable our time, our service, our life to the Gospel of Jesus Christ.

Since Christ has conquered Satan both personally and representatively, He has delegated His authority to the Church. The Church has been given power of attorney, the right to use His Name and to continue the ministry of Christ on earth. The ministry of the Church could be summarized in the Lord's commission to the Apostle Paul in (Acts 26:18: KJV) *18 To open their eyes, and to turn them from darkness to light, and from the power of Satan unto God, that they may receive forgiveness of sins, and inheritance among them which are sanctified by faith that is in me*

(Luke 9:1-2 KJV) *1 Then he called his twelve disciples together, and gave them power and authority over all devils, and to cure diseases. 2 And he sent them to preach the kingdom of God, and to heal the sick.*

(Matthew 24:14 KJV) *14 And this gospel of the kingdom shall be preached in all the world for a witness unto all nations; and then shall the end come.*

> Matthew 10:1-8; Mark 3:15; 6:7, 13; Luke 10:18-19; Mark 9:38-39; 16:15-20; Acts 19:13-18;Acts 1:1; 26:18; Luke 4:18-20; Matthew 28:19-20

The Kingdom of Darkness and the Believer

The believer needs to realize their position, responsibility, battleground and spiritual armor that God has provided for complete victory over the powers of evil. They should neither be fearful, nor ignorant of Satan's devices but avail themselves of the spiritual armor and weapons provided by Christ's victory.

(2 Timothy 1:7 KJV) *For God hath not given us the spirit of fear; but of power, and of love, and of a sound mind.*

(2 Corinthians 2:11 KJV) *11 Lest Satan should get an advantage of us: for we are not ignorant of his devices.*

Believer's Position → Legally	
In Christ we are partakers of the divine nature.	Ephesians 1:3-7; 2 Peter 1:4
New creatures in Christ.	2 Corinthians 5:17; Galatians 6:15
In the Kingdom of Light.	Colossians 1:13-14; Romans 8:38; Acts 26:18
Seated in heavenly places with Christ.	Ephesians 1:3; 2:2-8; 6:12
Believer's Responsibility → Experientially	

Must live victorious over the sins of the flesh, giving Satan no opportunity to position himself in a believers life.	John 16:31; Romans 6:7-8; Ephesians 4:27; Galatians 6:15
Must keep himself in the love of God so that the wicked one will not be able to touch him.	1 John 4:17-18; 5:18
Must submit to God and then resist the devil.	James 4:7; 2 Corinthians 2:11

Believer's Battleground – Personally

Spirit

When a person becomes a believer in Jesus Christ they become a living temple of God; their body, spirit and soul now is joined with the Holy Spirit opening up a relationship with God and they become an inner sanctuary. The believer's spirit is born again, born unto God, and is regenerated, justified and filled with the Holy Spirit and are one with the Spirit becoming children of God.

(1 Corinthians 6:17 KJV) [17] But he that is joined unto the Lord is one spirit

No true born again believer can be possessed by demon spirits. The Holy Spirit enters the believer to bring the believers spirit into total union with God, through Christ. There is no room left for a demon to reside there.

(Romans 8:16 KJV) [16] The Spirit itself beareth witness with our spirit, that we are the children of God:

Soul

The mind, will and emotions are all part of the soul which is the Holy Place of the Temple of God. The Living Word of God is needed to renew the soul. Romans 12:1-2 refers to the need of transforming the believer by renewing of the mind. The Word of God will bring the mind, will and emotions in harmony with the Spirit of God becoming a new creature in Christ.

(Romans 12; 1-2 KJV) [1] I beseech you therefore, brethren, by the mercies of God, that ye present your bodies a living sacrifice, holy, acceptable unto God, *which is* your reasonable service. [2] And be not conformed to this world: but be ye transformed by the renewing of your mind, that ye may prove what *is* that good, and acceptable, and perfect, will of God.

In this area, the soul is where the enemy will attack and the believer will experience their "fiery darts". Oppression, depression, fear, unbelief, evil thoughts, emotional and mental torment, satanic accusations and deception, are some of the "fiery darts" that have to be recognized, resisted and quenched by the spiritual weapons of God. The battle for the mind is the major area of conflict.

(Matthew 15:19-20 KJV) **19** For out of the heart proceed evil thoughts, murders, adulteries, fornications, thefts, false witness, blasphemies: **20** These are *the things* which defile a man: but to eat with unwashen hands defileth not a man.

There are three sources of thoughts that should be recognized. Thought from mankind or one's self, from God, and from Satan or evil spirits (Matthew 16:13-23). Recognizing where thoughts are originating from is something each believer should and must understand. Any thought that is not of God, contrary to His Word should not be entertained in the mind but dispelled immediately. There will be attacks upon believers from Satan and his evil spirits throwing what Scripture calls "fiery darts" in an attempt to confuse, cause depression, doubt, cover over the truth, feel sorry for one self, cause anger, cause one to consider gossip, and all that would cause a believer to take their focus off of the Word of God and focus on themselves in pity. This can only be avoided by walking daily in the ways of God always being watchful. Every imagination and thought that would exalt itself against the knowledge of Christ must be cast down and brought into captivity to the obedience of Christ. We must protect our mind with the Word of God.

(2 Corinthians 10:3-5 KJV) **3** For though we walk in the flesh, we do not war after the flesh: **4** (For the weapons of our warfare *are* not carnal, but mighty through God to the pulling down of strong holds;) **5** Casting down imaginations, and every high thing that exalteth itself against the knowledge of God, and bringing into captivity every thought to the obedience of Christ;

Sin entered the mind when the serpent tempted Eve.	2 Corinthians 11:3
Peter allowed thoughts to enter in his mind from Satan.	Matthew 16: 22-23
Judas accepted thoughts of betraying Jesus which came from the devil.	John 13:2,27
The mind has to be renewed.	Romans 12: 1-2
The believer must allow the mind of Christ to be in him.	Philippians 2:5-8
Must discipline his mind to think on divine things.	Philippians 4:8-9
The carnal and fleshly mind must be crucified.	Colossians 2:18; 1:21; Romans 8:7-9; Ephesians 4:17-23

Body

The Outer Court of the Temple of God is represented by the body. The body is capable of hearing, seeing, tasting, feeling, and smelling these being the five senses. This physical body is what allows mankind to have contact with the physical aspects of the world around them. The enemy attacks the instincts and appetites of this physical body of mankind. These attacks include sickness, disease, and infirmity. Believers must not try to lean on their understanding of why these attacks may be happening but put their full trust in God and allowing God to work in their lives. This earthly body is temporal but the spirit is eternal.

(1 Corinthians 6:19-20 NKJV) [19] Or do you not know that your body is the temple of the Holy Spirit *who is* in you, whom you have from God, and you are not your own? [20] For you were bought at a price; therefore glorify God in your body and in your spirit, which are God's.

Believer's Spiritual Armory

The Lord has given the Church and the believer, spiritual weapons which are mighty through God. These are not carnal weapons/tools but they come from the Lord's armory.

(2 Corinthians 10:3-5 KJV) For though we walk in the flesh, we do not war after the flesh: [4] (For the weapons of our warfare *are* not carnal, but mighty through God to the pulling down of strong holds;) [5] Casting down imaginations, and every high thing that exalteth itself against the knowledge of God, and bringing into captivity every thought to the obedience of Christ; [6] And having in a readiness to revenge all disobedience, when your obedience is fulfilled.

The Word of God – Essential to know the word of God – to overcome Satan.	(Revelation 12:11 KJV) [11] And they overcame him by the blood of the Lamb, and by the word of their testimony; and they loved not their lives unto the death. (John 8:32-34; Matthew 4:1-10; Psalm 119:130; Ephesians 1:15-22; 1 John 2:12-14)
The Name of Jesus – His name represents our power and authority. There is no higher authority, the power is not in us but in Him whose name we bear.	(Luke 9:1 KJV) Then he called his twelve disciples together, and gave them power and authority over all devils, and to cure diseases. (Matthew 10:1,8; Mark 3:15; 6:7,13; 16:17; Acts 16:18; Philippians 2:9-11; John 16: 23-24)
Christ in you – By new birth, the Holy Spirit indwells the believer – greater is He that is in the believer than he that is in the world.	(1 John 2:14 NKJV) [14] I have written to you, fathers, Because you have known Him *who is* from the beginning. I have written to you, young men, Because you are strong, and the word of God abides in you, And you have overcome the wicked one. (Galatians 4:6; Colossians 1:27; Ephesians 1:17-

	23; John 1: 12)
The Blood of Jesus - The sinless and incorruptible blood of Jesus is the cleansing power in the believer against sin.	(Revelation 12:11 KJV) [11] And they overcame him by the blood of the Lamb, and by the word of their testimony; and they loved not their lives unto the death.
The power of the Holy Spirit - The believer, who is filled with the Holy Spirit, is given equipment also to contend with and withstand all the power of the enemy.	(Matthew 12:28 KJV) [28] But if I cast out devils by the Spirit of God, then the kingdom of God is come unto you.
The Gifts of the Holy Spirit - Discerning of spirits is a weapon the church can use to discern what spirit is at work in a supernatural manifestation.	(1 Corinthians 12:9-11 KJV) [9] To another faith by the same Spirit; to another the gifts of healing by the same Spirit; [10] To another the working of miracles; to another prophecy; to another discerning of spirits; to another *divers* kinds of tongues; to another the interpretation of tongues: [11] But all these worketh that one and the selfsame Spirit, dividing to every man severally as he will.
The Whole Armor of God – God has provide all the armor needed by the believer in spiritual warfare – truth, righteousness, the gospel of peace, faith, salvation, Holy Spirit/Word of God, and praying always.	(Ephesians 6:10-18 KJV) [11] Put on the whole armour of God, that ye may be able to stand against the wiles of the devil. [12] For we wrestle not against flesh and blood, but against principalities, against powers, against the rulers of the darkness of this world, against spiritual wickedness in high *places*. [13] Wherefore take unto you the whole armour of God, that ye may be able to withstand in the evil day, and having done all, to stand. [14] Stand therefore, having your loins girt about with truth, and having on the breastplate of righteousness; [15] And your feet shod with the preparation of the gospel of peace; [16] Above all, taking the shield of faith, wherewith ye shall be able to quench all the fiery darts of the wicked. [17] And take the helmet of salvation, and the sword of the Spirit, which is the word of God: [18] Praying always with all prayer and supplication in the Spirit, and watching thereunto with all perseverance and supplication for all saints;

Bibliography

Connor Kevin, J, *The Foundations of Christian Doctrines*, Portland, Oregon, Bible Temple Publications, 1980

Geisler, Dr. Norman, *Systematic Theology*, Minneapolis, Minnesota, Bethany House, 2003

Towns, Elmer, L, *Concise Bible Doctrine*, Chattanooga, Tennessee, AMG Publishers, 1983, 2003

Horton, David, *The Portable Seminary*, Bloomington, Minnesota, Bethany House Publishers, 2006

Evans, Williams, *The Great Doctrines of the Bible*, Chicago, Illinois, Moody Publishers, 1912,1934,1949,1994

Erickson, Millard J, *Introducing Christian Doctrine*, Grand Rapids, Michigan., Baker Academic, 2006

Berkhof, Loouis, *Systematic Theology New Combined Edition*, Grand Rapids, Michigan,. Wm. B. Eerdmans Publishing Co, 1996

Carpenter, Eugine, E. and Comfort, Philip, W, *Holman Treasury of Key Bible Words*, Nashville, Tennessee, Broadman and Holman Publishers, 2000

Graham, Dr. Billy, *Angels*, Nashville, Tennessee, Thomas Nelson, 1995

Graham, Dr. Billy, *Death and the Life After*, Nashville, Tennessee, W Publishing Group, 1987

Martin, Walter, *The Kingdom of the Cults*, Bloomington, Minnesota, 2003

Boyd, Robert, *Boyd's Bible Handbook*, Eugene, Oregon, 1983

Thiessen, Henry Clarence., *Introductory Lectures in Systematic Theology*, Grand Rapids, Michigan, Wm. B. Eerman Publishing Company, 1949

Always Begin With Prayer

Breinigsville, PA USA
13 May 2010
237953BV00001B/6/P